HESI Live Review Workbook for the

NCLEX-RN® EXAM

8th Edition

Edited by

Amanda Churchman, MSN, RN

Program Director

Practical Nursing Program

Red River Technology Center

Duncan, Oklahoma

ELSEVIER

Elsevier
3251 Riverport Lane
St. Louis, Missouri 63043

HESI LIVE REVIEW WORKBOOK FOR THE NCLEX-RN EXAM, EIGHTH EDITION, ISBN: 978-0-323-79284-4

Content Strategist: Heather D. Bays-Petrovic
Content Development Manager: Lisa Newton
Content Development Specialist: Deborah Poulson
Senior Book Production Executive: Manchu Mohan
Book Designer: Bridget Hoette

Printed in India.

Last digit is the print number: 9 8 7 6 5 4 3 2

Reviewers

Sharon Mingo, DNP(c), MSN-Ed
Nursing Professor
Nursing Department
LaSalle University
Philadelphia, PA

Mary Judith Yoho, PhD, RN, CNE
Nurse Consultant
Grants Pass, Oregon

Contents

Chapter 1: Test-Taking Strategies and Study Guide, **1**

Chapter 2: Legal Aspects and Leadership Role of the Registered Nurse, **10**

Chapter 3: Clinical Concepts and Mechanisms of Disease, **19**

Chapter 4: Advanced Clinical Concepts and Disaster Management, **33**

Chapter 5: Oxygenation, Ventilation, Transportation, and Perfusion, **43**

Chapter 6: Ingestion, Digestion, Absorption, and Elimination, **64**

Chapter 7: Regulatory, Reproductive, and Urinary, **76**

Chapter 8: Movement, Coordination, and Sensory Input, **86**

Chapter 9: Pediatric Nursing, **104**

Chapter 10: Maternal-Newborn Nursing, **120**

Chapter 11: Mental Health Nursing, **134**

Appendix A: Normal Laboratory Values, **147**

Appendix B: Comparison of Three Types of Hepatitis, **153**

Appendix C: Compare and Contrast: Parkinson's Disease, Myasthenia Gravis, and Multiple Sclerosis, **154**

Appendix D: Practice Questions for the NCLEX-RN® Examination with NGN–Style Case Studies, **155**

1

Test-Taking Strategies and Study Guide

Goals of the Live Review Course

- Strengthen test-taking skills.
- Provide practice answering NCLEX-style questions.
- Incorporate recommended strategies to manage test anxiety.
- Formulate a study plan using tools such as the *HESI Live Review Workbook for the NCLEX-RN Exam.*
- Review basic curriculum content.

NCLEX-RN Examination

- The test covers essential nursing knowledge (based on entry-level nursing that reflects current nursing practice).
- The test plan is revised every 3 years, after a practice analysis with entry-level nurses is conducted (**New Test Plan: April 2023**).
- Information about the detailed test plan, including descriptions of content categories and related content for each category, can be found at www.ncsbn.org. The National Council of State Boards of Nursing (NCSBN) website also presents information for students, FAQs, and examples of alternate format test items (questions).

Organization of NCLEX-RN Test Plan: Client Need Categories

- **Safe and Effective Care Environment**
  - — Management of care
  - — Safety and infection control
- **Health Promotion and Maintenance**
- **Physiological Integrity**
  - — Basic care and comfort
  - — Pharmacological and parenteral therapies
  - — Reduction of risk potential
  - — Physiological adaptation
- **Psychosocial Integrity**

Organization of Test Plan: Integrated Processes

- Nursing Process
- Caring
- Communication and Documentation
- Teaching and Learning
- Culture and Spirituality

Test Administration: Computerized Adaptive Testing

- Difficulty level is tailored to the candidate's ability.
- The number of questions for the current NCLEX-RN test plan can range from 75-145 items. Of these items, 15 are pretest items that are not scored. The time limit for this examination is five hours.
- The number of questions for the new Next-Generation NCLEX (NGN) test plan (April 2023) can range from 85-150 items. Of these items, 15 are pretest items that are not scored. The time limit for this examination is five hours.

About Knowledge Test Questions

- Multiple Choice
  - — One question with four answer options
  - — Select one option
- Multiple Response
  - — Select one or more options
  - — Select all that apply (SATA)
- Fill in the Blank
  - — Type in one or more numbers
  - — If rounding is necessary, it is performed at the end of the calculation
- Hot Spot
  - — Identify one area in a graphic

Notes

— Measures skills related to safety, physical assessment, and other procedures and techniques

- Chart/Exhibit
  — Read information in the chart/exhibit to arrive at the correct option
  — Provides client history, laboratory data, and clinical data on tabs
- Ordered Response or Drag-and-Drop
  — Rank order or move options to provide the correct option
  — Instructs the individual to order the steps in the correct sequence
- Audio Item
  — Presents the candidate with an audio clip.
  — Individual uses headphones to listen to the question and options
  — Evaluates a candidate's competence in certain skills or assessment areas
- Graphic Options
  — May be used as all or part of an individual item, either in the question itself or as part of the response

Next-Generation NCLEX Examination (NGN)–Style Question Types

Question types were developed using the NCSBN Clinical Judgment Measurement Model (NCJMM), which is a valid measurement of a graduate nurse's level of clinical judgment and decision-making abilities using the context of a client scenario.

The following information was derived from Linda Silvestri and Donna Ignatavicius's "Next-Generation NCLEX® (NGN) Item Types and Descriptions."

- **Bowtie (for standalone item only)**
  — Items address more than one of the cognitive skills of the NCJMM in the one item. Visually, the item looks like a bowtie. There are five options for selection in the left side and five options in the right side of the bowtie (wells), and four options in the middle well.
- **Trend (for standalone case only)**
  — Trend items address multiple cognitive skills of the NCJMM by requiring the candidate to review information over time. Trend standalones can feature any item response type.
- **Matrix Multiple Choice**
  — Items have at least 4 rows and no more than 10 rows. There can be two options/columns or three options/columns. Each row must have one response item selected or the candidate will not be allowed to move on to the next item in the exam.
- **Multiple Response—Select All That Apply**
  — Items allow the candidate to select one or more answer options at a time. There may be only one correct response or multiple correct responses. There will be at least 5 options with no more than 10 options, but all 10 options could be correct.
- **Multiple Response—Select N**
  — Items allow the candidate to select one or more answer options and the question tells the candidate the number of items (N) that can be selected.
- **Multiple Response—Grouping**
  — Items will be presented in a table and the table will have a minimum of two groupings and a maximum of five groupings. Each grouping has a minimum of two options and a maximum of four options, and the number of options for each grouping will be the same. The candidate will need to select at least one option from each grouping.
- **Matrix Multiple Response**
  — Items will have response columns and each response column could have multiple correct responses. There can be between 2 and 10 columns and 4 to 7 rows. Each column must have one response option selected, but one or more check boxes per column can be selected.
- **Drop-Down Cloze**
  — Items include one or two sentences of information with one or more drop-down options from which to complete the sentence(s). There will be three to five options in each drop-down. There will be a minimum of one sentence with one drop-down per sentence and a maximum of five sentences with one drop-down per sentence.

Notes

- **Drop-Down Rationale**
  — Items include one sentence with one cause and one effect or one sentence with one cause and two effects. This can be a single dyad (one sentence with two drop-downs) or a single triad (one sentence with three drop-downs each). There can be three to five options in each drop-down.
- **Drop-Down Table**
  — Items include a table of information with drop-down options in different parts of the table. There will be a minimum of three columns and three rows and a maximum of five columns and four rows. One column will be a header column. There is one drop-down per row.
- **Drag-and-Drop Cloze**
  — Items will have a minimum of 4 selections (known as tokens) and a maximum of 10. There can be one or more response targets to which to drag a token. There is a minimum of one sentence with one target per sentence and a maximum of five sentences with one target per sentence.
- **Drag-and-Drop Rationale**
  — Items include one sentence with one cause and one effect or one sentence with one cause and two effects. This can be a single dyad (one sentence with two targets) or a single triad (one sentence with three targets).
- **Highlight Text**
  — Items will include a paragraph of information and the candidate will need to select parts of the text based on what the question is asking for the candidate to select. For example, the candidate could be asked to highlight significant information or what is critical for an action. There can be a maximum of 10 options in these question types.
- **Highlight Table**
  Items include a table from which the candidate will need to select parts of the text based on what the question is asking the candidate to select. There can be a maximum of 10 options. The table will include two columns (one being a header) and up to five rows.

(Examples of these NGN item types will be provided throughout this NCLEX review.)

Test-Taking Strategies: General Strategies

- Every question must be answered to move on to the next question. Make your best decision if unsure of the answer.
- Quickly eliminate the options that do not answer the question.
- Reread the question for qualifiers or other words that specify what the question asks.
- Decide what makes the responses different from each other.
- The options may contain correct information but may not answer the questions.
- Only use the information that the question provides. Never say, "But, what if…?" If the question does not state the information, you cannot assume that possible circumstance exists.

Test-Taking Strategies for Your Toolbox

- **Use ABCs**
  — Clients with airway problems or interventions are priority
  — Actual CPR = Circulation, Airway Breathing (CAB)
  — Acute before chronic
- **Maslow's Hierarchy of Needs**
  — Address physiological needs first, followed by safety and security needs, love and belonging needs, self-esteem needs, and, finally, self-actualization needs.
  — When a physiological need is not addressed in the question, look for the option that addresses safety.
- **Carefully determine the steps of the nursing process.**
  — **Assessment** requires gathering and verification of data.
  — **Analysis** requires interpreting data, communicating the diagnoses, and determining the health team's ability to meet needs.
  — **Planning** requires knowledge of prioritization and organization.
  — **Implementation** reflects delegation and assignment of tasks.
  — **Evaluation** compares actual outcomes with expected outcomes.

Notes

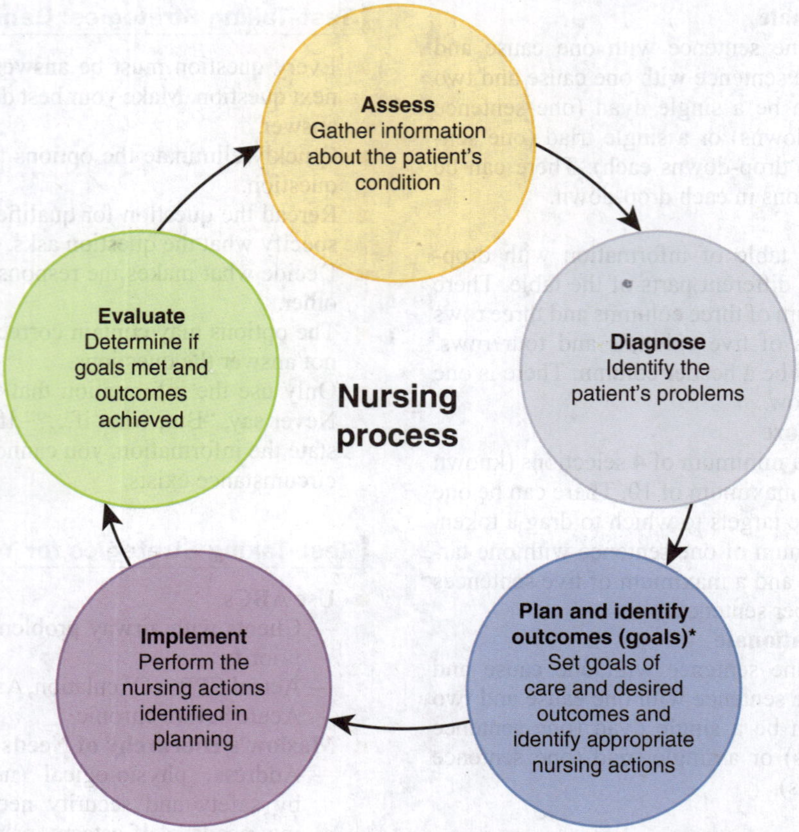

The Nursing Process. (Reprinted with permission from Cooper, K., & Gosnell, K. [2019]) *Foundations and adult health nursing* [8th ed.]. Elsevier.)

- **Think Safety, Safety, SAFETY!**
  — Perform the least invasive intervention first
  — Assess before taking action
  — Treat the client, not the machine!
  — Gather information and perform all relevant actions *before* calling the health care provider (HCP)
  — Determine which client to assess **first** (most at risk, most physiologically unstable)
  — Follow guidelines for delegating assignments (https://www.ncsbn.org/NGND-PosPaper_06.pdf)
  — Remember the differences between the Scope of Practice for the Licensed Nurse (RN), Licensed Practical Nurse (PN), and Unlicensed Assistive Personnel (UAP)

More Test-Taking Strategies

- Read the question first. Make sure to understand what the question is asking before reading the scenario.
  — This helps a candidate pick out the pertinent information in the scenario and eliminate distractors.
- The question may contain **red flag** words like *all, nothing*, *never*, and *always*.
- Notifying the HCP is a ***red flag item.*** Think about the appropriate nursing actions to take ***prior*** to notifying the HCP.
- Common nursing interventions includes:
  — Assess client status, vital signs, and/or lab values

Notes

— Review medication administration
— Provide small, frequent feedings
— Recommended fluid intake: "3 L/day"
— Alternate rest with activity
— Conserve energy with any activity

Teaching Points

- Risk factors: modifiable versus nonmodifiable
- Prevention and wellness promotion
- New medications and self-care instructions
- Client empowerment
- Anticipatory guidance
- Incorporating client education information into lifestyle, culture, and spiritual beliefs

Clarification of Acronyms

- **Health Care Provider (HCP)**
  — Physician
  — Physician assistant
  — Nurse practitioner
- **Prescriptions**
  — Orders written by licensed HCPs
- **Unlicensed Assistive Personnel (UAP)**
  — Client care technician
  — Nursing assistant
  — Nurse's aide
  — Medical assistant

Keep Memorization to a Minimum

- Growth and development milestones
- Crisis intervention
- Lab values
- Drug classifications
- Immunizations
- Stages of death and dying
- Principles of teaching/learning
- Stages of pregnancy and fetal growth
- Nurse Practice Act: Standards of Practice and Delegation

Strategies for Success in Answering NCLEX-RN Questions

- Essential Steps
  1. Determine if the style of the question is positive (+) or negative (–).
  2. Identify the key words in the question.
  3. Rephrase the question in your own words and answer the question.
  4. Rule out options.
- Is the Question in a Positive or Negative Style?
  — A *positive style* may ask what the nurse should do or the best or first action to implement.
  — A *negative style* may ask what the nurse should avoid, which prescription the nurse should question, or which behavior indicates the need for reteaching the client.

The Next Steps

- Identify key words or phrases that provide the critical information.
  — The age of the client, the setting, the timing, a set of symptoms or behaviors, diagnoses, medications, lab values, vital signs.
  — For example, the nursing actions for a 10-year-old, 1-day postoperative client are different from those for a 70-year-old, 1-hour postoperative client.
- Rephrase the Question
  — This helps eliminate nonessential information in the question and helps you determine the correct answer.
  — Ask yourself, "What is the question really asking?"
  — Before looking at the choices, rephrase the question in your own words. Then answer the question.
- Rule Out Options
  — Based on your knowledge, identify any options that are clearly incorrect.
  — Mentally mark through those options on the computer monitor.
  — Rule out options that delay treatment (e.g., continue to monitor, reassess in 15 minutes). Choose options that can be performed immediately.
  — Differentiate among the remaining options, using prior knowledge of the subject and related nursing principles (e.g., roles of the nurse, nursing process, ABCs, Maslow's Hierarchy of Needs).

Appropriate Knowledge

- Use the appropriate knowledge to answer questions.
  — Do not respond based on:
    - *Your* past client care experiences or agency
    - A familiar phrase or term

Notes

- "Of course, *I* would have already…"
- What *you* think is *realistic*
- *Your* children, pregnancies, parents, elders, personal response to a drug, and so on

— Do respond based on:
- ABCs
- Scientific, behavioral, sociological principles
- Principles of teaching/learning
- Maslow's Hierarchy of Needs
- Nursing process

— Answer based only on what the question asks—no more, no less.
- NCLEX-RN ideal hospital
- Basic anatomy and physiology
- Critical thinking

Study Break Box

1. A client has not had a bowel movement in 2 days and reports this information to the RN. Which intervention would the RN implement first?

1. Instruct the caregiver to offer a glass of warm prune juice at mealtimes.
2. Notify the HCP and request a prescription for a stool softener.
3. Assess the client's medical record to determine his normal bowel pattern.
4. Instruct the caregiver to increase the client's fluids to five 8-ounce glasses per day.

Correct Answer: 3

Rationale

Assessing the normal bowel pattern in a client with possible constipation provides the information to determine an appropriate response to the client's concern. Note that two interventions (A and D) are similar and can be eliminated. Nursing interventions to correct the constipation should be performed before notifying the HCP and requesting medical intervention.

Study Break Box—*cont'd*

2. A client who has chronic obstructive pulmonary disease (COPD) is resting in a semi-Fowler's position with oxygen at 2 L/min per nasal cannula. The client develops dyspnea. Which action would the RN take first?

1. Call the HCP.
2. Obtain a bedside pulse oximeter.
3. Raise the head of the bed higher.
4. Assess the client's vital signs.

Correct Answer: 3

Rationale

Remember to address ABCs first. The objective is to assist the client in using the accessory muscles of breathing. Raising the head of the bed farther will keep the spine straight, decrease pressure on the diaphragm, relax the abdominal muscle to improve breathing and will assist the client to breathe easier. This intervention addresses breathing, which would be the priority. Although the RN might call the HCP, obtain the pulse oximeter, and assess the client's vital signs, these would not be done **first**.

Specific Areas of Content: Lab Values

- Know the normal ranges for commonly used laboratory tests, what variations mean, and the best nursing actions
- Hemoglobin and hematocrit (H & H)
- White blood cells (WBCs), red blood cells (RBCs), platelets
- Electrolytes: Potassium (K^+), Sodium (Na^+), Calcium (Ca^2), Magnesium (Mg^{2+}), Chloride (Cl^-) Phosphorus (Po^4)
- Blood urea nitrogen (BUN) and creatinine
- Relationship of Ca^{2+} and PO_4
- Arterial blood gases (ABGs)
- Prothrombin time (PT), international normalized ratio (INR), partial thromboplastin time (PTT). Don't get them confused
- Glycosylated Hgb (A1c)

Notes

Study Break Box

1. In completing a client's perioperative routine, the RN finds that the consent form has not been signed. The client begins to ask more questions about the surgical procedure. Which action would the RN take?

1. Witness the client's signature on the consent form.
2. Answer the client's questions about the surgery.
3. Inform the HCP that the client has questions about the surgery.
4. Reassure the client that the surgeon will answer any questions before the anesthetic is administered.

Correct Answer: 3

Rationale

Informed consent must be obtained prior to performing any invasive or surgical procedure. The RN needs to notify the HCP that the client has questions concerning the procedure that must be addressed by the HCP. The consent form cannot be witnessed until all client questions have been clarified to obtain informed consent. It is not the nurse's responsibility to answer the questions. Reassuring the client that the surgeon will answer their questions does not address the issue and therefore should not be stated.

Complementary and Alternative Therapy

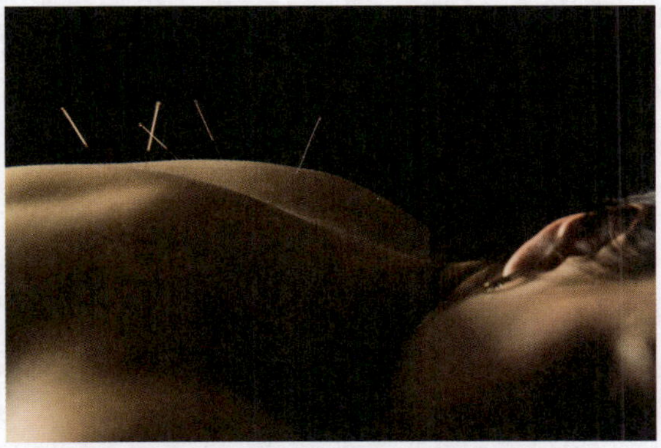

Accupuncture. (Reprinted with permission from Cooper, K., & Gosnell, K. [2019] *Foundations and adult health nursing* [8th ed.]. Elsevier.)

- Complementary and alternative therapy (CAM*) can be influenced by culture. It includes use of herbal medications as well as other treatments such as yoga, acupressure, acupuncture, Reiki, and aromatherapy.
  — Know the risks and benefits
  — Know the mechanisms of action, side effects, and drug interactions
  — Know the contraindications with traditional and other herbal medications

Nutrition

- Know the values and food sources of vitamins, minerals, proteins, carbohydrates, and fats.
- Be able to identify foods relative to their sodium content, potassium level, and levels of phosphate, iron, or vitamin K.
- Identify pregnancy and fetal growth needs.
- Introduce one food at a time for infants to determine allergies.
- Progression of diet as tolerated.
- Note client food allergies

Medication Administration and Pharmacology Think: Safety, *Safety*, SAFETY

- Safe medication administration is more than just knowing the action of the medications:
  — Reflect on the holistic picture of the client
  — Medication "Rights"—plus technique of skill execution
  — Drug interactions
  — Vulnerable organs: labs; what to assess
  — Allergies and presence of suprainfections
  — Concept of peak and trough
  — How you would evaluate:
    - The drug is effective?
    - There's a problem with the drug?
  — Special considerations
- Teach safety, empowerment, compliance!

Best Practices for Exam Success

- Manage test anxiety.
- Use positive self-talk ("I can do this!").
- Set up a study schedule and stick to it.

Notes

- Avoid negative people.
- Respect your body and your mind.
- Think positive—say to yourself: **"I will be successful!"**
- Establish a balanced lifestyle (i.e., a regular schedule for sleeping, eating, exercising, socializing, and working).

Develop a Study Plan

1. Organize resources.
2. Identify challenges.
3. Take practice tests or review NCLEX questions and rationales.
4. Establish and stick to a study schedule.
5. Pass the NCLEX!

Develop a Study Schedule

- Plan your schedule for the 4 to 8 weeks before the NCLEX exam date.
- Do you need a study group?
- Review key nursing content/concepts.
  — Growth and development
  — Lab results
  — Drug categories
  — Drug calculations
  — Immunization schedules

Exam Success: Take Care of Yourself

- **A Week Before the Exam**
  — Make a test drive to the site.
  — Be mindful of traffic patterns.
  — Familiarize yourself with the exam center.
  — Confirm that you have all of your documents.
- **The Day Before the Exam**
  — Allow only 30 minutes to review test-taking strategies.
  — Assemble all necessary materials:
    - Admission ticket
    - Directions to testing center
    - Identification
  — ***Do*** something you enjoy.
  — ***Do*** respect your body and your mind.
- **The Day of the Exam**
  — ***Do*** eat a healthy meal.
  — ***Do*** dress comfortably.
  — ***Do*** allow plenty of time to get there.
  — ***Do*** take ***only*** your identification forms into the examination room.
  — ***Do*** avoid distractions.
  — ***Do use positive self-talk.***

During the Exam

- Breathe deeply and regularly.
- Continue the positive self-talk.
- Be in the moment—**no regrets!**
- **Do not** allow the number of questions to influence your level of self-confidence.

Test-Taking Strategy

A word of advice: *do not* expect to achieve the maximum benefits of this review tool by "cramming" a few days before the examination. *It does not work!* Instead, organize planned study sessions in an environment that you find relaxing, free of stress, and supportive of the learning process well in advance of taking your NCLEX.

Notes

Next-Generation NCLEX® Examination (NGN)–Style Question

(Refer to the previous information regarding the different types of NGN questions. In each chapter of this review, we will give an example of each type of question so you can become familiar with this new NCLEX format.)

Drag & Drop Rationale

Scenario: The RN is caring for a client admitted with heart failure. The home medication list is obtained.

The medication ______(1)______ is contraindicated for clients with a history of heart failure and can worsen symptoms such as ______(2)______.

Home Med List (Option #1)	Symptoms (Option #2)
Furosemide 40 mg PO Daily	Exertional fatigue
Potassium chloride 20 mEq PO Daily	Hypotension
Pioglitazone 45 mg PO Daily	Hyperglycemia
Enalapril 5 mg PO BID	Unusual bleeding

Answer: #1 = Pioglitazone, #2 = exertional fatigue.

Rationale: Pioglitazone is a medication used to treat type 2 diabetes and has been known to cause or worsen heart failure. This medication is contraindicated in clients who have heart failure and can lead to worsening symptoms such as exertional fatigue; swelling of the hands, legs, and feet; hypertension; and shortness of breath.

Notes

2 Legal Aspects and Leadership Role of the Registered Nurse

Legal Systems

- Civil law is concerned with the protection of the client's private rights.
- Criminal law deals with the rights of individuals and society as defined by legislative laws.

Nursing Negligence and Malpractice

- **Nursing Negligence**
  - Failure to exercise the proper degree of care required by the circumstances that a reasonable, prudent person would exercise under the circumstances to avoid harming others *(careless act)*
- **Nursing Malpractice**
  - Failure to use that degree of care that a reasonable, prudent nurse would use under the same or similar circumstance *(professional negligence)*
- **Malpractice is found when:**
  - The nurse owed a duty to the client.
  - The nurse did not carry out that duty or breached that duty.
  - The client was injured.
  - The nurse's failure to carry out that duty caused the client's injury.

Standards of Care

- Nurses are required to follow standards of care, which originate in Nurse Practice Acts; state and federal law (US) and provincial, territorial, and federal laws (Canada); accreditation recommendations; the guidelines of professional organizations; and the written policy and procedures of the health care agency.
- Nurses are responsible for performing procedures correctly and exercising professional judgment when implementing health care providers' orders.
- Nurses retain the accountability and responsibility for delegated care/tasks.

Study Break Box

1. The unlicensed assistive personnel (UAP) reports to the staff RN that a client who had surgery 4 hours ago has had a decrease in blood pressure (BP), from 150/80 to 110/70, in the past hour. The RN advises the UAP to check the client's dressing for excess drainage and report the findings to the RN. Which factor is most important to consider when assessing the legal ramifications of this situation?

1. The parameters of the state's or province's nurse practice act.
2. The need to complete the hospital's adverse occurrence report.
3. Hospital protocol regarding the frequency of vital sign assessment every hour postoperatively.
4. The health care provider's prescription for changing the postoperative dressing.

Correct Answer: 1

Rationale

To delegate tasks to UAP, the RN must be knowledgeable regarding the parameters of the state's nurse practice acts. Delegation of an assessment that requires nursing judgment to a UAP is inappropriate. The other answer options do not apply to this scenario.

2. The newly licensed RN overhears two nurses talking in the elevator about a client who will lose her leg because of negligence of the staff. Which action by the newly licensed RN would be implemented first?

1. Monitor the nurses closely for further occurrences.
2. Advise them to cease their communication.
3. Inform the nurse manager of the conversation.
4. Submit an occurrence or variance report.

Correct Answer: 2

Rationale

Nurses should not discuss client information in public settings, as it is a violation of Health Insurance Portability and Accountability Act of 1996 (HIPAA). This is a violation of client privacy and confidentiality and should be stopped immediately. All other options should be completed, but advising them to cease their communication should occur **first**.

Notes

Practice Issues

- Nurses must follow the health care provider's orders unless the nurse believes that it is in error, violates hospital policy, or is harmful to the client.
- If the health care provider confirms the prescription/order and the nurse still believes the order is inappropriate, the nurse should contact the charge nurse, nurse manager, or nurse supervisor to intervene.
- The nurse must make a formal report explaining the refusal.
- The nurse should file an incident (occurrence; variance) report in any situation that will potentially cause harm to a client.

Advance Directives (AD)

- Assess the client's knowledge of AD.
- Provide the client with information about AD.
- The client's AD must be reviewed on admission.
- Integrate AD into the client plan of care.
- ADs can limit life-prolonging measures when there is little or no chance of recovery.
- **Living Will (LW)**
  - — LW is a written document that directs treatment in accordance with a client's wishes in the event of a terminal illness or condition that is activated when a client is no longer able to communicate his or her wishes independently.
- **Durable Power of Attorney for Health Care**
  - — A client appoints a representative (health care proxy) to make health care decisions based on the client's wishes.

Study Break Box

1. An awake, alert client with impending pulmonary edema is brought to the emergency department. The client provides the RN with a copy of a living will that states that "no invasive" medical procedures should be used to "keep her alive." The health care team is questioning whether the client should be intubated. Which information would guide the team's decision?

1. The living will removes the obligation to the client in any medical decision-making.

Study Break Box—*cont'd*

2. The client is awake and alert, which makes the living will irrelevant and nonbinding.
3. Lifesaving measures do not have to be explained to the client because of the signed living will.
4. The family should be contacted to determine who has durable power of attorney for health care for the client.

Correct Answer: 2

Rationale

This client is awake and alert and is capable of making decisions regarding health care procedures at this time. Therefore, the LW has not been activated, and all plans for care should be discussed with the client before intubation takes place.

A living will does not remove the client's ability to make medical decisions and all lifesaving procedures should still be explained to the client. The client should be asked if he or she has a durable power of attorney to make medical decisions. After the client has been intubated, they cannot communicate health care decisions.

Abuse

- The National Center on Elder Abuse identifies the two most important indicators of abuse as:
  - — Frequent unexplained crying by the older individual
  - — An older person's unexplained fear or suspicion of a particular person or persons in the home
- Obvious physical injury or neglect (e.g., evidence of malnutrition or presence of bruising on the extremities or trunk) are signs of possible abuse
- **Red Flag:** The injury does not match the story.
- The nurse has legal responsibilities to report incidents of abuse, neglect, or violence.
- Mandated reporting on vulnerable populations (e.g., elderly, pediatric, vulnerable adult)
- Health care professionals who do not report suspected abuse or neglect are liable for civil or criminal legal action.

Notes

Restraints/Safety Reminder Devices (SRDs)

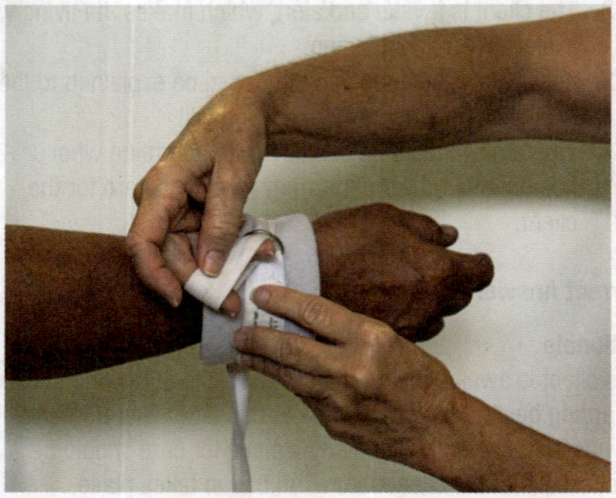

Wrist safety reminder device. (Reprinted with permission from Cooper, K., & Gosnell, K. [2019)] *Foundations and adult health nursing* [8th ed.]. Elsevier.)

- Used *only* to ensure the physical safety of the client or of other clients when less restrictive interventions fail.
- Must have a written prescription from a health care provider; must reassess prescription (i.e., at 8 or 24 hours).
- Nurse must follow agency policy and procedure to restrain any client.
- Documentation of restraint use and of follow-up assessments must detail the attempts to use less restrictive interventions.
- Liability for improper or unlawful restraint lies with the nurse and health care facility.
- The nurse must ensure that the UAP or PN working under the nurse's supervision uses restraints properly and according to health care facility policy and procedures.

Study Break Box

1. **A family member of a client who is in a Posey vest restraint (SRD) asks why the restraint was applied. Which response would the RN make?**
   1. The Posey vest restraint was prescribed by the health care provider.
   2. There is not enough staff to keep the client safe all the time.

Study Break Box—*cont'd*

   3. The other clients are upset when the client wanders at night.
   4. The client's actions place the client at high risk for self-harm.

Correct Answer: 4

Rationale

The client's behavior places the client at high risk for self-harm. Restraints may be applied to protect the client from injury after all other measures to protect the client have been attempted. The HCP can prescribe restraints only once all other less restrictive interventions have failed. Staffing issues are not legal indications for restraining a client. Wandering at night and other client concerns are also not reasons for applying restraints.

Legal Aspects of Mental Health

- Admissions
  - — Voluntary
  - — Involuntary
  - — Emergency
- Client rights
- Competency

Study Break Box

1. **Which nursing action has the highest priority when admitting a client to a psychiatric unit on an involuntary basis?**
   1. Reassure the client that this admission is only for a limited amount of time.
   2. Offer the client and family the opportunity to share their feelings about the admission.
   3. Determine the behaviors that resulted in the need for admission.
   4. Advise the client about the legal rights of all hospitalized clients.

Correct Answer: 3

Rationale

Think safety. An involuntary admission is based on the risk for harm to self or others; therefore, assessment of harmful behaviors is the highest priority. The other options are of lesser priority, but will be conducted during the admission process and assessment.

Notes

Confidential Health Care

- Confidentiality is the right of all clients. The American Nurses Association Code of Ethics for Nurses and the Canadian Nurses Association Code of Ethics for Registered Nurses assert the duty of the nurse to protect the confidentiality of clients.
- The HIPAA established standards for the verbal, written, and electronic exchange of private health information.
- HIPAA establishes the client's rights:
  - — To consent to use and disclosure of health information;
  - — To inspect and copy their medical records; and
  - — To amend mistaken or incomplete information.
- The Personal Information Protection and Electronic Documents Act (PIPEDA) (Canada) is federal legislation that protects personal information, including health information. PIPEDA delineates how private-sector organizations may collect, use, or disclose personal information.

Informed Consent

- Competent and of legal age.
- Voluntary.
- Risk, benefits, alternatives.
- Opportunity for questions.
- The HCP who is performing the procedure or treatment obtains informed consent.
- The registered nurse (RN) witnesses the signature. This task cannot be delegated to a UAP.
- Answers to any questions the client has about a procedure are the responsibility of the HCP.

Study Break Box

1. The RN enters the room of a preoperative client to obtain the client's signature on the surgical consent form. Which question is most important for the RN to ask the client?

1. "When did the surgeon explain the procedure to you?"
2. "Is any member of your family going to be here during your surgery?"
3. "Have you been instructed in postoperative activities and restrictions?"
4. "Have you received any preoperative pain medication?"

Study Break Box—*cont'd*

Correct Answer: 4

Rationale

Asking the client or knowing if the client has received pain medication prior to signing and witnessing the surgical consent form is essential. Pain medications can alter a client's ability to think clearly and make medical decisions. Consent should be obtained, if possible, before pain medications are administered. The other questions are components of the preoperative checklist and should be reviewed with the client and family prior to the procedure.

Good Samaritan Laws

- Limits liability if a nurse who offers assistance at the scene of an accident.
- Provide only care that is consistent with the nurse's level of expertise.
- Nurse is required to deliver care in a "reasonable and prudent manner."

Communication Skills: Types of Leadership

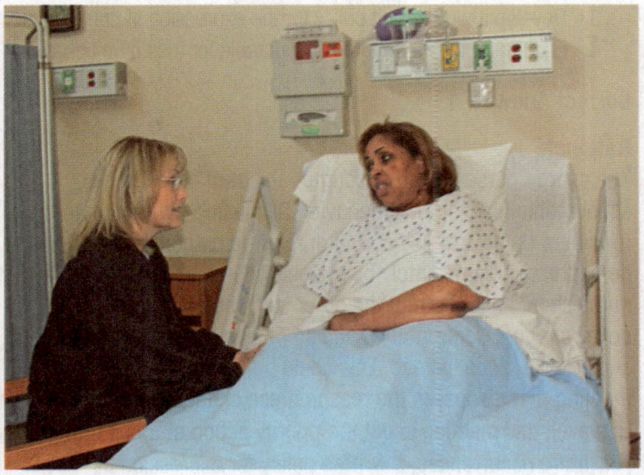

A nurse sitting at the same level as the client to foster communication. (Reprinted with permission from Cooper, K., & Gosnell, K. [2019)] *Foundations and adult health nursing* [8th ed.]. Elsevier.)

- Awareness of Speech and Body Language
  - — Reciprocal
  - — Two-way exchange
  - — Empathetic

Notes

- Authoritarian: Aggressive
- Laissez Faire: Passive
- Democratic: Assertive
- Consider the type of leadership indicated by these verbal examples:
  — "Do it my way."
    - Aggressive communication/authoritarian leader
  — "Whatever, as long as you like me."
    - Passive communication/laissez-faire leader
  — "Let's consider the options available."
    - Assertive communication/democratic leader

Study Break Box

1. The charge nurse confronts a staff nurse whose behavior has been resentful and negative since a change in unit policy was announced. The staff nurse states, "Don't blame me; nobody likes this idea." Which is the charge nurse's priority action?

1. Confront the other staff members involved in the change of unit policy.
2. Call a unit meeting to review the reasons the change was made.
3. Develop a written unit policy for the expression of complaints.
4. Encourage the nurse to be accountable for their own behavior.

Correct Answer: 4

Rationale

The charge nurse should encourage the staff nurse to be accountable for their own behavior. Displacing blame on other members of the staff is not an appropriate response and should be addressed immediately by the charge nurse. The charge nurse should not confront the other staff members about the policy change. Confrontation should be avoided and a discussion should take place instead. This could be handled in a unit meeting that discusses the reason these changes were made. However, this meeting is not the priority action at this moment. For future occurrences, a written policy for expression of complaints should be developed for the unit or facility.

Delegation and Supervision Skills

- The process by which responsibility and authority—but ***not accountability***—are transferred to another individual.
- The nursing process or any activity requiring nursing judgment may not be delegated to the UAP.
- **Five Rights of Delegation**
  1. Right task
  2. Right circumstance
  3. Right person
  4. Right direction/communication
  5. Right supervision
- **Supervision**
  — Direction/guidance
  — Evaluation/monitoring
  — Follow-up
- **Delegation Skills**
  — RN Responsibilities
    - Determine client needs and when to delegate.
    - Ensure proficiency and availability of delegatee.
    - Evaluate outcomes of and maintain accountability for delegated responsibility.
  — Delegatee Responsibility
    - Accept activities based on own competence level.
    - Maintain competence for delegated responsibility.
    - Maintain accountability for delegated activity.

Study Break Box

1. Which assignment should the RN delegate to a UAP in an acute care setting?

1. Checking blood glucose hourly for a client with a continuous insulin drip.
2. Giving PO medications left at the bedside for the client to take after eating.
3. Taking vital signs for an older client with left humeral and left tibial fractures.
4. Replacing a client's pressure ulcer dressing that has been soiled by incontinence.

Correct Answer: 3

Rationale

Measuring vital signs on the uninjured arm of an elder client does not require the expertise of the RN to be performed. The other actions are beyond the scope of practice for a UAP and should be completed by the RN.

Notes

Study Break Box—*cont'd*

2. The charge nurse is making assignments for each of four staff members, including a RN, a licensed practical nurse (PN), and two UAPs. Which task is best to assign to the PN?

1. Maintain a 24-hour urine collection.
2. Wean a client from a mechanical ventilator.
3. Perform sterile wound irrigation.
4. Obtain scheduled vital signs.

Correct Answer: 3

Rationale

Performing a sterile wound irrigation is within the scope of practice for the PN and is an appropriate assignment for the charge nurse to make. Maintaining a 24-hour urine collection can be performed by one of the UAPs and the other can gather the scheduled vital signs. A RN should be responsible for weaning a client from a mechanical ventilator.

3. Which situation warrants a variance (incident) report by the RN?

1. A client refuses to take prescribed medication.
2. A client's status improves before completion of the course of medication.
3. A client has an allergic reaction to a prescribed medication.
4. A client received medication prescribed for another client.

Correct Answer: 4

Rationale

Variance or incident reports are used for unusual circumstances that require investigation by the facility to prevent further occurrences. A client who receives medication that was prescribed to another client is an example of a medication variance and requires reporting using the facility's incident reporting procedure. This incident should be recorded and investigated to ensure that the occurrence does not reoccur to another client. An incident where a client refuses to take their medications or has status improvement does not require documentation via an incident report but should be documented in the chart. Although an allergic reaction is a concerning incident, this type of reporting is not appropriate. The HCP should be notified of the allergic reaction and the allergy should be noted on the client's chart.

Effective Team Communication

Team members collaborating. (Reprinted with permission from Cooper, K., & Gosnell, K. [2019)] *Foundations and adult health nursing* [8th ed.]. Elsevier.)

- **Communication focuses on:**
  - — Team building
  - — Facilitating collaboration
  - — Consulting
  - — Delegating
  - — Supervising
  - — Leading and managing
- Lateral violence refers to acts that occur among colleagues. Bullying is described as acts perpetrated by one in a higher level of authority that occur over time (ANA, 2015).
  - — These may affect client safety.
  - — Examples of the impact on client safety could include:
    - Delayed medication administration caused by failure to notify the nurse responsible for administering the medication of a change
    - Delayed notification of a change in prescriptions by the HCP
    - Nurse omits pertinent information re: client's care or prescriptions
- **Best practices for communication include:**
  - — Communicate clearly
  - — Treat others with respect
  - — Avoid gossip

Notes

— Rely on facts
— Collaborate
— Offer assistance when needed
— Speak directly to the individual with whom one has an issue

- **Handoff communication**
  — A transfer of communication along with authority and responsibility during transitions in care.
  — Important client information is shared at pertinent points of care
  — Ensures continuity of care and client safety
  — Improves communication and appropriate delegation

Study Break Box

1. The RN is preparing for change of shift. Which action by the RN is characteristic of ineffective handoff communication?

1. The RN states to the RN coming on duty, "The client is anxious about complications after surgery. Review the information I provided about how to use an incentive spirometer."
2. The RN refers to the electronic medical record (EMR) to review the client's medication administration record.
3. During rounds, the RN talks about the problem the UAP created by not performing a fingerstick blood glucose test on the client.
4. Before giving a report, the RN performs rounds on assigned clients so that there is less likelihood of interruption during handoff.

Correct Answer: 3

Rationale
The RN should not discuss or gossip about a problem with a fellow coworker during shift handoff. This incident should be addressed with the UAP to ensure the incident does not happen again. It is inappropriate to discuss the incident in the shift report and undermine the competency of the UAP. The oncoming RN should be made aware of client concerns and what client teaching has been performed. Using the EMR ensures accurate reporting during handoff communication and is recommended to provide accurate medication administration history information. Reducing the likelihood of interruptions during handoff is an effective communication technique.

S-BAR

- S-BAR is an interdisciplinary communication strategy that promotes effective communication about clients between caregivers.
  — S = **SITUATION:** State the issue or problem.
  — B = **BACKGROUND:** Provide the client's history.
  — A = **ASSESSMENT:** Give the most recent vital signs and current findings.
  — R = **RECOMMENDATIONS:** State what should be done.

Culturally Sensitive Care

- The client's culture, religious group, and country of origin influence health care beliefs.
- The cultural assessment answers questions such as:
  — Primary language spoken
  — Pain management expectations
  — Support systems
  — Feelings toward self-care (for example, client's feelings regarding the gender of the caregiver; does the client follow customs of giving family members control of decision making?)
  — Diet preferences
- Explain to the client and interpreter that confidentiality will be maintained.
- Value different styles of communication used by clients, families, and health care providers.
- Employ culturally relevant and language appropriate teaching materials and techniques.

Notes

Study Break Box

1. **The charge nurse is planning client assignments for the shift. The care team includes a RN, a PN, and a UAP. Which client is appropriate to be assigned to the PN? (Select all that apply.)**

   1. A client scheduled for a STAT x-ray after a fall from a stretcher.
   2. A client receiving IV vancomycin through a peripherally inserted catheter (PICC) line.
   3. A client with sickle cell crisis who was transferred from the intensive care unit (ICU) to the acute care area and who is receiving hydromorphone via a client-controlled analgesia (PCA) pump.
   4. A client with a pressure ulcer who was prescribed negative pressure (wound Vacuum-assisted closure (VAC)) care.
   5. A postoperative client who has been prescribed 2 units of packed red blood cells.

Correct Answer(s): 2, 4

Rationale

A client receiving IV vancomycin and a client with a wound VAC would be appropriate assignments to give to the PN. The client needing an x-ray can be assigned to the UAP. A client on a PCA of hydromorphone could need more advanced monitoring, which would be more appropriate for the RN. Also, blood transfusions must be initiated and supervised by an RN.

Study Break Box—*cont'd*

2. **A charge nurse is making assignments for five clients. The nursing team has a RN, a PN, and two UAPs. Which client is appropriate to assign to the RN? (Select all that apply.)**

   1. A client from the previous shift with unstable angina.
   2. A client with a stage 3 pressure ulcer who needs a bed bath.
   3. A client with an enteral feeding infusing at 30 mL/h.
   4. A cardiotomy client who is day 2 postoperative and who has chest tubes.
   5. A client with quadriplegia for whom urinary catheterization is prescribed.

Correct Answer(s): 1, 4

Rationale

The client with unstable angina and the client with chest tubes need advanced monitoring and assessment that are most appropriate for the RN. The client needing a bed bath can be assigned to the UAP. The client with the enteral feeding and the client needing urinary catheterization could be assigned to the PN.

Test-Taking Strategy

Do not second guess yourself and do not change your answers. Your first answer is usually the correct one if you have taken the time to break down and understand the question. Read each answer option carefully and chose the best option based on your gut instinct.

Notes

Next-Generation NCLEX® Examination (NGN)–Style Question

Drop-Down Cloze

Scenario: A hospice nurse is admitting a new client to the company's services. The client is a 68-year-old divorcee with three grown daughters who was diagnosed with small cell lung carcinoma over 1 year ago. The client underwent chemotherapy and radiation, but treatment was unsuccessful. The hospice nurse is discussing end-of-life plans with the client and the family. The client wishes to make decisions for care so that the family will not have to when the time comes.

Question: Complete the following sentence by choosing from the options.

The nurse would advise the client complete a(n) ________ (1)________ to officially document all wishes for end-of-life care to be implemented once the client is no longer able to make decisions. The client will also be advised to appoint a(n) ________ (2)________ to carry out the client's medical wishes.

Drop-Down Option 1	Drop-Down Option 2
Death with Dignity Consent	Attorney-in-fact
Informed Consent	Power of Attorney
Last Will & Testament	Health Care Proxy
Advanced Directive	Estate Planner

Answer: 1 = Advanced Directive, 2 = Health Care Proxy

Rationale 1: An advanced directive is a legal document that details a client's wishes for health care to be instated if/when said client becomes incapacitated or unable to make decisions independently. Death with Dignity Consent is used for physician-assisted suicides in states where this is allowed. Informed consent is required before all invasive procedures but does not pertain to this situation. A last will & testament discusses how a client's possessions will be dispersed but does not address medical issues.

Rationale 2: A health care proxy is the appropriate term for the individual who is appointed by a client to make health care decisions for the client if/when the client becomes unable to make decisions for themselves. The proxy should have a detailed understanding of the client's wishes for end-of-life care and should be willing to see that those plans are carried out accordingly. This person is only entitled to make health care decisions and is not involved in financial decisions or estate planning. An attorney-in-fact is a person who assumes responsibility for making financial, legal, and business matter decisions for the client and is another term for someone with general power of attorney. An estate planner helps in designating who will handle a client's assets and responsibilities after death.

Notes

Clinical Concepts and Mechanisms of Disease

3

Operative Care: Preoperative Care

- **Preparation**
  — Obtain a complete history, including the following:
  - Physical assessment
  - List of current medications (prescriptions, over the counter [OTC], complementary) and allergies
  - Previous surgical experiences (response to anesthetic)
  - Signed consent (confirm informed consent **before** client is sedated)
  - Confirm labs and diagnostics
  - Skin preparation
  - Preop checklist and preprocedure verification
- **Preoperative Teaching**
  — Diet restrictions (typically NPO [nothing by mouth] after midnight before surgery)
  — Teach coughing and deep breathing, incentive spirometry
  — Review methods of pain control
  — Use of thromboembolic deterrent stockings, sequential compression devices (SCDs), and expected outcomes
  — Complete preoperative verification process

Postoperative Care

- ABCs and hemodynamic stability (monitor for signs and symptoms of shock).
- Position client on side.
- Manage pain.
- Manage temperature.

Nursing and Collaborative Care

- **Urinary retention**
  — Check for distention
- **Urinary tract infection (UTI) Prevention**
  — Remove urinary catheter Post-operative Day (POD) #1 or #2
- **Pulmonary problems**
  — Check breath sounds
  — Check O_2 saturation
- **Bowel sounds**
  — Decreased peristalsis
  — Paralytic ileus
- **Wound management**
  — Incisions, drains, skin integrity
  — Wound dehiscence or evisceration
- **Venous thromboembolism (VTE)**
  — Antiembolism stockings (TED Hose)
  — Early mobilization

Study Break Box

1. A 72-year-old client returned from surgery 6 hours ago. The client received hydromorphone 2 mg IV 30 minutes ago for pain rating 8/10. The family member requests her father be checked immediately. On arrival to the room, the RN finds the client difficult to arouse, with a respiration rate of 6. Which is the priority nursing action?

1. Elevate the head of the bed.
2. Administer naloxone 0.4 mg IV.
3. Assess breath sounds.
4. Check vital signs and pulse oximetry.

Correct Answer: 2

Rationale

The client's respiratory rate is 6. The RN should administer naloxone 0.4 mg IV immediately. One of the side effects of hydromorphone is respiratory depression. The other nursing interventions need to be completed but are not the priority.

Notes

Teaching postoperative care with a client. (Reprinted with permission from Potter, P. A., Perry, A. G., Stockert, P. A., & Hall, A. [2021]. *Fundamentals of Nursing* [10th ed.]. Elsevier.)

Pain

- Pain management is client centered.
- Pain is whatever the client says it is, existing whenever he or she reports pain.
- Pain occurs in all clinical settings.
- Nurses have both a legal and ethical responsibility for managing clients' pain and suffering (be aware of any personal bias or misconceptions about pain management).
- **Pain Assessment and Management**
  - — Assessment includes:
    - **P**: precipitating or palliative
    - **Q**: quality
    - **R**: relief measures/region (location)
    - **S**: severity (using a scale appropriate for age and client condition: numerical, descriptive, a set of faces with expressions)
    - **T**: timing (onset, duration)
    - **U**: effect of pain on client
  - — Assess for nonverbal behaviors, which may indicate pain (moaning, grimacing, clenched teeth, pacing, or inactivity)
  - — Wong-Baker FACES Pain Rating Scale recommended for persons 3 years of age and older

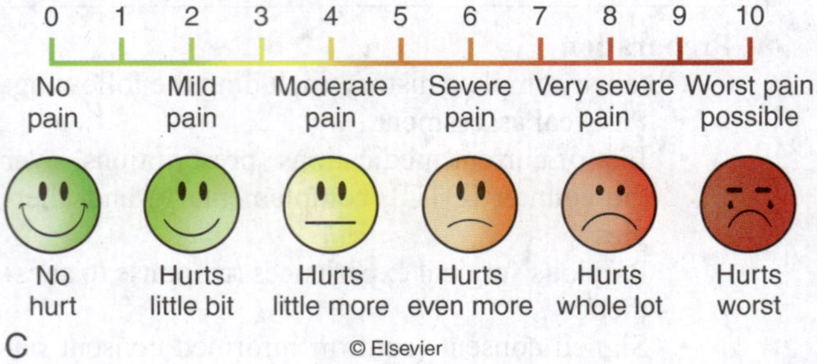

C

Sample pain scales. A, Visual analog. B, Verbal descriptive. (Reprinted with permission from Cooper, K., & Gosnell, K. [2019]. *Foundations and adult health nursing* [8th ed.]. Elsevier.)

  - — Assess personal cultural, spiritual, and ethical beliefs that may influence the perception of pain
  - — Consider special populations: palliative care, end of life
  - — Documentation includes pain assessment data (preintervention and postintervention rating), interventions (both nonpharmacological and pharmacological), and client teaching
  - — Controlled substance disposal must be documented per regulatory guidelines (ask another nurse to witness the waste of a tablet fragment, discarded injection contents, or discarded liquid contents)
- **Nonpharmacological Noninvasive Pain Relief Techniques**
  - — Repositioning
  - — Cutaneous stimulation: heat and cold application, massage therapy, transcutaneous electrical nerve stimulation (TENS)
  - — Relaxation techniques
  - — Guided imagery
  - — Complementary and alternative medicine (CAM) (e.g., acupressure or yoga)
- **Pharmacological Types of Pain Medications**
  - — *Nonopioids* for mild pain or use in combinations for moderate pain
  - — *Opioids* for moderate to severe pain
  - — *Coanalgesic* or *adjuvant drugs* (i.e., anticonvulsants, antidepressants) for neuropathic pain

Notes

- **Types of Pain Medications: Nonopioid Analgesics**
  - **Acetaminophen**
    - Maximum recommended dosage is 4000 mg/24 h
    - Monitor liver and renal function
    - Antidote: acetylcysteine
  - **Nonsteroidal Anti-inflammatory Drugs (NSAIDs)**
    - **Nonselective**
      - Salicylates
      - Ibuprofen
      - Ketorolac
      - Indomethacin
    - Selective (cyclooxygenase-2 [COX-2] inhibitors)
      - Celecoxib
- **Types of Pain Medications: Opioid Analgesics and Adjuvant Drugs**
  - **Mu Agonists**
    - Morphine
    - Hydromorphone
    - Meperidine
    - Methadone
    - Levorphanol
    - Fentanyl
    - Oxycodone
    - Hydrocodone
    - Codeine
  - **Partial Agonists**
    - Buprenorphine hydrochloride
    - Butorphanol
    - Nalbuphine hydrochloride
    - Pentazocine hydrochloride
  - **Adjuvant Drugs (used for neuropathic pain)**
    - Anticonvulsants, antidepressants, anesthetics
      - Prescribed alone or in combination with opioids
    - Corticosteroids
- **Nonpharmacological Invasive Pain Relief Techniques**
  - Nerve blocks
  - Interruption of neural pathways
  - Spinal cord stimulation
  - Acupuncture

Study Break Box

1. A client has an order for hydromorphone intravenous (IV) push 1 mg every 3 hours. The drug is available as 4 mg/mL per vial. The RN administers _____ mL of hydromorphone for one dose. (Fill in the blank.)

Answer = 0.25

Rationale

$$\frac{1\ \text{mg}}{4\ \text{mg}} \times 1\ \text{mL} = 0.25\ \text{mL}$$

Fluids and Electrolytes

- **Fluid Balance**
  - Changes in osmolarity cause shifts in fluid. The osmolarity of the extracellular fluid (ECF) is almost entirely due to sodium
  - The osmolarity of intracellular fluid (ICF) is related to many particles, with potassium being the primary electrolyte
  - The pressures in the ECF and the ICF are almost identical. If either ECF or ICF changes in concentration, fluid shifts from the area of lesser concentration to the area of greater concentration
- **Fluid Volume Excess**
  - Causes
    - Congestive heart failure (CHF) (most common), renal failure, cirrhosis, overhydration
  - Symptoms
    - Peripheral edema, periorbital edema, elevated blood pressure (BP), dyspnea, altered Level of Consciousness (LOC)

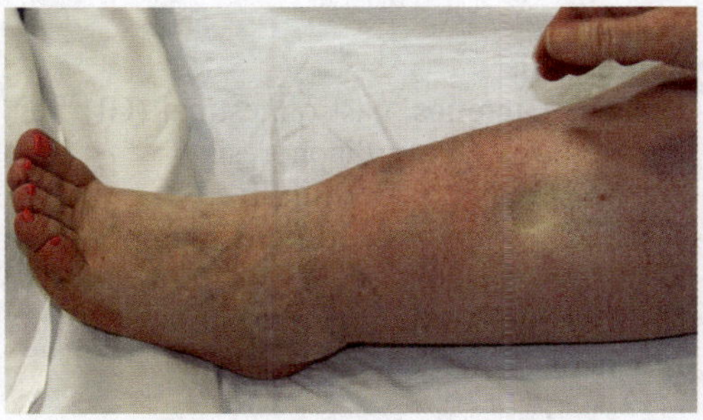

Pitting edema. (Reprinted with permission from Cooper, K., & Gosnell, K. [2019]. *Foundations and adult health nursing* [8th ed.]. Elsevier.)

Notes

— Lab findings
  - ↓ Blood urea nitrogen (BUN)*, ↓ Hemoglobin (Hbg), ↓ Hematocrit (Hct), ↓ serum osmolality, ↓ urine specific gravity
— Treatment
  - Diuretics, fluid restrictions, weigh daily, monitor K^+

■ **Fluid Volume Deficit**

— Causes
  - Inadequate fluid intake, hemorrhage, vomiting, diarrhea, burns, massive edema
— Symptoms
  - Weight loss, oliguria, postural hypotension, dry mucus membranes
— Lab findings
  - ↑ BUN and ↑ or normal creatinine, ↑ Hgb, ↑ Hct, ↑ urine specific gravity
— Treatment
  - Strict Intake and Output (I&O), replace with isotonic fluids, monitor BP, weigh daily

■ **Types of IV Fluids**

— *Isotonic* fluids expand the ECF volume (osmolarity between 250 and 300 mOsm/L): 0.9% normal saline (NS), LR (lactated Ringer's solution)
— *Hypotonic* fluids move water into the cell by osmosis, causing them to swell (osmolarity less than 250 mOsm/L): 0.45NS
— *Hypertonic* fluids pull fluid from cells, causing them to shrink (osmolarity >300 mOsm/L): D10; 3% saline, D5 in 0.45NS

Electrolyte Imbalances

Sodium: skeletal muscle contraction, cardiac contraction, nerve impulse transmission, normal osmolarity, and volume of ECF

■ **Hyponatremia**

— *Causes:* Diuretics, gastrointestinal (GI) fluid loss, hypotonic IV fluids, diaphoresis
— *Diagnostic:* Na^+ <135 mEq/L
— *Signs & symptoms:* Muscle cramps, confusion, weakness, seizures
— **Nursing and Collaborative Care**
  - Check BP frequently
  - Restrict fluids
  - Diet (foods high in Na^+ content)
    - □ Cheese
    - □ Table salt
    - □ Seafood
    - □ Processed meat
    - □ Canned foods
    - □ Ketchup
    - □ Salty snack foods

■ **Hypernatremia**

— *Causes:* Water deprivation, diabetes insipidus, renal failure, Cushing syndrome
— *Signs & symptoms:* Dry mucous membranes, thick mucus, low urinary output, tissue turgor, restlessness, agitation, confusion, flushed skin, pulmonary edema, seizures, thirst, fever
— *Diagnostic:* Na^+ >145 mEq/L (>145 mmol/L)
— **Nursing and Collaborative Management**
  - No IVs that contain sodium
  - Restrict dietary sodium
  - Weigh daily

Potassium: depolarizes and generates action potentials, regulating protein synthesis and glucose use and storage

■ **Hypokalemia**

— *Causes:* Diuretics, vomiting, diarrhea, Cushing syndrome, gastric suction
— *Diagnostic:* K^+<3.5 mmol/L (mEq/L)
— *Signs & Symptoms:* Rapid, thready pulse, flat T waves, anorexia, muscle cramps, weakness, fatigue, tingling, numbness, nausea, vomiting, constipation, GI bloating, palpitations
— **Nursing and Collaborative Management**
  - IV potassium
  - Diet: foods high in K^+
    - □ Oranges
    - □ Bananas
    - □ Apricots
    - □ Cantaloupe
    - □ Legumes
    - □ Leafy vegetables
    - □ Potatoes
    - □ Meat

■ **Hyperkalemia**

— *Causes:* Oliguria, acidosis, renal failure, Addison disease
— *Diagnostic:* K^+ >5 mmol/L (mEq/L)

*The normal BUN/Cr ratio is ~10:1. With prerenal azotemia, it may increase to 20:1.

Notes

— *Signs & symptoms:* Tall tented T waves, bradycardia, muscle weakness, tiredness, numbness, tingling, nausea, vomiting, respiratory distress, angina, palpitations, irregular heartbeat

— **Nursing and Collaborative Management**
- 10% to 20% glucose with regular insulin
- Sodium polystyrene sulfonate is used to treat hyperkalemia
- IV loop diuretics
- Renal dialysis

Calcium: maintains bone strength and density, activates enzymes, allows skeletal and cardiac muscle contraction, controls nerve impulse transmission, and allows for blood clotting

■ **Hypocalcemia**

— *Causes:* Renal failure, hypoparathyroidism malabsorption, pancreatitis, alkalosis

— *Diagnostic:* Ca^{++} <2.25 mmol/L (<9 mEq/L)

— *Signs & symptoms:* Positive Trousseau sign (carpopedal spasm which occurs when a BP cuff is inflated above systolic BP [SBP] for 3 minutes); diarrhea; numbness; convulsions; numbness and tingling of fingers, toes, and circumoral (around mouth) region; positive Chvostek's sign (contraction of facial muscles when facial nerve is tapped); hyperactive reflexes; muscle twitching and cramping; carpal and pedal spasms; tetany; seizures; laryngospasm; dysrhythmias

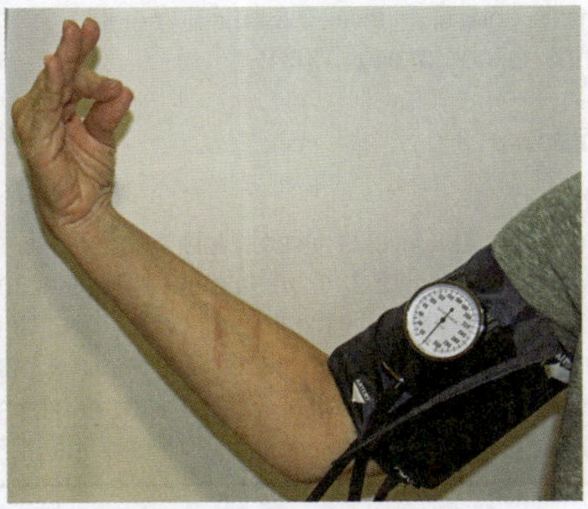

Trousseau sign. (Reprinted with permission from Cooper, K., & Gosnell, K. [2019]. *Foundations and adult health nursing* [8th ed.]. Elsevier.)

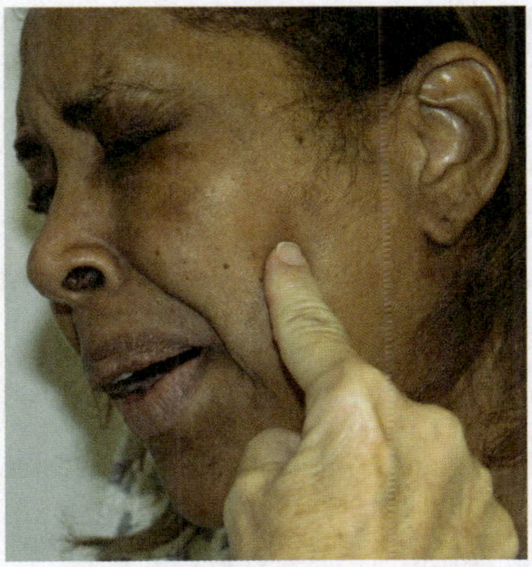

Chvostek sign. (Reprinted with permission from Cooper, K., & Gosnell, K. [2019]. *Foundations and adult health nursing* [8th ed.]. Elsevier.)

— **Nursing and Collaborative Management**
- Administer calcium supplements
- Administer IV calcium slowly
- Encourage calcium-rich foods, vitamin D, protein
- For acute hypocalcemia, keep a tracheostomy tray and resuscitation bag at bedside in case of laryngeal spasms

■ **Hypercalcemia**

— *Causes:* Hyperparathyroidism, malignant bone disease, excessive supplementation

— *Diagnostic:* Ca^{++} >2.75 mmol/L (>10.5 mEq/L)

— *Signs & symptoms:* Muscle weakness, constipation, nausea and vomiting, dysrhythmias, behavioral changes, anorexia, fatigue, diminished reflexes, lethargy, decreased level of consciousness, confusion, personality change, cardiac arrest if severe

— **Nursing and Collaborative Management**
- Limit vitamin D intake
- Avoid calcium-based antacids
- Administer calcitonin to reduce calcium
- Renal dialysis may be required

Notes

Magnesium: controls skeletal muscle contraction, carbohydrate metabolism, adenosine triphosphate (ATP) formation, vitamin activation, and cell growth

- **Hypomagnesemia**
  - *Causes:* Alcoholism, malabsorption, diabetic ketoacidosis, diuretics
  - *Diagnostic:* Mg^{2+} <0.65 mmol/L (<1.3 mEq/L)
  - *Signs & symptoms:* Skeletal muscle weakness; hyperactive deep tendon reflexes; numbness and tingling; painful muscle contractions; decreased GI motility; nausea
  - **Nursing and Collaborative Management**
    - Administer oral supplements
    - Increase dietary intake of magnesium
    - IV magnesium via infusion pump
    - Monitor vital signs
- **Hypermagnesemia**
  - *Causes:* Renal failure, adrenal insufficiency, excess replacement
  - *Diagnostic:* Mg^{2+} >1.05 mmol/L (>2.1 mEq/L)
  - *Signs & symptoms:* Bradycardia; peripheral vasodilation; hypotension; prolonged PR interval with a widened QRS complex; decreased to absent deep tendon reflexes
  - **Nursing and Collaborative Management**
    - No magnesium drugs for chronic kidney disease (CKD) clients
    - IV administration of calcium chloride or calcium gluconate

Phosphorous: activates vitamins and enzymes, forms ATP for energy supplies, assists in cell growth and metabolism, maintains acid-base balance and calcium homeostasis

- **Hypophosphatemia**
  - *Causes:* Alcohol withdrawal, diabetic ketoacidosis, respiratory alkalosis
  - *Diagnostic:* Phosphate <0.97 mmol/L (<3.0 mg/dL)
  - *Signs & symptoms:* ↓ Cardiac output, weak peripheral pulses, skeletal muscle weakness
  - **Nursing and Collaborative Management**
    - Oral supplementation
    - Diet high in phosphorus
- **Hyperphosphatemia**
  - *Causes:* Renal failure, excess intake
  - *Diagnostic:* Phosphate >1.45 mmol/L (>4.5 mg/dL)
  - *Signs & symptoms:* include signs of hypocalcemia
  - **Nursing and Collaborative Management**
    - Phosphate binders
    - Diet low in phosphorus

Study Break Box

1. A client is receiving an infusion of dobutamine hydrochloride. The order reads: Infuse dobutamine IV at 5 mcg/kg/min available in 500 mg in 250 mL D_5W. The client weighs 65 kg. Calculate the flow rate in mL/hr.

______________ mL/hr

Calculation: Ordered amount of drug × client's weight × 60 (minutes/hour) ÷ Drug Vehicle (amount of drug available)

ANS: 9.75 mL/hr

Rationale:

500 mg = 500,000 mcg/250 mL = 2000 mcg/1 mL

$$\frac{5\text{ mcg} \times 65\text{ kg} \times 60\text{ min}}{2000\text{ mcg}/1\text{mL}} = 9.75\text{ mL/hr}$$

2. Which laboratory result for a preoperative client would prompt the RN to contact the health care provider?

1. Platelet count: 151 × 10^9/L (151,000/mm³).
2. White blood cell (WBC) count: 85 × 10^9/L (8500/mm³).
3. Serum potassium level: 2.8 mEq/L (mmol/L).
4. Urine specific gravity: 1.031.

Correct Answer: 3

Rationale:

The serum potassium level is severely low. Normal potassium level is between 3.6 and 5.2 mEq/L (mmol/L). This electrolyte imbalance can lead to deadly dysrhythmias and must be resolved prior to starting an operative procedure. This requires immediate contact of the health care provider (HCP). The other labs are within normal limits and do not require contact of the HCP.

Acid Base

- Acid-Base Balance
  - pH
    - Normal = 7.35 to 7.45
    - <7.35 = acidosis

Notes

• >7.45 = alkalosis

— pCO_2

• Normal = 35 to 45 mm Hg
• >45 = acidosis
• <35 = alkalosis

— HCO_3

• Normal = 21 to 28 mEq/L
• <21 = acidosis
• >28 = alkalosis

— PaO_2

• Normal = 83 mm Hg–102 mm Hg

— Anion gap

• 10–16 mmol/L

Arterial Blood Gas Interpretation Practice

1. Determine whether the pH value is normal, acidic, or alkalotic.
   1. 7.31 ______
   2. 7.47 ______
   3. 7.36 ______

Rationale

1. 7.31 ***Acidic***
2. 7.47 ***Alkalotic***
3. 7.36 ***Normal***

2. Determine whether the client is hypoventilating, hyperventilating, or has normal ventilation.
   1. $pCO_2 = 42$
   2. $pCO_2 = 33$
   3. $pCO_2 = 55$

Rationale

1. $pCO_2 = 42$, Normal ventilation
2. $pCO_2 = 33$, Hyperventilating: blowing off CO_2
3. $pCO_2 = 55$, Hypoventilating: retaining CO_2

3. Determine whether this reading indicates a state of acidosis, alkalosis, or normal.
   1. $HCO_3 = 20$
   2. $HCO_3 = 33$
   3. $HCO_3 = 21$

Rationale

1. $HCO_3 = 20$ **Acidosis**
2. $HCO_3 = 33$ **Alkalosis**
3. $HCO_3 = 21$ **Normal**

Steps for Interpreting Arterial Blood Gas (ABG) Results

1. Is there alkalosis or acidosis present? First look at pH results.
   pH <7.35 = acidosis
   pH >7.45 = alkalosis
2. What is the respiratory (pCO_2) component?
   ■ The number is the amount of CO_2 in the blood
   ■ CO_2 is the respiratory component in the blood measured by millimeters of Mercury (mm Hg)
   ■ Normal CO_2 level is between 35-45 mm Hg
   ■ Respiratory alkalosis is pCO_2 below 35 mm Hg; symptom is hyperventilation
   ■ Respiratory acidosis is pCO_2 above 45 mm Hg; symptom is confusion or restlessness
3. Check your blood gas report for the bicarbonate (HCO_3) level. It is the renal component in the acid-base balance. The normal level for these ions is between 21 and 28 mEq/L.
4. Determine whether there is compensation for the pH imbalance. Generally, the pulmonary and renal systems compensate for each other to return the pH to normal. The lungs will compensate for metabolic instability by changing CO_2 excretion and the kidneys will compensate for the respiratory instability by altering bicarbonate retention and H^+ secretion.

Arterial Blood Gas Interpretation Practice

1. ■ pH = 7.32
   ■ $pCO_2 = 50$
   ■ $HCO_3 = 25$
   This client has ______________.
   Rationale: pH = acidosis, pCO_2 = acidic, HCO_3 = normal. This client has <u>uncompensated respiratory acidosis</u>.

2. ■ pH = 7.28
   ■ $pCO_2 = 35$
   ■ $HCO_3 = 18$
   This client has ______________.
   Rationale: pH = acidosis, pCO_2 = normal, HCO_3 = acidic. This client has <u>uncompensated metabolic acidosis</u>.

Notes

____

____

____

____

____

3. ■ pH = 7.43
■ pCO_2 = 40
■ HCO_3 = 24

This client has ___________.

Rationale: pH = normal, pCO_2 = normal, HCO_3 = normal. This client has normal ABG reading.

4. ■ pH = 7.56
■ pCO_2 = 44
■ HCO_3 =38

This client has ___________.

Rationale: pH = alkalosis, pCO_2 = normal, HCO_3 = alkalotic. This client has uncompensated metabolic alkalosis.

5. ■ pH = 7.33
■ pCO_2 = 50
■ HCO_3 = 29

This client has ___________.

Rationale: pH = acidosis, pCO_2 = acidic, HCO_3 = alkalotic. This client has partially compensated respiratory acidosis.

Safety: Sentinel Events

- An unexpected outcome involving a death or serious injury.
- Signals the need for immediate investigation and response.
- Accredited hospitals are expected to identify and respond to all sentinel events.
- **Examples of Sentinel Events**
  - Client suicide
  - Operative/postoperative complication
  - Wrong-site surgery
  - Medication error
  - Client fall
  - Client death or injury in restraints
  - Transfusion error
- **Response to Sentinel Events**
  - Analyzing root cause
  - Designing action plan to implement improvements to ↓risk
  - Implementing improvements
  - Monitoring effectiveness of those improvements

Safety: Falls

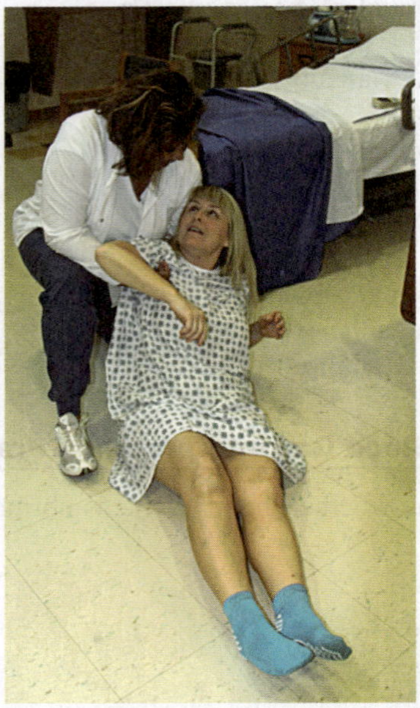

A nurse easing a client to the floor during a fall. (Reprinted with permission from Cooper, K., & Gosnell, K. [2019]. *Foundations and adult health nursing* [8th ed.]. Elsevier.)

- **Risk Factors**
  - **Adults**
    - Stroke
    - Depression
    - Mobility
    - History of seizures, falls
    - Use of assistive devices
    - Polypharmacy
    - Environmental issues
    - Forgetting or ignoring mobility issues
  - **Infants and Children**
    - Length of stay
    - IV or saline lock
    - Use of antiseizure medications
    - Acute or chronic orthopedic diagnosis
    - Receiving physical or occupational therapy
    - History of falls
  - **Nursing and Collaborative Management**
    - Fall prevention
    - Safety surveillance

Notes

- Assess need for pain relief, toileting, and positioning
- Frequent reorientation
- Client and family education
- Address environmental concerns
- Client sitter

High-Alert Medications

- Most likely to cause significant harm to a client even when used as intended.
  - Types of Drugs
    - Anticoagulants, narcotics and opiates, insulin, chemotherapeutic drugs, and sedatives
  - Types of Harm
    - Hypotension, bleeding, hypoglycemia, delirium, lethargy, bradycardia
  - Prevention Strategies
    - Built-in redundancies
    - Double-checking
    - Smart pumps
    - Standardized or protocol-driven order sets

Death and Grief

- **Stages of Grief**
  - Denial
  - Anger
  - Bargaining
  - Depression
  - Acceptance
- Encourage client to express anger.
- Do not take away the defense mechanisms for coping that the client uses in crisis.
- Customs surrounding death and dying vary among cultures.
- Make every attempt to understand and accommodate the family's cultural traditions when caring for the dying client.

Infection

- Infection is the invasion of the body by a pathogen.
- Response to the invasion can be:
  - Localized
  - Systemic
- Nosocomial, or hospital-acquired, nfections
  - Acquired as a result of exposure to a microorganism in a hospital setting

Human Immunodeficiency Virus (HIV)

- **Routes of Transmission**
  - Unprotected sexual contact
    - Most common mode of transmission
  - Exposure to blood through drug-using equipment
  - Perinatal transmission
    - During pregnancy
    - At the time of delivery
    - Breastfeeding
- **Nursing Assessment**
  - Laboratory Testing for HIV
    - Positive result on enzyme-linked immunosorbent assay (ELISA)
    - Confirmed Western blot test
    - Fourth-generation HIV assay that detects HIV-immunoglobulin M (IgM) and immunoglobulin G (IgG) antibodies
    - Positive p24 antigen assay
    - Polymerase chain reaction (PCR) (used with neonate)
    - In-home HIV test: Positive result is only preliminary; it must be confirmed by an HCP
  - Diagnosis of AIDS (HIV-III)
    - HIV-positive and a CD4+ T-cell count <200 cells/mm^3 or an opportunistic nfection
  - Primary HIV infection
    - Earliest stage: begins with flulike symptoms and antibodies may develop in weeks 1 to 12
  - Early (symptomatic) HIV disease signs and symptoms may not be present until 10 to 14 years after initial exposure without treatment
    - Fatigue, severe weight loss, swollen glands, unexplained fever, night sweats, dry cough
  - Parasites, fungi, bacteria, and viruses: cause of opportunistic diseases
    - Candidiasis: lungs, bronchi, esophagus
    - Invasive cervical cancer
    - Cytomegalovirus (CMV)
    - HIV-related encephalopathy
- **Nursing and Collaborative Management**
  - Monitor disease progression and immune function

Notes

— Initiate and monitor antiretroviral therapy (ART)
— Prevent development of opportunistic diseases
— Detect and treat opportunistic diseases
— Manage symptoms
— Prevent or decrease complications of treatment
— Prevent transmission of HIV
— Encourage proper nutrition
— Refer to mental health counseling
— Encourage safe sex practices

- **HIV Drug Therapy**
  - — Initiate and monitor highly active antiretroviral therapy (HAART)
  - — Three Goals of Drug Therapy:
    - Decrease the viral load
    - Maintain or raise CD4+ T-cell counts
    - Delay the development of HIV-related symptoms and opportunistic diseases
  - — Nursing and Collaborative Management
    - The client should have regular blood counts to track CD4 levels and the viral load
    - Side effects are common, and there are many drug-drug interactions
  - — HIV Medications
    - Nucleoside reverse transcriptase inhibitors (NRTIs)
    - Non–nucleoside reverse transcriptase inhibitors (NNRTIs)
    - Protease inhibitors
    - Integrase inhibitors
    - Fusion inhibitors
    - Entry inhibitor
    - See review book for complete list of meds.

Pediatric HIV

- **Clinical Manifestations**
  - — Recurrent infections such as thrush
  - — Unexplained fever
  - — Lymphadenopathy
  - — Hepatosplenomegaly
  - — Oral candidiasis
  - — Failure to thrive
  - — Developmental delay
- **Evaluation**
  - — For children 18 months of age and older, use HIV ELISA Western blot immunoassay.
  - — For infants younger than 18 months, use HIV PCR.
  - — In infants born to HIV-infected mothers, these assays will be positive because of the presence of maternal antibodies derived transplacentally.
- **Nursing and Collaborative Management**
  - — Teach transmission and control of infectious diseases.
  - — Safety issues include appropriate storage of special medications and equipment.
  - — Prevention is a key component of HIV education.
  - — Aggressive pain management is essential.
  - — Common psychosocial concerns include disclosure of the diagnosis.
  - — Do not administer live viruses.
  - — Address psychosocial concerns.
  - — If an HIV-infected mother is treated with zidovudine during pregnancy and the neonate is treated after birth, the probability of HIV infection of the child decreases.

Study Break Box

1. A client, who is HIV positive, asks why it is necessary to have a viral load study performed every 3 to 4 months. Which information would the RN provide?

1. To determine the progression of the disease.
2. To evaluate the ELISA.
3. To monitor the effectiveness of the treatment.
4. To track the effectiveness of the vaccine.

Correct Answer: 3

Rationale

Viral load testing directly measures the actual amount of HIV viral RNA particles in blood and is used to monitor the effectiveness of treatment. CD4+ T cells are monitored to determine progression of the disease. The ELISA test confirms a diagnosis of HIV. There is currently no vaccine for HIV.

Cancer

- The leading sites of primary cancer in men are the prostate, lungs, colon, and rectum. The leading sites of primary cancer in women are the breasts, lungs, colon, and rectum.

Notes

- Lung cancer is the leading cause of cancer-related deaths in both men and women.
- The incidence of cancer is highest amongst African Americans.
- **Primary Prevention**
  - — Education about lifestyle changes and risk factors
    - Smoking/smokeless tobacco
    - Dietary habits
    - Ultraviolet radiation
    - Excessive alcohol use
  - — Cancer risk assessment
  - — Genetic counseling
- **Health Promotion**
  - — The National Cancer Institute has recommended including at least five servings of fruits and vegetables in the daily diet. In addition are the following recommendations:
    - Eat foods from protein sources such as lean meat, fish, and skinned poultry
    - Choose low-fat dairy products, including white cheese rather than yellow
    - Eat whole grains
    - Include beans in the diet
    - Limit intake of saturated fat and added sugars
- **Contact the HCP if the client has:**
  - — Changes in bowel or bladder habits
  - — A wound that does not heal
  - — Unusual bleeding or discharge
  - — Thickening or lump in breast or elsewhere, etc.
  - — Indigestion or difficulty swallowing
  - — Obvious change in warts or moles
  - — Nagging cough or hoarseness
- **Screening Recommendations**
  - — **Breast**: Breast self-examination (BSE) (early 20s; educate about the benefits and limitations); emphasis is on reporting any new breast symptoms to the HCP; clinical breast examination (CBE) every 3 years and annually after age 40; mammography at age 40
  - — **Cervix**: Pap test; human papillomavirus (HPV) DNA test ages 21–29 every 3 years; ages 30–65: every 5 years with both the HPV/Pap test and every 3 years with Pap test alone
  - — **Colorectal**: Fecal occult blood test (FOBT); stool DNA; flexible sigmoidoscopy every 5 years, or barium enema every 5 years, or colonoscopy every 10 years, or computed tomography (CT) colonography every 5 years
  - — **Endometrial**: Report any unexpected bleeding or spotting to the HCP.
  - — **Lung**: Low-dose helical CT
  - — **Prostate**: Digital rectal examination (DRE) and prostate-specific antigen test (PSA)
  - — **Testicular**: Testicular Self Examination (TSE) monthly
- **Diagnosis of Cancer**
  - — Considerations for use in the diagnosis of cancer
    - Biopsy
    - Endoscope
    - Diagnostic imaging
    - Radioisotope studies
    - Laboratory tests
      - □ Alkaline phosphatase blood levels
      - □ Calcitonin
      - □ Carcinoembryonic antigen (CEA)
      - □ Tumor markers
      - □ Stool for occult blood
- **Cancer Therapies**
  - — **Surgery:** may be preventative, diagnostic, curative, or palliative
    - Nursing considerations: teaching specific to surgery
  - — Chemotherapy
  - — Bone Marrow Transplant
  - — External Radiation
    - Keep the skin dry
    - Do not apply lotions, ointments, creams, and powders in marked areas. Any lotions used must be prescribed by the physician
    - Protect the radiated area from direct sunlight
    - Instruct the client not to remove the markings
    - Avoid applications of heat or cold
    - Encourage 2 to 3 L of fluids per day
    - Encourage a diet high in protein and calories
  - — **Internal Radiation**
    - Sealed radioactive materials (radioactive implant [brachytherapy])
      - □ Client in private room
      - □ Limit time with client
      - □ Keep lead-lined container in room

Notes

- ☐ Wear dosimeter film badge when providing care
- Unsealed internal radiation: e.g., radioactive iodine for thyroid cancer
  - ☐ Client in a private room
  - ☐ Limit time spent with client
  - ☐ Wear dosimeter when in client room

Study Break Box

1. The RN is assigning rooms for four new clients. Only one private room is available in the oncology unit. Which client would be placed in the private room?

1. The client with ovarian cancer who is receiving chemotherapy.
2. The client with breast cancer who is receiving external beam radiation.
3. The client with prostate cancer who has just had a transurethral resection.
4. The client with cervical cancer who is receiving intracavity radiation.

Correct Answer: 4

Rationale

The client receiving intracavity radiation must be place in a private room due to the chance of radiation contamination. All other clients have little to no chance of transmitting radioactive material to other clients.

■ **Chemotherapy**

- — Strict guidelines must be followed
- — These drugs normally are administered by chemotherapy-certified nurses
- — Pregnant nurses should not administer most of these agents
- — Wear personal protective equipment for hazardous drug handling
  - Gowns: disposable, made of fabric that has low permeability to the agents in use, with closed front and cuffs
  - Gloves: powder free, labeled for use with chemotherapy drugs, latex, nitrile, or neoprene
  - Face and eye protection when splashing is possible
  - An approved respirator when there is a risk of inhaling drug aerosols (during spill or cleanup)
- — **Chemotherapeutic Agents**
  - Monitor for extravasation during infusion, and notify the HCP immediately if this occurs.
  - Types of IV access devices used for administration:
    - ☐ Hickman
    - ☐ Broviac
    - ☐ Port-a-cath
  - Side effects to monitor after chemotherapy
    - ☐ Leukopenia (WBC <4000 mm)
    - ☐ Neutropenia
    - ☐ Anemia
    - ☐ Thrombocytopenia
    - ☐ Stomatitis
    - ☐ Alopecia
    - ☐ Anorexia
    - ☐ Diarrhea
    - ☐ Tumor lysis syndrome

Study Break Box

1. The complete blood count (CBC) results for a client receiving chemotherapy are hemoglobin 85 mmol/L (8.5 g/dL); hematocrit, 32%; WBC count, 6.5 × 10^9/L (6500 cells/mm^3). Which meal choice is best for this client?

1. Grilled chicken, rice, fresh fruit salad, milk.
2. Broiled steak, whole wheat rolls, spinach salad, coffee.
3. Smoked ham, mashed potatoes, applesauce, iced tea.
4. Tuna noodle casserole, garden salad, lemonade.

Correct Answer: 2

Rationale

This client has low hemoglobin and low hematocrit, which indicate anemia due to chemotherapy. The client should eat a diet rich in iron. Steak, spinach, and grains are good sources of iron. The other foods are not the highest sources of iron.

Notes

Study Break Box—*cont'd*

2. The RN is caring for a client who is 24 hours postprocedure for a hemicolectomy with a temporary colostomy placement. The RN assesses the client's stoma, which is dry and dark blue. Which action should the RN take based on this finding?

1. Notify the HCP of the finding.
2. Document the finding in the client record.
3. Replace the pouch system over the stoma.
4. Place petrolatum gauze dressing on the stoma.

Correct Answer: 1

Rationale
A normal stoma is pink and moist. A dry, dark red stoma after surgery may indicate infection or other complication such as decreased blood flow. The RN should notify the HCP of the finding immediately. All other interventions do not address the complication noted with the stoma appearance.

3. After the change of shift report, the RN reviews assignments. Which client would the RN assess first?

1. The elderly client receiving palliative care for heart failure who complains of constipation and nervousness.
2. The adult client who is 48 hours postoperative for a colectomy and who is reported to be having nausea and vomiting.
3. The middle-aged client with chronic renal failure whose urinary catheter has been draining 95 mL for 8 hours.
4. The client who is 2 days postoperative for a thoracotomy and who has chest tubes, is on oxygen at 3 L/min, and has a respiratory rate of 12 breaths/min.

Correct Answer: 2

Rationale
The client who is 48 hours postoperative and is complaining of nausea and vomiting would need to be assessed first. These symptoms could be an indication of a paralytic ileus which is a medical emergency and would need to be reported to the HCP immediately. All the other clients are not experiencing symptoms that could be life-threatening and would need to be assessed following this client.

Study Break Box—*cont'd*

4. A practical nurse (PN) is assigned to care for an 82-year-old client who had a total right hip replacement with cement 2 days ago. Which observation would the PN immediately report to the RN? (Select all that apply.)

1. The client complains of incisional pain, rating it an 8 on a scale of 0 to 10.
2. The client has had a change in orientation to person but not to time or place.
3. Swelling and redness have developed in the client's lower left leg.
4. The practical nurse (PN) emptied 15 mL of bloody drainage from the Jackson-Pratt drain.
5. The client's last set of vital signs was temperature 37.9°C (100.2°F), pulse 87, respirations 12, blood pressure 108/74, and O_2 saturation 93%.

Correct Answer(s): 2, 3, 5

Rationale
A change in mental status and swelling/redness to the client's lower left leg could indicate serious postoperative complications and should be reported immediately to the RN. The client's vital signs indicate a low-grade fever that needs to be reported as well. Pain is a concern but can be assessed by the PN. The amount of drainage is small and does not need to be reported to the RN.

Test-Taking Strategy

As you review for the NCLEX, write down common lab values to memorize. Flashcards work very well for studying the various lab values and can be reviewed frequently. Candidates should be familiar with normal ranges for the following laboratory tests: ABGs (pH PO_2, PCO_2, SaO_2, HCO_3), cholesterol (total), BUN, creatinine, glucose, HgbA1C, WBC, RBC, H&H, INR, platelets, potassium, sodium, calcium, chloride, magnesium, prothrombin time (PT), partial thromboplastin time (PTT), and activated partial thromboplastin time (APTT).

Notes

Next-Generation NCLEX® Examination (NGN)–Style Question

Drag Drop Box

Drag & Drop Table: Complete the table by moving the correct options from the list of arterial blood gas findings used to assess the listed acid base imbalances.

Respiratory Acidosis	Respiratory Alkalosis	Metabolic Acidosis	Metabolic Alkalosis
(1)	(3)	(5)	(7)
(2)	(4)	(6)	(8)

Options:

pH >7.45	pH <7.35	CO_2 <35	HCO_3 >26
pH <7.35	CO_2 >45	HCO_3 <22	pH >7.45

Answer:

Respiratory Acidosis	Respiratory Alkalosis	Metabolic Acidosis	Metabolic Alkalosis
pH <7.35	pH >7.45	pH <7.35	pH >7.45
CO_2 >45	CO_2 <35	HCO_3 <22	HCO_3 >26

Notes

Advanced Clinical Concepts and Disaster Management

4

Acute Conditions: Shock

Interaction of blood volume and the size of the capillary bed affecting mean arterial pressure (MAP).

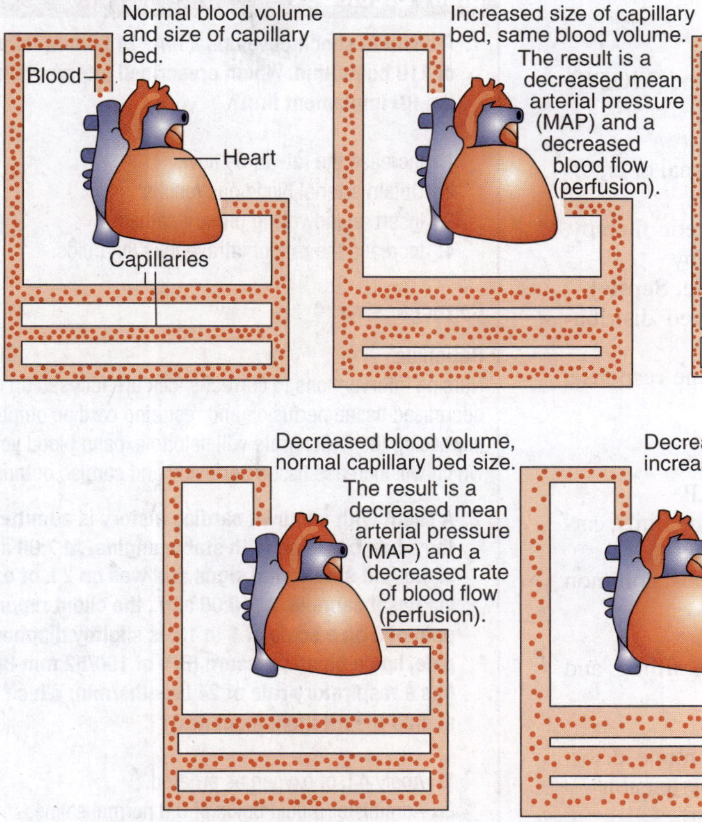

Interaction of blood volume and the size of the capillary bed affecting mean arterial pressure (MAP). (Reprinted with permission from Ignatavicius, D. D., Workman, M. L., Rebar, C. R., & Heimgartner, N. M. [2021]. *Medical-Surgical Nursing: Concepts for Interprofessional Collaborative Care* [10th ed.]. Elsevier.).

- **Stages of Shock**
  - — **Stage 1: Nonprogressive**
    - Restlessness
    - MAP ↓ 10 to 15 mm Hg from baseline
    - ↑ Heart rate (HR)
    - Pulse oximetry 90% to 95%
    - ↑ Respiratory rate
  - — **Stage 2: Progressive**
    - Pallor/cyanosis of mucosa/nail beds
    - MAP ↓ >20 mm Hg

Notes

- ↓ pH, ↑ lactate
- ↓ Urine output (oliguria)
- Rapid, weak thread pulse
- Cool, moist skin
- Pulse oximetry 75% to 80%
- Anuria

— **Stage 3: Refractory**
- Rapid Level of Consciousness (LOC) change
- Toxic metabolite release leads to unresponsiveness to shock correction
- Slow, shallow respirations
- Pulse oximetry <70%
- Multiple organ dysfunction syndrome (MODS)

■ **Types of Shock**

— **Hypovolemic**
- ↓ Circulating volume related to internal or external blood loss or dehydration
- Older adults at risk related to diuretic therapy, ↓ thirst reflex, anticoagulation therapy

— **Vasogenic (Anaphylactic, Neurogenic, Septic)**
- Excessive vasodilation and impaired distribution of blood flow
- Older adult risk related to ↓ immune response, malignancies, malnutrition

— **Cardiogenic**
- Pump failure
- Results in ↓ cardiac output and MAP
- Older adult risk related to diabetes mellitus, cardiomyopathies, cognitive impairment
- Myocardial infarction (MI) is the most common cause

— **Obstructive**
- Physical obstruction that impedes filling and pumping of the heart
- Pericarditis, cardiac tamponade
- Older adult risk related to autoimmune disorders, malignancies, pulmonary hypertension

■ **Nursing and Collaborative Management**

— Correct decreased tissue perfusion and restore cardiac output
- Optimize oxygenation and ventilation
- Fluid resuscitation
- Correct positioning, monitoring

— In cardiogenic shock, volume expanders may precipitate pulmonary edema

— Assessment data
- Vital signs
- Mental status
- Urine output

■ **Treatment of Shock**

— Drug Therapy
- Restore cardiac function based on effect of shock on preload, afterload, and contractility
- Replace blood volume or fluid loss
- Administer medications

■ Vasodilators

■ Vasoconstrictors

Study Break Box

1. A client in shock develops a MAP of 60 mm Hg and a HR of 110 beats/min. Which prescribed intervention would the RN implement first?

1. Increase the rate of O_2 flow.
2. Obtain arterial blood gas results.
3. Insert an indwelling urinary catheter.
4. Increase the rate of intravenous (IV) fluids.

Correct Answer: 4

Rationale

Nursing interventions to correct shock are focused on correcting decreased tissue perfusion and restoring cardiac output. Increasing the IV fluid rate will help to expand blood volume, which will increase tissue perfusion and cardiac output.

2. A client with a known cardiac history is admitted to the acute care unit with stable angina. At 7:00 a.m., the client had stable vital signs and was on 2 L of oxygen via nasal cannula. At 10:00 a.m., the client reports chest pain of 6 on a scale of 1 to 10, is slightly diaphoretic and pale, has a blood pressure (BP) of 100/52 mm Hg, and has a respiratory rate of 24 breaths/min. Which action should the RN implement first?

1. Apply 4 L of oxygen as ordered.
2. Administer a fluid bolus of 0.9 normal saline.
3. Administer the prescribed opioid for pain control.
4. Obtain a full set of vital signs, including temperature.

Correct Answer: 1

Rationale

This is a client with a known cardiac history whose symptoms align with cardiac problems. The client has increased work of breathing with respiratory rate of 24. The priority in this client is to maximize perfusion to the myocardium. The RN should ensure adequate oxygenation before implementing other interventions.

Notes

Study Break Box—*cont'd*

3. A client with burn injuries has lost a significant amount of body fluid. An IV of Lactated Ringer's solution is infusing at 200 mL/hr, and the client's urine output for the past 8 hours is 400 mL. Which sign or symptom is the highest priority in early distributive shock?

1. A change in BP from 118/60 to 102/68.
2. A change in level of consciousness from awake to restless.
3. A decrease in O_2 saturation from 98% to 93%.
4. A decrease in urine output over 8 hours from 400 to 240 mL.

Correct Answer: 2

Rationale

In hypovolemic shock, the body conserves fluids, leading to decreased urine output. A key word in this question is "early." All of the other signs and symptoms occur later in the decompensated stage of shock.

Continuum of Sepsis

- Systemic inflammatory response syndrome (SIRS)
- Sepsis
- Severe sepsis
- Septic shock
- Multiple Organ Dysfunction Syndrome (MODS)

Sepsis

- SIRS is an assortment of insults, including sepsis, ischemia, infarction, and injury.
- Generalized inflammation occurs in organs remote from the initial insult.
- SIRS usually starts with an infection.
- Septic shock is one component of the SIRS.
- Syndrome starts with an infection that progresses to bacteremia, then sepsis, then severe sepsis, then septic shock, and finally MODS.
- The prognosis for MODS is poor.
- **Nursing and Collaborative Management**
  - — The most important goal is to prevent the progression of SIRS to MODS
  - — The nursing role is attentive data collection and ongoing monitoring to detect early signs of organ dysfunction
  - — Collaborative care focuses on:
    - Prevention strategies
    - Early recognition of subtle changes in HR, systolic BP, respiratory rate, oxygen saturation, urinary output, and central nervous system (CNS) changes
    - Serum lactate and glucose levels
    - Prevention and treatment of infection
    - Blood culture before antibiotics
    - Broad-spectrum antibiotics within 1 to 3 hours of admission
    - Maintenance of tissue oxygenation
    - Nutritional and metabolic support
    - Support of individual failing organs

DIC: Disseminated Intravascular Coagulation

- DIC is a serious disorder of homeostasis resulting from overstimulation of clotting factors followed by anticlotting processes in response to diseases or injury.
- Astute ongoing evaluation and assessment are needed.
- Faster clotting + ↓ in clotting factors and platelets + hemorrhage and clotting = DIC
- DIC may lead to uncontrollable hemorrhage.
- Early detection of bleeding, both occult and overt, is the primary goal.
- D-dimer assay measures the degree of fibrinolysis (fibrin products in the blood).
- Assess the client for signs of external and internal bleeding.
- Be alert for manifestations of the syndrome.
- Heparin infusion (early in DIC, when clots are forming).
- Blood, fresh frozen plasma (FFP) transfusions, and cryoprecipitate.
- Appropriate treatment measures can be challenging and sometimes paradoxic.

Acute Respiratory Distress Syndrome (ARDS)

- A severe form of respiratory failure
  - — Considered to be present if the client has hypoxemia that doesn't improve with oxygen
  - — A predisposing condition for ARDS within 48 hours of clinical manifestations
  - — New interstitial or alveolar infiltrates on a chest x-ray (whiteout or white lung)
- Progression
  - — Is marked by alveolar capillary membrane damage with subsequent leakage of fluids into the interstitial spaces and alveoli
  - — As ARDS progresses, profound respiratory distress develops, requiring endotracheal intubation, and positive-pressure ventilation (PPV)

Notes

- Nursing Assessment
  - — Hypoxemia
  - — Dyspnea
  - — Scattered crackles
  - — Increased work of breathing
  - — Intercostal retractions
  - — Respiratory acidosis (early)
  - — Pleural effusions
  - — Decreased cardiac output
  - — Cyanosis
- Nursing and Collaborative Management
  - — Overall Goals
    - PaO_2 of at least 60 mm Hg
    - Adequate lung ventilation to maintain normal pH
  - — Goals for Recovering Client
    - PaO_2 within normal limits for age or baseline values on room air
    - SaO_2 >90%
    - Patent airway
    - Clear lungs on auscultation

Delirium

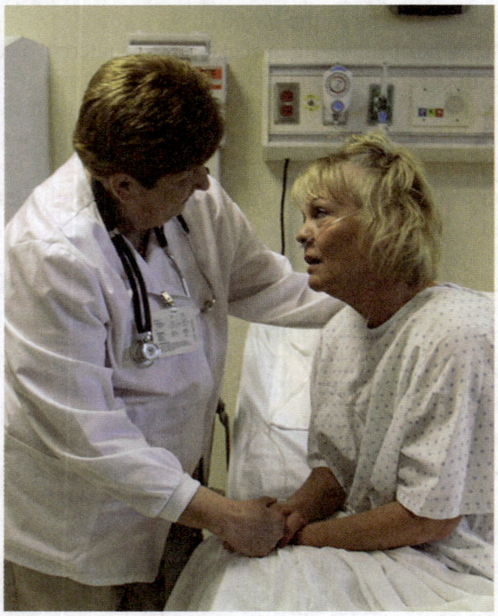

Nurse using touch as a therapeutic technique while caring for a client at risk for delirium. (Reprinted with permission from Cooper, K., & Gosnell, K. [2019]. *Foundations and adult health nursing* [8th ed.]. Elsevier.)

- An **acute state** of confusion, and difficulty concentrating
  - — Common among elderly, hospitalized clients
  - — May indicate an impending change in condition (i.e., sepsis, urinary tract infection [UTI])
- Risk Factors
  - — Sleep deprivation, advanced age, or vision and hearing impairment
  - — Use of opioids and/or corticosteroids
  - — Drug or alcohol abuse
  - — UTI, fluid and electrolyte imbalance
  - — Postoperative (unscheduled surgery), intensive care unit (ICU), or emergent delirium
- Nursing and Collaborative Management
  - — Prevention and early recognition (monitor neurological status)
  - — Protect the client from harm
  - — Provide a low-stimulation environment (calm)
  - — Provide the appropriate level of supervision/surveillance
  - — Reorient the client and communicate with simple statements
  - — Consider management with neuroleptic drugs (e.g., haloperidol [Haldol]) as prescribed
  - — Encourage family visibility and support

Study Break Box

1. A client recovering from ARDS is awake and alert but has residual fatigue and generalized weakness. The client's current vital signs are HR 83 beats/min, BP 104/64 mm Hg, respiratory rate 25 breaths/min, and SpO_2 92% on 2 L/min oxygen via nasal cannula. Which vital sign requires the RN to take action?

1. HR of 83 beats/min.
2. BP of 104/64 mm Hg.
3. Respiratory rate of 25 breaths/min.
4. SpO_2 92% of 2 L/min O_2 via nasal cannula.

Correct Answer: 3

Rationale

This respiratory rate is high, especially for a client on oxygen. The RN should take action on this finding. The other findings do not require immediate nursing attention.

Notes

Study Break Box—*cont'd*

2. A client is admitted with a 2-day history of cough, fever, and fatigue. The medical history is positive for type I diabetes and recent upper respiratory infection (URI). Vital signs are HR 109 beats/min, BP 102/58 mm Hg, respiratory rate 24 breaths/min, temperature 104°F (40°C), and SpO_2 92% on 2 L oxygen via nasal cannula. Which prescription has the highest priority in this client's care?

1. Initiate large-bore IV access.
2. Draw two sets of blood cultures.
3. Administer the ordered IV antibiotics.
4. Draw serum lactate and glucose levels.

Correct Answer: 2

Rationale

The top priority would be to draw two sets of blood cultures for this client with suspected sepsis. The pathogen needs to be identified to initiate treatment to eradicate the endotoxins. The other nursing interventions are not the priority.

3. A client with a history of uterine fibroids had a cesarean delivery 12 hours earlier and delivered healthy twins. At shift change, the RN assesses the client and notes shortness of breath, cool extremities, and oozing of blood from the incision site. Based on the client's presentation, which nursing action has the highest priority?

1. Assess the client's temperature.
2. Notify the health care provider.
3. Clean the blood from the incision site.
4. Draw labs for prothrombin time (PT), partial thromboplastin time (PTT), complete blood count (CBC), and fibrinogen.

Correct Answer: 2

Rationale

The client is in shock and showing signs of DIC. The client requires immediate attention from the health care provider. The other nursing interventions are not the priority.

Life Support

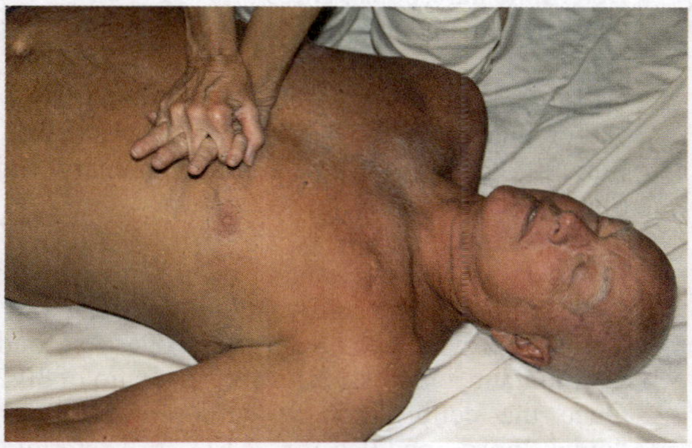

Proper hand placement for chest compressions. (Reprinted with permission from Cooper, K., & Gosnell, K. [2019]. *Foundations and adult health nursing* [8th ed.]. Elsevier.)

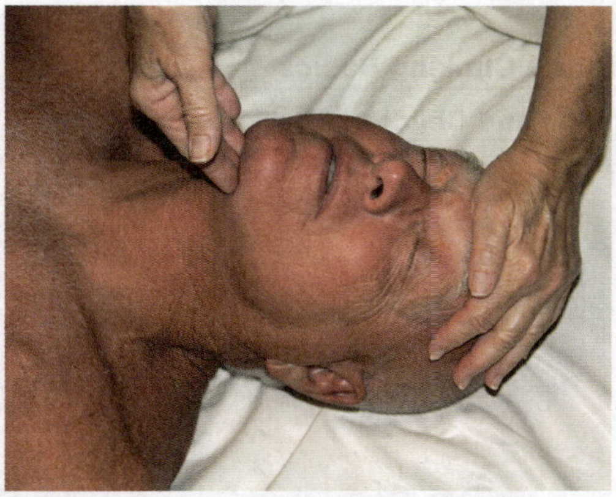

Head-tilt/chin-lift maneuver. (Reprinted with permission from Cooper, K., & Gosnell, K. [2019]. *Foundations and adult health nursing* [8th ed.]. Elsevier.)

- Cardiac arrest is the most common event requiring cardiopulmonary resuscitation (CPR).
- CAB: *C*hest compressions–*A*irway–*B*reathing
  - — High-quality chest compressions
  - — Push hard and push fast.
  - — Adult: 100 to 120 compressions/min

Notes

- **In-Hospital Cardiac Arrest**
  - — Determine unresponsiveness
  - — Activate emergency response or cardiac arrest team
  - — Call for an automated external defibrillator (AED) and/or emergency crash cart (do not leave client)
  - — Initiate CPR with Basic Cardiopulmonary Life Support (BCLS) guidelines
  - — Initiate compressions
    - After 30 compressions, open airway with head-tilt-chin lift and ventilate with bag-valve mask (provide two breaths, each over 1 second)
    - Maintain compressions-to-breaths ratio of 30:2
  - — Once the defibrillator or AED arrives, apply "quick-look" paddles or AED to determine whether defibrillation is necessary; defibrillate as indicated according to hospital policies and procedures
  - — Resume CPR

CPR and Choking Basics

Neonates and Children Ages 1 to 8

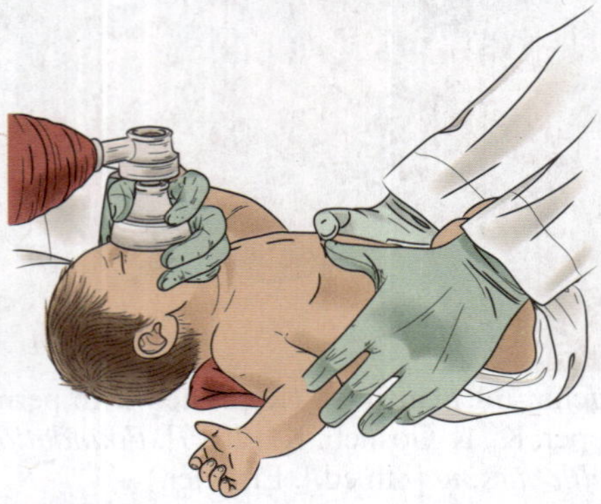

Position of fingers for proper compression technique for two-rescuer CPR in an infant. (Reprinted with permission from Cooper, K., & Gosnell, K. [2019]. *Foundations and adult health nursing* [8th ed.]. Elsevier.)

- Indications for CPR in children are different than those for adults.
  - — **Neonates and infants:** hypoxia, hypoglycemia, hypothermia, acidosis, hypercoagulability
  - — **Children:** respiratory arrest, prolonged hypoxemia secondary to respiratory insult or shock, including septic shock
- Guidelines vary based on the age of the child.
  - — If no response occurs, call a "code," or cardiac arrest, to initiate response of cardiac arrest team
  - — Obtain AED or emergency crash cart with defibrillator
- Guidelines vary based on the age of the child.
  - — Check for pulse
    - Infant aged <1 year: brachial pulse
    - Children aged 1 year to puberty: carotid or femoral
  - — Compressions (begin within 10 seconds)
    - *Infants*: Compressions cover one-third of the anterior/posterior diameter of the chest; depth is 1½ inches
    - *Children*: Compressions cover one-third of the anterior/posterior diameter of the chest; depth is 2 inches
    - *Compression-to-Breath Ratio*: For infants and children the ratio is 30:2 when only one rescuer is available. When two or more rescuers are available to assist with resuscitation, then the ratio changes to 15:2
  - — Deliver each breath over 1 second

Study Break Box

1. The RN finds a client slumped in a chair. Place the RN's actions in order of priority from first to last for this client.

1. Activate the code team and obtain defibrillator.
2. Assess unresponsiveness.
3. Assess the cardiac rhythm using the "quick-look" paddles.
4. Assess for a carotid pulse.
5. Open airway and give two rescue breaths by bag-valve mask.
6. Move the client to a flat position in bed or on the floor.
7. Begin compressions.

Correct Answer: The order in which actions would be performed according to BCLS guidelines is 2, 4, 1, 6, 7, 5, 3

Rationale

First determine the client's level of responsiveness, breathing adequacy and if there is a pulse present. Then initiate a call for help by activating code team. Then move the client to the floor so you can begin high quality chest compressions. You deliver 30 compressions followed by 2 breaths. Once the defibrillator arrives, you will check the rhythm using the quick-look paddles.

Disaster Management

- The nurse is an active team member in the event of biological, chemical, radioactive, mass trauma, and natural disasters.

Notes

- The nurse plays a role at all three levels of disaster management (primary, secondary, tertiary).
- Levels of prevention in disaster management:
  - Primary: planning, training, and educating personnel and the public

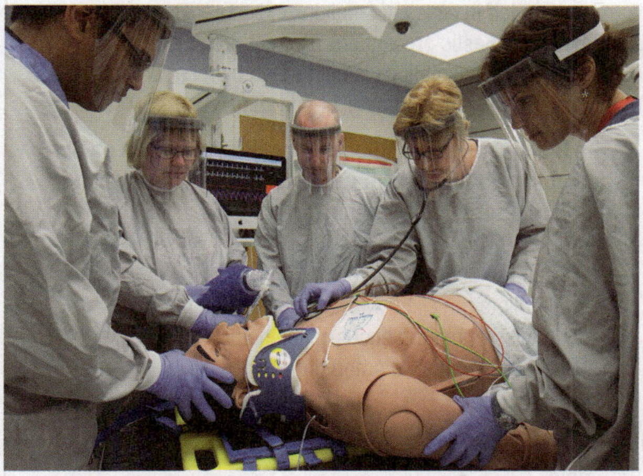

A trauma team participates in a realistic trauma resuscitation simulation. (Reprinted with permission from Ignatavicius, D. D., Workman, M. L., Rebar, C. R., & Heimgartner, N. M. [2021]. *Medical-Surgical Nursing: Concepts for Interprofessional Collaborative Care* [10th ed.]. Elsevier.)

  - Secondary: triage, treatment, shelter supervision
  - Tertiary: follow-up, recovery assistance, prevention of future disasters
- **Triage**
  - The goal of triage is to maximize the number of survivors by sorting the injured as treatable and untreatable, using the criteria of potential for survival and availability of resources
  - Color-coded system (in order of priority)
    - *Red*: life-threatening, need immediate intervention
    - *Yellow*: injuries with systemic effects and complications
    - *Green:* minor injuries, no systemic complications
    - *Black*: dying or deceased—catastrophic injuries
  - START (**S**imple **T**riage **A**nd **R**apid **T**reatment) method
  - Identify the walking wounded; move them to an area where they can be evaluated later.
  - Three-step evaluation of others, done one at a time:
    - Assess respirations
    - Assess circulation
    - Assess mental status

Study Break Box

1. Four clients arrive in the emergency department after an explosion. In which order should they be assessed? All options must be used.

1. A 70-year-old who is complaining of a pain level of 8/10 from a hand burn.
2. A 35-year-old with partial and full-thickness burns to the anterior and posterior chest.
3. A 25-year-old with a superficial burn to the right anterior arm and lateral chest.
4. A 42-year-old with a partial-thickness burn to the anterior lower extremity and confusion.

Correct Answer: The correct order is 2, 4, 1, 3

Rationale

Clients are assessed using the SMART method of triage.

2. The RN is assessing clients at the site of a community disaster. Using the color-code system for triage, which client would the RN tag with a red code?

1. A client with a large head injury that is bleeding, an open chest wound, cyanotic skin, no capillary refill, and agonal respirations.
2. A client with bruising and swelling of the right forearm, assorted lacerations to the face and neck, dry skin, normal capillary refill, and a respiratory rate of 18.
3. A client with scratches and scrapes to the head and face who is limping and helping other clients at the scene.
4. A client with an open wound to the abdomen, and a deformed right femur, pulse 125, delayed capillary refill, respiratory rate 32, who is moaning.

Correct Answer: 4

Rationale

A red tag would be assigned to the client with an open wound to the abdomen, and a deformed right femur, pulse 125, delayed capillary refill, respiratory rate 32, and who is moaning. The other clients are not the priority in a disaster situation.

Bioterrorism

- Review exposure information, assessment, findings, and treatment for various agents.
- Questions may deal with disasters and bioterrorism as they affect the individual victims, families, and the community.

Notes

Study Break Box

1. The RN is assigned to receive a client in the emergency department with suspected anthrax exposure predecontamination. Which transmission precautions would be most appropriate for the client? (Select all that apply.)

1. Airborne.
2. Contact.
3. Aplastic.
4. Droplet.
5. Standard.

Correct Answer(s): 1, 2, 5

Rationale

Since this client has not been decontaminated yet, health care providers would observe airborne, contact, and standard precautions. There is no such thing as aplastic precautions. Droplet precautions are not necessary because anthrax is not spread by respiratory droplets from a person talking, coughing, or sneezing.

2. The emergency department RN is assessing a client with a vesicular rash as a result of suspected smallpox exposure. Which transmission precautions would be most appropriate for this client? (Select all that apply.)

1. Airborne.
2. Contact.
3. Aplastic.
4. Droplet.
5. Standard.

Correct Answer(s): 1, 2, 5

Rationale

A combination of airborne, contact, and standard precautions is recommended in cases of smallpox exposure. There is no such thing as aplastic precautions. Droplet precautions are not necessary because smallpox is not spread by respiratory droplets from a person talking, coughing, or sneezing.

3. The RN is caring for a client in shock of unknown etiology and observes the rhythm below on the monitor. Which is the RN's priority intervention?

1. Check for a carotid pulse.
2. Defibrillate the client with 360 joules of energy.
3. Administer an intravenous saline bolus.
4. Give two breaths via Ambu bag.

Correct Answer: 1

Rationale

First assess the client by checking for a carotid pulse before performing an intervention. If no pulse is present, then the RN would follow BCLS guidelines. The other nursing interventions are not the priority.

Notes

Study Break Box—*cont'd*

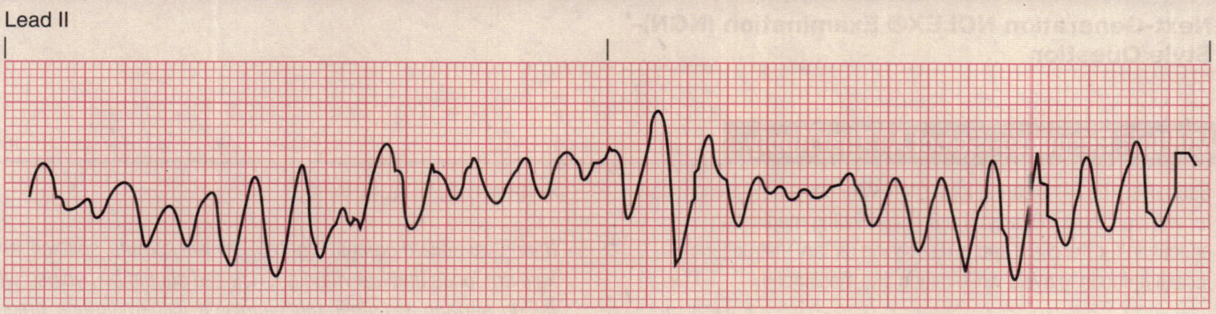

A

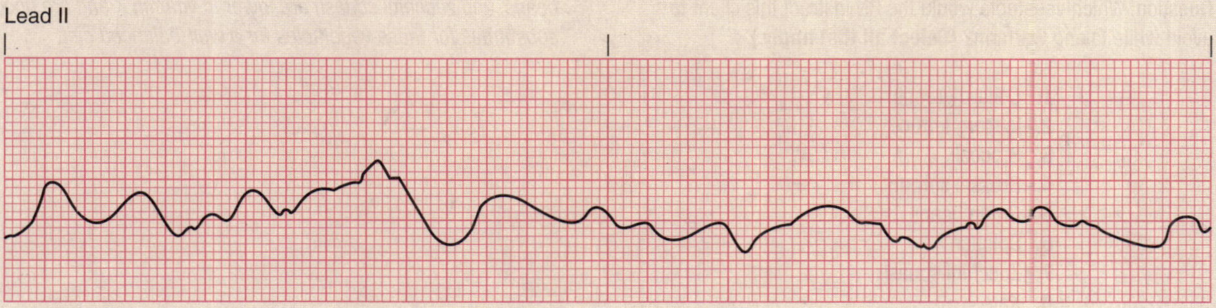

B

4. The RN admits a client with suspected early DIC. Which symptom would indicate early organ ischemia? (Select all that apply.)

1. Slight gingival bleeding.
2. Alterations in mental status.
3. Petechial hemorrhage to chest.
4. Slight decrease in urine output.
5. Bluish discoloration of fingertips.

Correct Answer(s): 2, 3, 4

Rationale

Alterations in mental status, petechial hemorrhage to chest, and slight decrease in urine output would indicate early signs of organ ischemia. Gingival bleeding and bluish discoloration of fingertips are results of the effects of DIC but are not related to organ ischemia.

Test-Taking Strategy

Reviewing food sources for specific nutrients can come in very handy while preparing for the NCLEX. Having a basic knowledge of foods that are rich in potassium, sodium, calcium, iron, and vitamins C, D and K is recommended for providing client nutrition education.

Notes

Next-Generation NCLEX® Examination (NGN)–Style Question

Multiple Response–Select All That Apply

Scenario: The RN is caring for a client who has a new prescription for warfarin 2 mg PO daily. The RN is providing medication education for the client and is discussing dietary instructions including foods to avoid while taking this medication.

Question: Which vegetable would the RN instruct this client to avoid while taking warfarin? **(Select all that apply.)**

1. Collard greens
2. Iceberg lettuce
3. Broccoli
4. Brussel sprouts
5. Green beans
6. Spinach
7. Zucchini squash
8. Kale

Answer: 1, 3, 4, 6, 8.

Rationale: Collard greens, broccoli, brussel sprouts, spinach, and kale are foods that are vitamin K rich and should be avoided while taking warfarin and other anticoagulants. Iceberg lettuce, green beans, and zucchini squash are lower in vitamin K and are good substitutes for these vegetables for a well-balanced diet.

Notes

Oxygenation, Ventilation, Transportation, and Perfusion

5

Chest Tubes and Water or Dry Seal Management

- Chest tubes are inserted into the pleural space to remove air/fluid and restore intrathoracic pressure, which allows the lung to reexpand.
- A chest collection drainage system has three compartments or chambers.
- **Collection Chamber**
  - — Air and fluid are collected from the pleural or mediastinal space
  - — Fluid remains, and air is vented to the second compartment, the water-seal chamber
- **Water-Seal Chamber**

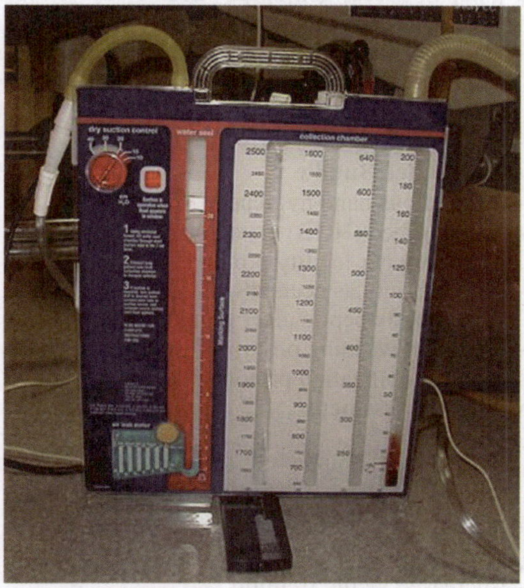

A commonly used disposable chest drainage system. (Reprinted with permission from Vincent, J.L., Abraham, E., Moore, F.A., Kochanek, P.M., & Fink, M.P. (2017). *Textbook of critical care* (7th ed.). Elsevier.)

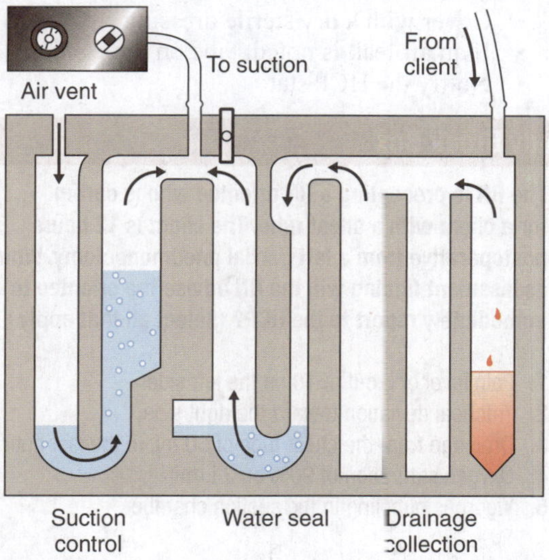

Diagram of chambers of water seal chest drainage. (Reprinted with permission from Ignatavicius, D. D., Workman, M. L., Rebar, C. R., & Heimgartner, N. M. [2021]. *Medical-Surgical Nursing: Concepts for Interprofessional Collaborative Care* [10th ed.]. Elsevier.)

  - — Contains 2 cm of water, which prevents backflow and acts as a one-way valve
  - — Fluctuations in the water level are known as tidaling; fluid should move upward with each inspiration and downward with each expiration
- **Suction Control Chamber**
  - — Water suction uses 20 cm of water to aid in draining air/fluid from the chest
  - — Dry suction provides an effective level of vacuum by continuously balancing the forces of suction control and atmosphere
- **Nursing and Collaborative Management**
  - — Check that water level is accurate at 2 cm every shift; add sterile water to the chamber if needed
  - — Keep the unit lower than the client's chest
  - — Keep the unit straight and all tubing loosely coiled below chest level, with all connections tight and taped
  - — Monitor the fluid drainage and mark the time of measurement and the fluid level; notify health care provider (HCP) if there is >70 mL/hr drainage

Notes

— Monitor respiratory effort and pain levels
— Assess for tidaling; observe for air bubbling in the water-seal chamber and fluctuations (tidaling)
— Replace the unit when collection chamber is full
— If the chest tube is accidentally dislodged, then:
  • Cover with a dry sterile dressing
  • If an air leak is noted, tape on three sides
  • Notify the HCP stat

Study Break Box

1. The RN is precepting a RN orientee who is caring for a client with a chest tube. The client is 12 hours postoperative from a left partial pneumonectomy. Which assessment finding will the RN advise the orientee to immediately report to the HCP? (Select all that apply.)

1. Pain level of 6 out of 10 on the left side.
2. Tracheal deviation toward the right side.
3. Drainage from the chest tube of 50 mL in the last hour.
4. Oxygen saturation of 90% on 2 L/min.
5. Vigorous bubbling in the suction chamber.

Correct Answer(s): 2, 4, 5

Rationale

The most common cause of tracheal deviation is a pneumothorax. Oxygen saturation should be at least 95%. Bubbling in the suction chamber should be gentle; vigorous bubbling could indicate an air leak. The other answer options do not reflect situations that require the RN to notify the HCP.

2. The RN palpates a crackling sensation around the insertion site of a chest tube in a client who has had thoracic surgery. Which action would the RN take?

1. Return the client to surgery.
2. Prepare for insertion of a larger chest tube.
3. Increase the water-seal suction pressure.
4. Continue to monitor the insertion site.

Correct Answer: 4

Rationale

Small amounts of subcutaneous emphysema (crackling sensation) after thoracic surgery are common and will be absorbed, causing no problem. The RN should continue to monitor the insertion site for worsening that includes swelling of the neck and chest. Other actions are not indicated at this time.

Pneumonia

- Inflammation of lung tissue, causing consolidation of exudate.
- **Etiology**
  — Bacterial (Gram-negative is the most severe), viral, fungal (rare), or aspiration
  — Community-acquired pneumonia (CAP) or hospital-acquired pneumonia (HAP)
  — Ventilator-associated pneumonia (VAP)
- **Risk Factors**
  — Age >65 years or residents in long-term care
  — Recent surgery (abdominal, thoracic)
  — Altered consciousness: alcoholism, head injury, seizures, smoking, splenic dysfunction, anesthesia, drug overdose, cerebrovascular accident (CVA)
  — Prolonged immobility
  — Immunosuppression
- **Prevention**
  — Pneumococcal conjugate vaccine for young children aged >2 years and adults aged ≥65 years
  — Pneumococcal polysaccharide (Pneumovac) for all adults aged ≥65 years and children aged ≥2 years at increased risk for pneumonia
  — Influenza vaccine yearly
- **VAP Practice Bundle**
  — Meticulous hand hygiene
  — Head of bed (HOB) elevation 30–45 degrees
  — Oral care per facility protocol
  — Suction only as needed with sterile technique
  — Use routine peptic ulcer prophylaxis
  — Sedation/weaning protocols
  — Early mobilization protocols
- **Nursing Assessment**
  — Tachypnea
  — Productive cough
  — Pleuritic pain
  — Fever of abrupt onset
  — Dyspnea
  — Increased tactile fremitus
  — Mental status changes
  — Crackles, decreased breath sounds
  — Dullness on percussion
  — Arterial blood gases (ABGs) indicative of hypoxemia
- **Nursing and Collaborative Management**
  — Hand washing to reduce cross-contamination
  — Blood and sputum cultures

Notes

— Isolation if prescribed
— Administer and encourage fluids if not contraindicated
— Administer antipyretics as ordered
— Administer empiric anti-infectives as prescribed.
— Manage pain
— Monitor O_2 saturation and administer humidified O_2 as appropriate
— Teach coughing, turning, and deep breathing techniques
— Encourage use of incentive spirometry
— Individualize rest and activity; mobility increases diaphragm movement, chest expansion, and secretion mobilization

- **Anti-infectives**
  - — **Penicillins**
    - semisynthetic penicillins
    - oxacillin
  - — **Antipseudomonal penicillins**
    - piperacillin sodium
  - — **Tetracyclines Aminoglycosides**
    - gentamycin (rarely used)
    - vancomycin
  - — **Cephalosporins**
    - ceftriaxone sodium
    - cefepime hydrochloride
  - — **Macrolides**
    - clarithromycin (Biaxin)
  - — **Fluoroquinolones**
    - ciprofloxacin (Cipro)

Study Break Box

1. A client who is 1 day postoperative after a left pneumonectomy is lying on his right side with the HOB elevated 10 degrees. The RN assesses his respiratory rate at 32 breaths/min. In what order would the RN perform the following actions?

1. Elevate the HOB.
2. Assist the client into the supine position.
3. Measure the client's O_2 saturation.
4. Administer intravenous (IV) PRN morphine.

Correct Answer: 3, 2, 1, 4

Rationale

The RN should measure the client's O_2 saturation, then assist the client into a supine position for repositioning and full lung expansion. After turning the client supine, elevate the HOB to help with breathing. Finally, the RN should administer IM morphine as needed.

2. The RN is orienting a graduate nurse (GN) caring for a client dependent on a ventilator. Which action by the GN demonstrates understanding of VAP care? (Select all that apply.)

1. Administers a proton pump inhibitor as prescribed.
2. Rinses the client's oral cavity with chlorhexidine every 2–4 hours.
3. Elevates the HOB 60 degrees.
4. Implements spontaneous breathing trial.
5. Performs hand hygiene before and after care.

Correct Answer: 1, 2, 4, 5

Rationale

VAP prevention guidelines recommend use of routine peptic ulcer prophylaxis such as proton pump inhibitors, oral care per facility protocols which may include chlorhexidine rinses, use of weaning protocols and spontaneous breathing trials, and meticulous hand hygiene before and after care. The HOB should be elevated 30–45 degrees, not 60 degrees

Notes

Chronic Airflow Limitation (CAL)

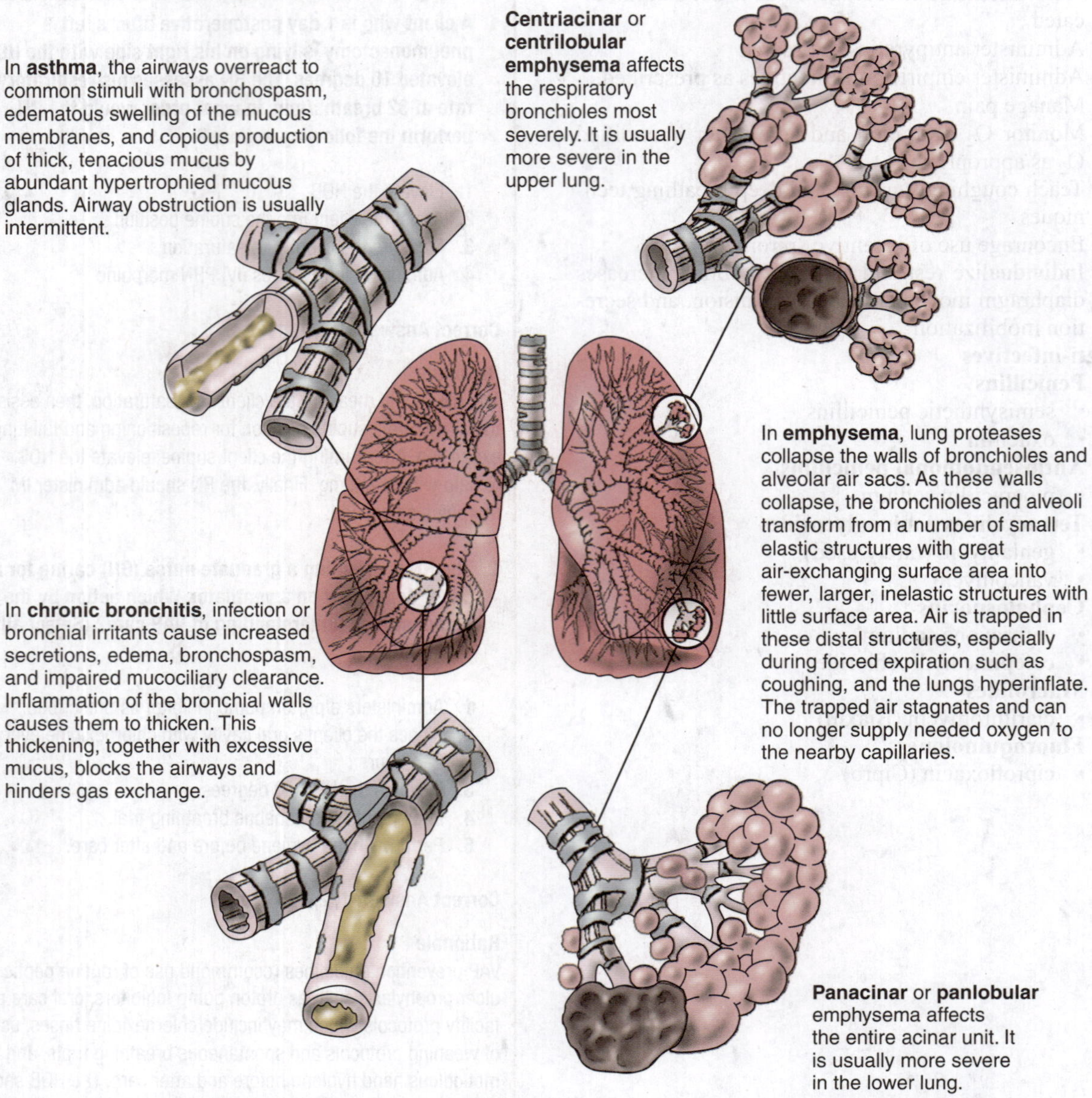

Causes of narrowed airways. (Reprinted with permission from Ignatavicius, D. D., Workman, M. L., Rebar, C. R., & Heimgartner, N. M. [2021]. *Medical-Surgical Nursing: Concepts for Interprofessional Collaborative Care* [10th ed.]. Elsevier.)

Notes

- **Asthma**
  - Reversible inflammatory airway disease
- **Chronic obstructive pulmonary disease (COPD)**
  - Chronic progressive disease
  - Emphysema
  - Chronic bronchitis
  - Etiology and Prescription Factors
    - Cigarette smoking
    - Environmental exposure
    - Occupational exposure
    - Genetic predisposition
- **Chronic Bronchitis: Pathophysiology**
  - Chronic sputum with cough production on a daily basis for a minimum of 3 months/year
  - Chronic hypoxemia/cor pulmonale
  - Increased mucus production
  - Increased bronchial wall thickness (obstructs air flow)
  - Exacerbations usually due to infection
  - Increased CO_2 retention/acidemia
  - Reduced responsiveness of respiratory center to hypoxemic stimuli
- **Emphysema**
  - Abnormal enlargement of the air spaces distal to the terminal alveolar walls
  - Increased dyspnea/work of breathing
    - Reduced gas exchange surface area
    - Increased air trapping (increased anterior-posterior diameter)
    - Decreased capillary network
    - Increased work/increased O_2 consumption
- **COPD: Nursing Assessment**
  - **Inspection**
    - Bronchitis
      - ☐ Right-sided heart failure (HF)
      - ☐ Cyanosis, distended neck veins
    - Emphysema
      - ☐ Pursed-lip breathing
      - ☐ Noncyanotic, thin
  - **Auscultation**
    - Bronchitis
      - ☐ Crackles
      - ☐ Rhonchi
      - ☐ Inspiratory/expiratory wheezes
    - Emphysema
      - ☐ Distant breath sounds
      - ☐ Diminished breath sounds
      - ☐ Wheezes
- **COPD: Nursing and Collaborative Management**
  - Keep SaO_2 to >90% during rest, sleep, and exertion, or the PaO_2 >60 mm Hg
  - Long-term continuous O_2 therapy (LTOT) more than 15 hours per day:
    - Increases survival, exercise tolerance, and improved mental status in clients with hypoxemia
    - Maintain infection control techniques
  - Monitor for signs and symptoms (S/S) of fluid overload
  - Baseline ABGs for CO_2 retainers
  - Teach the client pursed-lip breathing
  - Orthopneic position
  - Nutrition consult
  - Acute exacerbation management

Study Break Box

1. A client with pneumonia has impending respiratory failure. Which set of ABG values demonstrate acute respiratory failure?

1. pH–7.30 PCO_2–52 PO_2–56 HCO_3–26.
2. pH–7.35 PCO_2–44 PO_2–86 HCO_3–25.
3. pH–7.35 PCO_2–62 PO_2–66 HCO_3–31.
4. pH–7.30 PCO_2–39 PO_2–88 HCO_3–20.

Correct Answer: 1

Rationale

The findings for Option A reflect respiratory acidosis, indicating respiratory failure. The PO_2 is below normal the PCO_2 is high, indicating retention of acid; and the HCO_3 is normal. pH–7.35 PCO_2–44 PO_2–86 HCO_3–25 indicates a normal ABG finding. pH–7.35 PCO_2–62 PO_2–66 HCO_3–31 indicates compensated respiratory acidosis which would not be seen in acute respiratory failure. pH–7.30 PCO_2–39 PO_2–88 HCO_3–20 indicates metabolic acidosis.

Reactive Airway Disease

- **Asthma**
  - Reversible inflammatory disorder of the airways characterized by an exaggerated bronchoconstrictor response to a wide variety of stimuli
    - Allergens
    - Environmental irritants

Notes

- Cold air
- Exercise
- Beta-blockers
- Respiratory infection
- Emotional stress
- Reflux esophagitis

Drug Therapy for Asthma and COPD

- **Asthma Medication Goals**
  - Quick-relief medications
  - Long-term control medications
- **COPD Medication Goals**
  - Reduce exacerbations.
  - Long-acting beta-agonists
  - Intercostal space inhaled corticosteroids internal carotid stenosis (ICS)
- **Bronchodilators**
  - Short-acting inhaled β_2-adrenergic agonists
  - Long-acting inhaled β_2-adrenergic agonists
  - Long-acting oral β_2-adrenergic agonists
  - Anticholinergics (inhaled)
    - Ipratropium
    - Aclidinium bromide
- **β_2-Adrenergic Agonists**
  - **Inhaled: Short Acting**
    - metaproterenol: nebulizer, oral tablets, elixir, metered-dose inhaler (MDI)
    - Salbutamol sulfate: nebulizer, MDI, oral tablets
    - levalbuterol: nebulizer, MDI
    - terbutaline: oral tablets, nebulizer, subcutaneous, MDI
    - bitolterol: MDI, nebulizer
  - **Inhaled: Long Acting**
    - salmeterol xinafoate: dry powder inhaler (DPI)
    - formoterol fumarate: DPI
  - **Immediate Acting**
    - epinephrine hydrochloride: (1:1000) subcutaneous
- **Corticosteroids**

COPD: Assessment and Collaborative Management

- **Nursing Assessment**
  - Dyspnea, wheezing, chest tightness
  - Assess precipitating factors
  - Medication history
  - Determine need for ventilatory support
- **Collaborative Management**
  - Monitor levels of control of COPD symptoms.
  - Monitor respirations and assess breath sounds
  - Monitor oxygen saturation
  - Monitor mental status
  - Chest physiotherapy
  - Assess peripheral pulses and warmth and color of extremities
  - Position for maximum ventilation
  - Encourage slow, pursed-lip breathing
  - The efficacy of diaphragmatic breathing (DB) in rehab with COPD remains unclear
  - Administer humidified oxygen therapy
  - Nutritional therapy
  - Provide education on peak flow meter monitoring, importance of medication compliance, and trigger avoidance

Notes

Pulmonary Tuberculosis (TB)

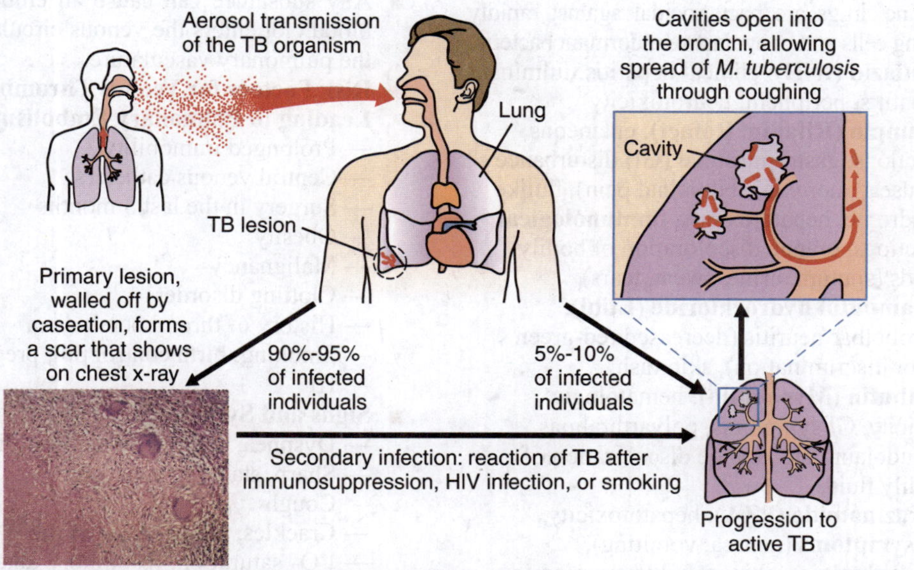

Primary TB infection with progression to secondary infection and active disease. *HIV,* Human immune deficiency virus; *M. tuberculosis, Mycobacterium tuberculosis; TB,* tuberculosis. (Illustration from Workman, M. L., & LaCharity, L. [2016]. Understanding pharmacology [2nd ed.]. St. Louis: Saunders; photo from Kumar, V., Abbas, A., & Aster, J. [2015]. *Robbins and Cotran pathologic basis for disease* [9th ed.]. Philadelphia: Saunders.)

- TB is a communicable disease caused by the *Mycobacterium tuberculosis* or the tubercle bacillus, an acid-fast organism, spread by airborne transmission.
- Primary infection (PBI)
  - — Bacteria inhaled
- Latent TB infection (LTBI)
- **Risk Factors**
  - — Immunocompromised states
  - — Multidrug-resistant TB
  - — Disproportionately in poor, underserved, and minorities
  - — Underserved working in institutions
- **Nursing Assessment and Collaborative Management**
  - — **Nursing Assessment**
    - Low-grade fever
    - Pallor
    - Chills
    - Night sweats
    - Easy fatigability
    - Anorexia
    - Weight loss
  - — **Nursing and Collaborative Management**
    - Diagnosis with Nucleic acid amplification test (NAAT), QuantiFERON-TB or purified protein derivative (PPD) (Mantoux test)
    - Notify local public health department.
    - Airborne precautions isolation
    - Single-occupancy room with negative pressure
    - High-efficiency particulate air (HEPA) masks
    - Sputum specimens
    - Teach the client to cover his or her nose and mouth with paper tissues whenever coughing, sneezing, or producing sputum
    - Emphasize careful hand washing after handling sputum and soiled tissues
    - If the client needs to be out of the negative-pressure room, he or she must wear a standard isolation mask to prevent exposure to others

Notes

- **TB Drugs and Side Effects**
  - **First-Line Drugs**
    - First-line drugs are bacteriocidal against rapidly dividing cells and/or against semidormant bacteria.
      - **isoniazid (INH)**: clinical hepatitis, fulminant hepatitis, peripheral neurotoxicity
      - **rifampin (Rifadin, Rofact)**: cutaneous reactions, gastrointestinal (GI) disturbance (nausea, anorexia, abdominal pain), flulike syndrome, hepatotoxicity, **immunological** reactions, orange discoloration of bodily fluids (sputum, urine, sweat, tears)
      - **ethambutol hydrochloride (Etibi)**: retrobulbar neuritis (decreased red-green color discrimination), skin rash
      - **rifabutin (Mycobutin)**: hematologic toxicity, GI symptoms, polyarthralgias, pseudojaundice, orange discoloration of bodily fluids
      - **pyrazinamide (PZA)**: hepatotoxicity, GI **symptoms** (nausea, vomiting), polyarthralgias, skin rash, hyperuricemia, dermatitis
  - **Managing Active TB**
    - 8 weeks with INH, rifampin, ethamutol, and PZA
    - Followed by 18 weeks of INH and rifampin

Study Break Box

1. The RN is preparing to administer a PPD test to a client who is entering nursing school. Which action is the RN's highest priority?

1. Prepare 0.1 mL solution for tuberculin syringe.
2. Assess the skin condition on the forearm.
3. Teach the client about positive findings.
4. Inquire about bacillus Calmette-Guérin (BCG) vaccine history.

Correct Answer: 4

Rationale

The highest priority is assessing for a history of BCG vaccine because administering a PPD to a client who has received the vaccine will be positive and result in a large reaction at the site. Those clients will need to have a chest x-ray (CXR) and avoid PPD screening for at least 10 years after administration. The other options are appropriate but not the highest priority.

Pulmonary Embolus

- Any substance can cause an embolism. Typically, a blood clot enters the venous circulation and lodges in the pulmonary vasculature.
- **Risk Factors for Venous Thromboembolism (VTE) Leading to Pulmonary Embolism (PE)**
  - Prolonged immobility
  - Central venous catheters
  - Surgery in the last 3 months
  - Obesity
  - Malignancy
  - Clotting disorders
  - History of thromboembolism
  - Smoking, birth control pill, pregnancy
  - HF
- **Signs and Symptoms**
  - Dyspnea, tachypnea, tachycardia
  - Sharp, stabbing chest pain
  - Cough
  - Crackles, pleural friction rub
  - ↓ O_2 saturation, respiratory alkalosis, then respiratory acidosis
  - Pleural friction rub
  - S_3 or S_4 heart sound
  - Feeling of impending doom
  - Low-grade fever
  - Hemoptysis
  - Hypoxemia
  - Elevated D-dimer level
  - Diagnosed by findings: spiral computed tomography (CT), transesophageal echocardiography (TEE), V/Q scan
- **Nursing and Collaborative Management**
  - **Prevention**
    - Range-of-motion exercises
    - Ambulate and turn
    - Avoid popliteal pressure
    - Use antiembolism and pneumatic compression stockings
    - Assess peripheral circulation
    - Administer prescribed prophylactic anticoagulant and antiplatelet drugs
    - Teach the client and family about precautions
    - Encourage the client to stop smoking and to exercise
  - **Acute Management**
    - Oxygen therapy
    - Monitor ABG and pulse oximetry
    - Check vital signs, lung sounds, and cardiac status.

Notes

- Embolectomy
- Inferior vena cava filtration with placement of a vena cava filter

— **High-Risk Medications**
- **Anticoagulants** are used to prevent embolus enlargement and the formation of new clots; use with caution with active bleeding, stroke, and recent trauma
- **Warfarin (Coumadin)** should be initiated within the first 3 days of heparinization and is continued for 3 to 6 months post-PE
- **Low-molecular-weight heparin** is usually used unless the PE is massive or occurs with hemodynamic instability
- Alteplase (Activase, Cathflo), fibrinolytic drugs
  - ◻ Therapeutic activated partial thromboplastin time (aPTT) values usually range from 1.5 to 2.5 times
- IV heparin for more severe cases
- Both heparin and fibrinolytic drugs are high-alert drugs

Hematologic Problems: Anemia and Its Many Causes

- ↓ Erythrocyte production
- ↓ Hemoglobin synthesis
- Iron deficiency
- Defective DNA synthesis
- B_{12} and folic acid deficiency
- ↓ Number of erythrocyte precursors
- Chronic diseases or disorders
- Chemotherapy
- Blood loss
- Blood vessel rupture
- Chronic gastritis
- Trauma
- Menorrhagia
- Hemorrhoids

Anemia

- **Nursing Assessment**
  - — Pallor, fatigue
  - — Exercise intolerance
  - — Tachycardia, dyspnea
  - — Complete blood count
  - — Assess for risk factors
  - — Diet low in iron, vitamin B_{12} deficiency, history of bleeding, medications taken
  - — Hemoglobin (Hbg) <10 g/dL (100 mmol/L), Hematocrit (Hct) <36%, red blood cell (RBC) <4 × 10^{12}/L
- **Nursing and Collaborative Management**
  - — Treatment of underlying pathology
  - — Folic acid for sickle cell
  - — Vitamin B_{12} for GI disorders, especially gastric bypass
  - — Epoetin alfa, iron for iron deficiency
  - — Administer blood products as prescribed
  - — Encourage diet high in iron-rich foods, folic acid, vitamin B_{12}, vitamin B_6, amino acids, and vitamin C
  - — Give parenteral iron via Z-track technique

Study Break Box

1. The charge nurse is planning client assignments for the unit. The collaborative care team consists of a registered nurse (RN), a practical nurse (PN), and an unlicensed assistive personnel (UAP). Which client would be assigned to the RN? (Select all that apply.)

1. A client awaiting a blood transfusion for GI bleeding with a Hgb 7.0 mg/dL (70 g/L).
2. A client with pernicious anemia who is awaiting vitamin B_{12} injection.
3. A client with resolving sickle cell crisis awaiting IV fluid conversion to saline lock.
4. A client with a pressure ulcer who has been prescribed negative pressure wound (vacuum-assisted closure [VAC]) care.
5. A client who received two blood transfusions yesterday and is awaiting morning care.

Correct Answer(s): 1, 3

Rationale

The only client in this list that must be assigned to the RN is the client awaiting a blood transfusion for GI bleeding with a Hgb 7.0 mg/dL (70 g/L). An RN must initiate a blood transfusion and observe the client for S/S of transfusion reaction. A PN can assist with ongoing assessment of the client after the transfusion has been initiated by the RN. A PN can be assigned to administer the B_{12} injection, converting the Intravenous fluids (IVFs) to a saline lock, and manage the client with the wound VAC. The UAP can provide morning care to the client who had previously received blood transfusions.

Notes

Blood Transfusions

- **Blood Groups and Types**
  - — ABO system includes A, B, O, and AB blood types
  - — Rh factor is an antigenic substance in the erythrocytes
  - — If blood is mismatched during transfusion, a transfusion reaction occurs
    - Transfusion reaction is an antigen-antibody reaction
    - It can range from a mild response to severe anaphylactic shock
- **Types of Reactions**
  - — Acute hemolytic, febrile, nonhemolytic (most common), mild allergic, anaphylactic, delayed hemolytic
- **Nursing and Collaborative Management**
  - — Perform assessment before, during, and after, including the IV site
  - — Determine two identifiers
  - — Confirm informed consent
  - — Identify the compatibility
  - — Initiate a transfusion slowly, then maintain the infusion rate
- **Types of Blood Products**
  - — RBCs
    - Packed RBCs (PRBCs)
    - Autologous PRBCs
    - Washed RBCs
    - Frozen RBCs
    - Leukocyte-poor RBCs
  - — Other cellular components
    - Platelets
    - Granulocytes
  - — Plasma components
    - Fresh frozen plasma (FFP)
    - Cryoprecipitate

Study Break Box

1. A client who is receiving a transfusion of packed red blood cells has an inflamed IV site. Which action would the RN take?

1. Double-check the blood type of the transfusing unit of blood with another nurse.
2. Discontinue the transfusion and send the remaining blood and tubing to the lab.
3. Immediately start a new IV at another site and resume the transfusion at the new site.
4. Continue to monitor the site for signs of infection and notify the HCP.

Correct Answer: 3

Rationale

The RN would immediately start a new IV at another site and resume the transfusion at the new site. This is not a sign of a transfusion reaction but rather phlebitis. If the client remains free of S/S of a transfusion reaction, the transfusion should be continued. However, the previous site should be monitored for signs of infection and reported per facility policy. The other interventions should be completed if a transfusion reaction is suspected.

Hypertension (HTN)

- Persistent blood pressure (BP) elevation >140/90 mm Hg
- **Risk Factors**
  - — Nonmodifiable: family history, gender, age, ethnicity
  - — Modifiable: use of alcohol, tobacco, caffeine; sedentary lifestyle; obesity
- **Medications**
  - — Diuretics, antihypertensives, angiotensin-converting enzyme (ACE) inhibitors, calcium channel blockers
- **HTN Education**
  - — The number 1 cause of stroke (CVA, brain attack) is nonadherence to HTN medications

Notes

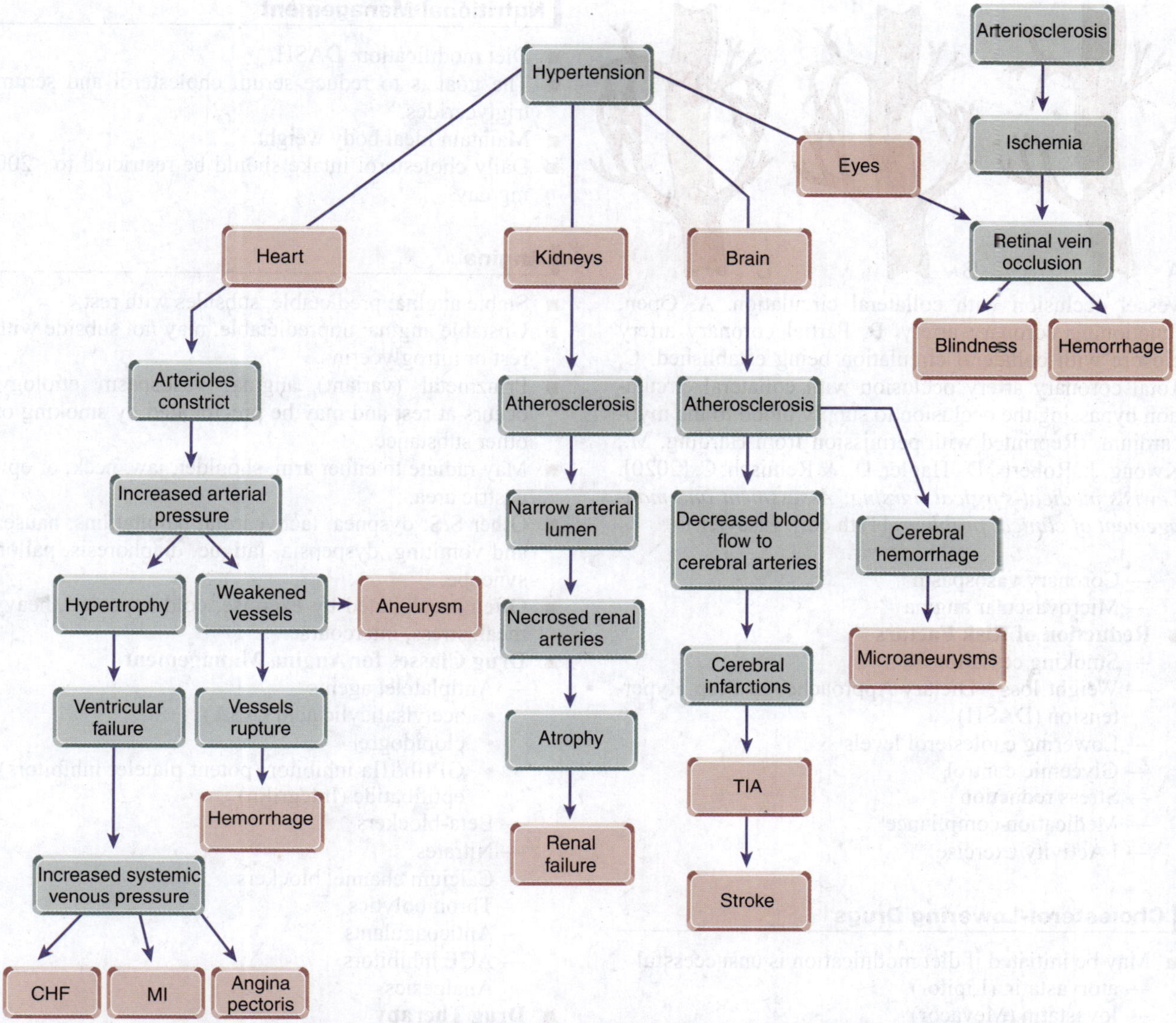

How hypertension affects major target organs. *CHF,* Congestive heart failure; *MI,* myocardial infarction; *TIA,* transient ischemic attack. (Reprinted with permission from Monahan, F.D., Drake, D.T., Neighbors, M. [eds.]. [1998]. *Medical-surgical nursing: foundations for clinical practice* [2nd ed.]. Philadelphia: Saunders.)

Coronary Artery Disease (CAD)

- CAD is one of the leading causes of morbidity and mortality in the United States and Canada.
- CAD results in ischemia and infarction of myocardial tissue.
- LAD (left anterior descending artery) is most commonly affected.
- Diagnostic: Highly sensitive C-reactive protein (hsCRP)
- **Prevalent Etiologies of CAD**
  — Atherosclerosis: partially or completely blocked coronary arteries

Notes

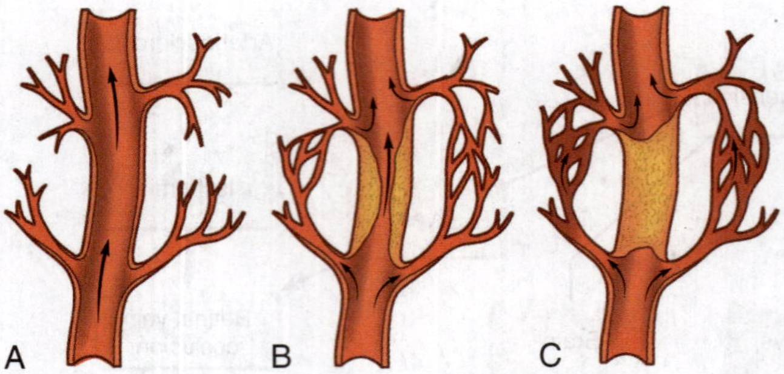

Vessel occlusion with collateral circulation. A, Open, functioning coronary artery. B, Partial coronary artery closure with collateral circulation being established. C, Total coronary artery occlusion with collateral circulation bypassing the occlusion to supply blood to the myocardium. (Reprinted with permission from Harding, M., Kwong, J., Roberts, D., Hagler, D., & Reinisch, C. [2020]. *Lewis's medical-surgical nursing: Assessment and management of clinical problems* [11th ed.]. Elsevier.)

- — Coronary vasospasm
- — Microvascular angina

- **Reduction of Risk Factors**
  - — Smoking cessation
  - — Weight loss—Dietary Approaches to Stop Hypertension (DASH)
  - — Lowering cholesterol levels
  - — Glycemic control
  - — Stress reduction
  - — Medication compliance
  - — ↑ Activity/exercise

Cholesterol-Lowering Drugs

- May be initiated if diet modification is unsuccessful
  - — atorvastatin (Lipitor)
  - — lovastatin (Mevacor)
  - — pravastatin (Pravachol)
  - — rosuvastatin (Crestor)
  - — simvastatin (Zocor)
  - — ezetemibe (Ezetrol)
  - — gemfibrozil (Lopid)
  - — niacin (nicotinic acid)
- Risk of statin medications: Rhabdomyolysis = medical emergency.

Nutritional Management

- Diet modification: DASH.
- The goal is to reduce serum cholesterol and serum triglycerides.
- Maintain ideal body weight.
- Daily cholesterol intake should be restricted to <200 mg/day.

Angina

- Stable angina: predictable, subsides with rest.
- Unstable angina: unpredictable, may not subside with rest or nitroglycerin.
- Prinzmetal (variant) angina: vasospasm etiology, occurs at rest and may be precipitated by smoking or other substance.
- May radiate to either arm, shoulder, jaw, neck, or epigastric area.
- Other S/S: dyspnea, tachycardia, palpitations, nausea and vomiting, dyspepsia, fatigue, diaphoresis, pallor, syncope.
- Often precipitated by exercise, cold exposure, heavy meal, stress, intercourse.
- **Drug Classes for Angina Management**
  - — Antiplatelet agents
    - acetylsalicylic acid (ASA)
    - clopidogrel
    - GPIIb/IIIa inhibitor (potent platelet inhibitors): eptifibatide (Integrilin)
  - — Beta-blockers
  - — Nitrates
  - — Calcium channel blockers
  - — Thrombolytics
  - — Anticoagulants
  - — ACE inhibitors
  - — Analgesics
- **Drug Therapy**
  - — Oxygen
    - Administer oxygen (4–6 L/min via nasal cannula) and titrate as appropriate to assist in oxygenating myocardial tissue, especially in clients who are high risk, in respiratory distress, or hypoxic
  - — Nitroglycerin
    - Dilates the coronary arteries
    - ↑ Blood flow to the damaged area of myocardium

Notes

— Dose: 0.4 mg/tablet
— One tablet sublingual every 5 minutes × 3 doses
— Morphine Sulfate
- Analgesic; ↓ anxiety; ↓ tachypnea; relaxes bronchial smooth muscle; improves gas exchange

— Beta-Blockers
- ↓ Heart rate; ↓workload of heart; ↓ oxygen demand of myocardium

— Calcium Channel Blockers
- ↓ Conduction through atrioventricular (AV) node; slow heart rate; ↓ oxygen demand by myocardium

— Thrombolytic Therapy (within protocol guidelines)
- Useful when infarction is diagnosed early; streptokinase and tissue plasminogen activator (tPA); administered IV
- Most effective if given within 6 hours of onset of chest pain; heparin therapy will usually follow thrombolytic therapy

- **Medical Interventions**
  — Percutaneous transluminal coronary angioplasty (PTCA)
  — Balloon angioplasty
  — Intracoronary stents
  — Coronary artery bypass graft (CABG)

Acute Myocardial Infarction (MI)

- Destruction of myocardial tissue due to lack of blood and oxygen supply.
- Begins with occlusion of the coronary artery.
- Ischemia, injury, infarction.
- ST-elevation MI (STEMI) (traditional MI).
- Non-STEMI (common in women).

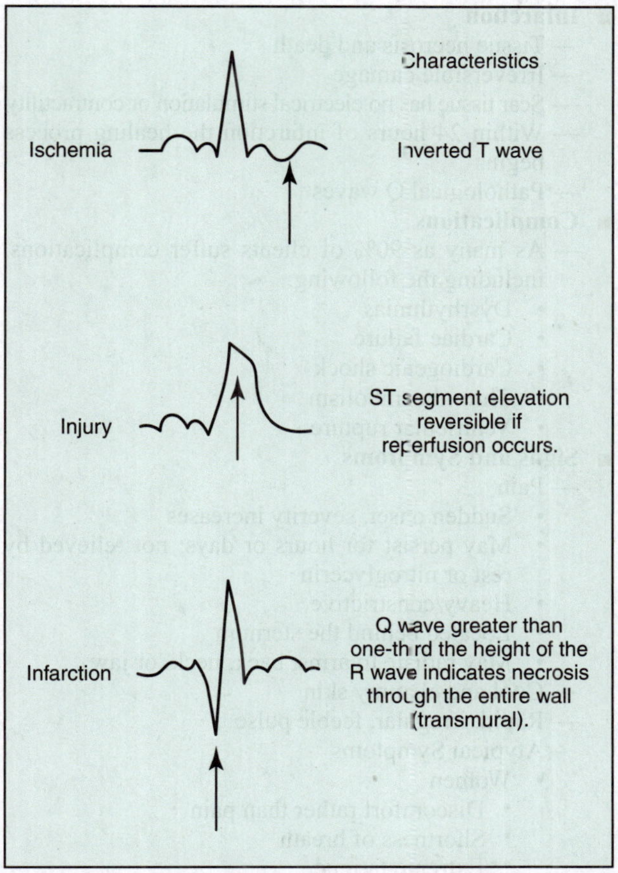

Electrocardiographic changes with myocardial infarction. (Reprinted with permission from Linton, A. D., & Matteson, M. A. [2020]. *Medical-Surgical Nursing* [7th ed.]. Elsevier.)

- **Ischemia**
  — Results from reduced blood flow and oxygen to the coronary arteries
  — If not reversed, then injury occurs
  — Ischemia lasting 20 minutes or more is sufficient to produce irreversible tissue damage
  — T wave inversion on electrocardiogram (ECG)
- **Injury**
  — Prolonged interruption of oxygen supply and nutrients
  — Cells are still salvageable
  — ST elevation

Notes

- **Infarction**
  - Tissue necrosis and death
  - Irreversible damage
  - Scar tissue has no electrical stimulation or contractility
  - Within 24 hours of infarction the healing process begins
  - Pathological Q waves
- **Complications**
  - As many as 90% of clients suffer complications, including the following:
    - Dysrhythmias
    - Cardiac failure
    - Cardiogenic shock
    - Thromboembolism
    - Ventricular rupture
- **Signs and Symptoms**
  - Pain
    - Sudden onset; severity increases
    - May persist for hours or days; not relieved by rest or nitroglycerin
    - Heavy/constrictive
    - Located behind the sternum
    - May radiate to arms, back, neck, or jaw
  - Cool and clammy skin
  - Rapid, irregular, feeble pulse
  - Atypical Symptoms
    - Women
      - Discomfort rather than pain
      - Shortness of breath
      - Extreme fatigue
    - Clients with Diabetes
      - Asymptomatic
      - Neuropathy
      - Dyspnea
    - Elderly Clients
      - Confusion/delirium
      - Dizziness
      - Shortness of breath
- **Medical Diagnosis**
  - ECG (12-lead)
  - Confirm by Biomarkers
    - Troponin
    - Myoglobin
    - Cardiac enzymes
- **Cardiac Lab Tests**
  - Troponin
    - Found only in cardiac muscle
    - May present as early as 1 hour after injury
    - Peaks within 24 hours
    - Returns to normal in 5 to 14 days
  - Myoglobin
    - Released 1 hour after an acute MI
    - Rises before creatine kinase-MB levels
    - Returns to normal within 24 hours
- **Treatment: Preserve Myocardial Tissue**
  - The overall goal is to preserve myocardial tissue within 90 minutes of arrival to the health care facility with the following:
    - Drug therapy
      - Oxygen
      - Nitroglycerin
      - Beta-blockers
      - Morphine
    - Thrombolytic therapy via catheterization
    - Percutaneous coronary intervention (PCI) and stents within 90 minutes of presentation for care
    - If PCI unavailable, risk versus benefit of intravenous thrombolytic therapy is completed
    - CABG
    - Severe CAD detected
    - Can be emergent or elective

Heart Failure

- **Etiology**
  - CAD, prior MI
  - Chronic HTN
  - Cardiomyopathy
  - Dilated, idiopathic
  - Hyperthyroidism
  - Diabetes
  - Valvular and congenital heart disease
  - Pulmonary diseases
- **Left-sided Heart Failure (LHF)**
  - **Causes**: left ventricular (LV) infarct, cardiomyopathy, hypertension
  - **Symptoms**: dyspnea, cough, orthopnea, pulmonary edema, paroxysmal nocturnal dyspnea
  - **Signs:** S_3 gallop, tachycardia, inspiratory rales
  - **Laboratory findings**: ABGs reveal hypoxemia, CXR shows pulmonary edema or pleural effusions, ↑ B-type natriuretic peptide (BNP) >500 ng/mL
- **Right-sided Heart Failure (RHF)**
  - **Causes:** LHF, right ventricular (RV) infarct, pulmonary or tricuspid valve disease, pulmonary HTN, COPD, PE
  - **Symptoms**: Systemic congestion, dyspnea on exertion, fatigue, weight gain, fluid retention

Notes

- **Signs**: ↑ central venous pressure (CVP), jugular venous distention (JVD) >3 to 4 cm, hepatomegaly, ascites, peripheral or sacral edema, and pleural and pericardial effusions

■ **Right HF Laboratory Tests**
- **Sodium and Volume Homeostasis**
  - As cardiac output decreases, renal perfusion decreases, activating the renin-angiotensin-aldosterone system (RAAS), causing fluid retention
- **Laboratory Tests**
  - Liver function shows hepatic congestion
  - Increased liver enzymes, increased PT and international normalized ratio (INR)
  - Hyponatremia (fluid restriction only if Na^+ is <132 mEq/L)
  - Increased blood urea nitrogen (BUN)/creatinine = decreased renal perfusion

■ **Pharmacological Management**
- ACE inhibitors
- Diuretics
- Inotropes
- Phosphodiesterase inhibitors
- Natriuretic peptides
- Beta-blockers
- Angiotensin II receptor blockers (ARBs)
- Vasodilators
- Dopamine agonist
- Anticoagulants/antiplatelets/aspirin

■ **Nursing and Collaborative Management**
- Administer oxygen as prescribed
- Reposition and perform coughing, deep breathing exercises every 2 hours
- Limit sodium intake
- Fluid restriction only if Na^+ <132 mmol/L (mEq/L)
- Avoid excessive fluid intake
- Avoid alcohol—depresses myocardial contractility
- With CAD, low cholesterol, low fat, low Na^+
- Educate on signs of worsening condition such as weight gain 1.36 kg (3 lb) weekly or 0.45 to 0.9 kg (1–2 lb) overnight; increasing dyspnea on exertion (DOE), orthopnea, or paroxysmal nocturnal dyspnea (PND)
- Regular exercise is strongly encouraged—improves the function of skeletal muscle more than changes in myocardial function

Study Break Box

1. The RN is administering 0900 medications to three clients on a telemetry unit when the UAP reports that another client is complaining of a sudden onset of substernal discomfort. Which action would the RN take?

1. Ask the UAP to obtain the client's vital signs.
2. Assess the client's discomfort.
3. Advise the client to rest in bed.
4. Observe the client's ECG pattern.

Correct Answer: 2

Rationale

A client with a complaint of sudden onset of substernal discomfort must be assessed immediately by the RN. All other interventions listed are inappropriate for this client.

2. A client with a history of coronary heart disease was admitted to the acute care unit 2 days ago for management of angina. During the assessment, the client states, "I feel like I have indigestion." In which order would the RN implement care? (Arrange from first action to last.)

1. Notify the rapid response team.
2. Administer PRN nitroglycerin prescription.
3. Assess the pulse, respirations, BP, and oxygen saturation.
4. Document assessment in the electronic medical record.
5. Provide 2 L of oxygen via nasal cannula.

Correct Answer: 3, 5, 2, 1, 4

Rationale

For emergency care of the client with chest pain, it is important to quickly gather vital signs, provide O_2, administer nitroglycerin, notify the rapid response team, and finally, document: 3, 5, 4, 2, 1, 4.

Notes

Study Break Box—*cont'd*

3. For which dysrhythmia would the RN implement defibrillation? (Select all that apply.)

1. Asystole.
2. Pulseless electrical activity.
3. Ventricular fibrillation.
4. Pulseless ventricular tachycardia.
5. Ventricular tachycardia.
6. Atrial fibrillation.

Correct Answer(s): 3, 4

Rationale

Ventricular fibrillation and pulseless ventricular tachycardia are life-threatening rhythms that require defibrillation. Stable ventricular tachycardia can be treated with medication or cardioversion. The other rhythms do not require defibrillation.

4. The RN is caring for a client when the client suddenly becomes unconscious. The RN identifies the following rhythm on the monitor. Which action is the highest priority?

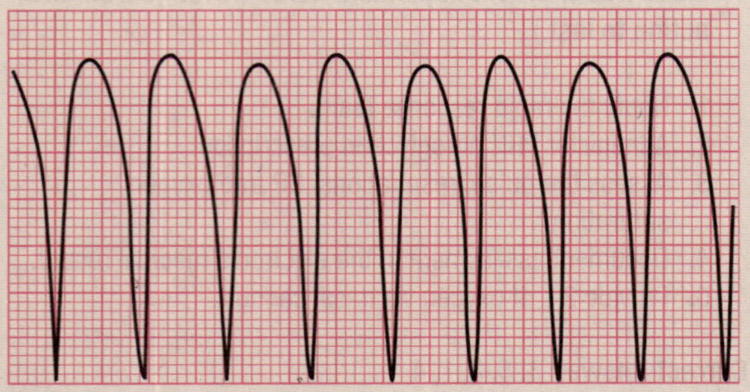

(Reprinted with permission from Harding, M., Kwong, J., Roberts, D., Hagler, D., & Reinisch, C. (2020). *Lewis's medical-surgical nursing: Assessment and management of clinical problems* (11th ed.). Elsevier)

1. Check for a carotid pulse.
2. Begin chest compressions.
3. Administer epinephrine 1:10,000 IV.
4. Initiate bag-valve mask ventilations.

Correct Answer: 1

Rationale

Per Basic Cardiopulmonary Life Support (BCLS) guidelines, when a person is found to be unconscious, the first step the RN would take is to assess for responsiveness and checking for a carotid pulse. This action is the highest priority at this time. Then the RN would proceed with the subsequent steps in the BCLS guidelines.

Dysrhythmias: Interpretation and Management

- Standard ECG uses 12 leads
  - — Provides best overall evaluation
- Telemetry
  - — Usually three leads show one view of the heart
- Holter monitor
  - — Usually worn for 24-hour continuous reading
- Client may be asymptomatic until cardiac output is altered.
- Client may complain of palpitations, syncope, pain, dyspnea, and diaphoresis.
- Changes in pulse rate/rhythm and ECG will be seen.
- Always treat the client and **NOT** the monitor!

Notes

Electrocardiogram (ECG)

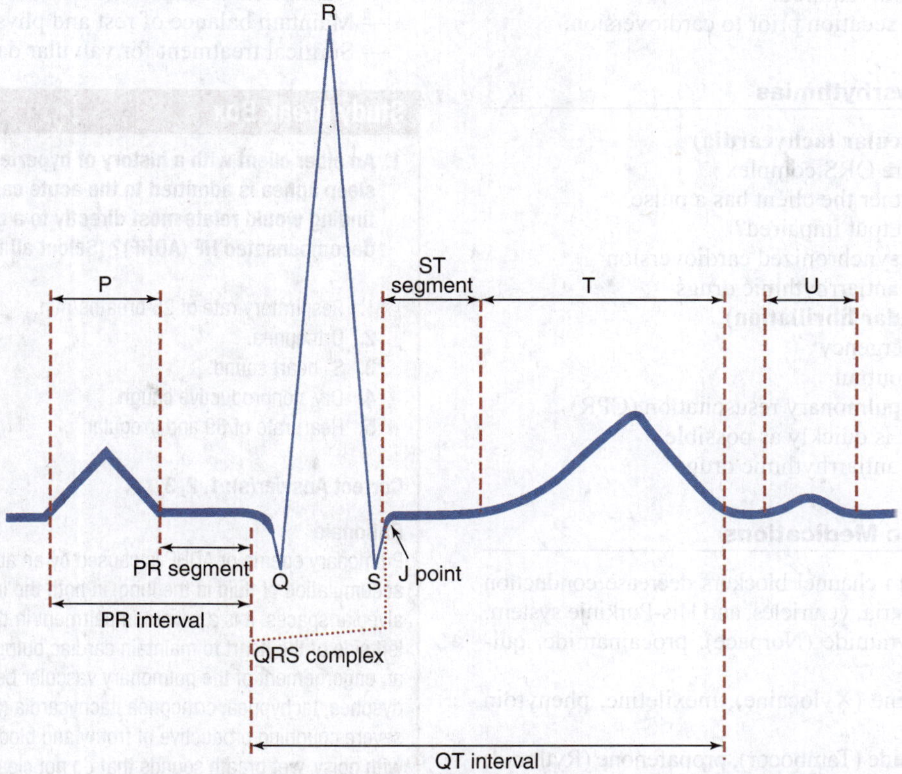

Components of a normal electrocardiogram. (Modified with permission from Ignatavicius, D. D., Workman, M. L., Rebar, C. R., & Heimgartner, N. M. [2021]. *Medical-Surgical Nursing: Concepts for Interprofessional Collaborative Care* [10th ed.]. Elsevier.

- **P wave**
  - Atrial depolarization
- **QRS complex**
  - Ventricular depolarization
  - Normal <0.11 second
- **ST segment**
  - Early ventricular repolarization
- **T wave**
  - Ventricular repolarization
- **PR interval**
  - Time for impulse to travel through the sinoatrial (SA) node
  - Normal: 0.12 to 0.2 second
- **R-R interval**
  - Measure the regularity of heartbeat

Atrial Dysrhythmias

- **A-fib (atrial fibrillation)**
  - Chaotic activity in the AV node
  - No true P waves visible
  - Irregular R-R intervals
  - Risk for CVA
  - Anticoagulant therapy is necessary
- **Atrial Flutter**
  - Sawtoothed waveform (F waves)
  - Regular/irregular R-R interval
  - Fluttering in the chest
  - Ventricular rhythm regular
- Cardioversion may be used for either.
- Focus is on rate control.

Notes

- If onset is >48 hours, then Transesophageal echocardiogram (TEE) is required.
- Always ensure sedation prior to cardioversion.

Ventricular Dysrhythmias

- **V-tach (ventricular tachycardia)**
  - Wide, bizarre QRS complex
  - Assess whether the client has a pulse
  - Is cardiac output impaired?
  - Prepare for synchronized cardioversion
  - Administer antiarrhythmic drugs
- **V-fib (ventricular fibrillation)**
  - Cardiac emergency
  - No cardiac output
  - Start cardiopulmonary resuscitation (CPR)
  - Defibrillate as quickly as possible
  - Administer antiarrhythmic drugs

Antiarrhythmic Medications

- **Class I:** Sodium channel blockers decrease conduction velocity in the atria, ventricles, and His-Purkinje system.
  - **IA**—disopyramide (Norpace), procainamide, quinidine
  - **IB**—lidocaine (Xylocaine), mexiletine, phenytoin (Dilantin)
  - **IC**—flecainide (Tambocor), propafenone (Rythmol)
  - **Other**—moricizine
- **Class II:** Beta-adrenergic blockers decrease automaticity of the SA node, decrease conduction velocity in AV node.
  - acebutolol, atenolol (Tenormin), metoprolol (Lopressor)
- **Class III:** Potassium channel blockers delay repolarization.
  - amiodarone, dofetilide (Tikosyn), sotalol (Betapace)
- **Class IV:** Calcium channel blockers decrease automaticity of SA node, delay AV node conduction.
  - diltiazem (Cardizem), verapamil (Calan)

Inflammatory Heart Disease

- **Endocarditis**
  - **Signs/symptoms:** fever, positive blood cultures, murmur, hemorrhages, HF symptoms, often with IV drug abuse
  - Infective endocarditis can lead to damaged heart valves
  - Assess for right- or left-sided HF
  - Administer IV antibiotics for 4 to 6 weeks
  - Maintain balance of rest and physical activity
  - Surgical treatment for valvular damage

Study Break Box

1. An older client with a history of hypertension, HF, and sleep apnea is admitted to the acute care unit. Which finding would relate most directly to a diagnosis of acute decompensated HF (ADHF)? (Select all that apply.)

1. Respiratory rate of 25 breaths/min.
2. Orthopnea.
3. S_3 heart sound.
4. Dry, nonproductive cough.
5. Heart rate of 69 and irregular.

Correct Answer(s): 1, 2, 3

Rationale

Pulmonary edema or ADHF is caused by an abnormal accumulation of fluid in the lung, in both the interstitial and alveolar spaces. It is a severe impairment in the ability of the left side of the heart to maintain cardiac output, thereby causing an engorgement of the pulmonary vascular bed, leading to dyspnea, tachypnea, orthopnea, tachycardia (S_3, S_4 gallop), and severe coughing productive of frothy and blood-tinged sputum with noisy, wet breath sounds that do not clear with coughing. A dry, nonproductive cough and heart rate of 69 beats/min and irregular are not characteristics of ADHF.

  - Teach clients to request prophylactic antibiotics for every invasive procedure (dental included)
- **Pericarditis**
  - **Signs/symptoms:** pain—hurts more with deep breaths or supine, pericardial friction rubs
  - Monitor for ST-segment elevation
  - Monitor hemodynamic status
  - Facilitate a leaning-over position and nonsteroidal anti-inflammatory drugs (NSAIDs) for pain control measures

Valvular Heart Disease

- **Valves may be unable to:**
  - Fully open (stenosis)
  - Fully close (insufficiency or regurgitation)

Notes

- **Causes**
  - Rheumatic fever
  - Congenital heart disease
  - Syphilis
  - Endocarditis
  - Hypertension
- **Mitral Valve Stenosis**
  - Early period: may have no symptoms
  - Later: excessive fatigue, dyspnea on exertion, orthopnea, dry cough, hemoptysis, or pulmonary edema
  - Rumbling apical diastolic murmur and a-fib are common
- **Nursing and Collaborative Management**
  - HF care
  - Monitor for a-fib with thrombus formation
  - Prophylactic antibiotic therapy before any invasive procedures (dental, surgical, childbirth)
  - May require surgical repair or valve replacement
  - Teach that there may not be a need for lifelong anti-coagulant therapy if valve replacement done

Study Break Box

1. The RN has just received report on four clients. Which client would the RN assess first?

1. A client with pericarditis with pain relieved by leaning forward.
2. A client with fractured ribs with pain reported at 6/10 on a 1 to 10 scale.
3. A client with stable angina who is awaiting discharge instructions.
4. A client with HF who needs transporting for an echocardiogram.

Correct Answer: 1

Rationale

Pain is sometimes alleviated by leaning forward, but it requires further assessment because this also is symptomatic of cardiac tamponade. Pain is to be expected with a rib fractures. A client with stable angina who is awaiting discharge does not require immediate attention. A client with HF who needs transporting for an echocardiogram does not require immediate attention.

Vascular Disorders

- **Arterial**
  - Smooth, shiny skin
  - Pallor on elevation
  - Weak peripheral pulses
  - Sharp or tingling pain
  - Cool to touch
  - Intermittent claudication
  - Painful, nonedematous ulcers
  - Bruits
- **Venous**
  - Monitor for history of deep vein thrombosis.
  - Bluish-purple skin discoloration
  - Normal peripheral pulses
  - Warm to touch
  - Slightly painful ulcers with marked edema
  - Capillary refill <3 seconds
  - Pruritus
- **Nursing and Collaborative Management**
  - **General**
    - Encourage smoking cessation
    - Encourage regular exercise
    - Achieve or maintain ideal body weight
    - Follow DASH diet
    - Tight glycemic control in diabetes
    - Tight BP control
    - Treatment of hyperlipidemia and hypertriglyceridemia
    - ACE (angiotensin converting enzyme inhibitors) **or** ARBs (angiotensin-receptor blockers)
  - **Arterial**
    - Bed rest
    - Keep extremity below the level of the heart
    - Topical antibiotics
    - Antiplatelet agent (clopidogrel)
    - Surgical grafting intervention
  - **Venous**
    - Wound care
    - Diet that promotes wound healing; zinc and vitamins A and C
    - Compression stockings day and evening
    - Teach the client to elevate the legs (at least 20 minutes, four to five times daily)

Notes

Abdominal Aortic Aneurysm

- Pulsating abdominal mass.
- Bruit heard over the abdomen.
- Hypotension, Jugular Vein Distention (JVD), widening pulse pressure.
- Confirmed on x-ray.
- If ruptures: S/S of hypovolemic shock.
- **Postoperative care:**
  - — Monitor for S/S of renal failure, MI, ARDS, or postoperative ileus
  - — Changes in pulses, S/S of occluded graft (changes in pulse, pain, cyanotic extremities)

Venous Thromboembolism (VTE)

- **Inflammation of the venous wall with clot formation**
  - — S/S: calf pain, induration (hardening) along the blood vessel, warmth, and redness
  - — Restrict ambulation
  - — Elevate extremity
  - — Antiembolic stockings
  - — Refrain from massaging leg muscles
- **Medications**
  - — Heparin therapy: Monitor partial thromboplastin time (PTT); antidote is protamine sulfate
  - — Coumadin therapy: Monitor prothrombin time (PT), INR; antidote is vitamin K
  - — Antiplatelet agents
  - — Clopidogrel bisulfate (Plavix)

Study Break Box

1. The RN begins their shift by reviewing the status of their clients. Which client would the RN assess first?

1. The client receiving oxygen per nasal cannula who is dyspneic on mild exertion and has a hemoglobin of 7 g/dL (70 mmol/L).
2. The client receiving IV aminoglycosides per Central Venous Catheter (CVC) who complains of nausea and has a trough level below therapeutic levels.
3. The client with a chest tube that drained 150 mL in the last hour.
4. The client receiving chemotherapy whose temperature is 37.2°C (98.9°F) and who has a white blood cell (WBC) count of 2.5×10^9/L (2500/mm^3).

Correct Answer: 3

Rationale

The HCP should be notified if chest tube drainage is >100 mL/hr. The first client does not require the RN's immediate attention. The client receiving IV aminoglycosides should be assessed, but this is not the priority client. The client receiving chemotherapy should be assessed, but this is not the priority client.

Test-Taking Strategy

Candidates for the NCLEX should focus on obtaining knowledge of related nursing procedures for clients needing or undergoing diagnostic testing. A basic understanding of what diagnostic results can determine about a client's condition can help a candidate anticipate HCP orders.

Notes

Next-Generation NCLEX® Examination (NGN)–Style Question

Multiple Response Grouping

Scenario: A 51-year-old client experiencing chest pain is brought to the ED by paramedics. Client states pain started after a quick lunch from a taco truck. The client reports having chest pain after eating which is relieved by "chugging" antacids, though this time the pain was not relieved.

Select the physician orders the RN would anticipate from each of the following categories. (Note: Each category must have at least one option selected.)

Laboratory tests		CBC
		BMP
		Cardiac enzymes
		Lipid panel
Diagnostics		CXR
		12-lead EKG
		ULS of abdomen
		EGD
Medications		Nitroglycerin spray
		Acetaminophen
		Magnesium hydroxide
		Lisinopril

Answer:

Select the physician orders the RN would anticipate from each of the following categories. (Note: Each category must have at least 1 option selected.)

Laboratory tests	X	CBC
	X	BMP
	X	Cardiac enzymes
	X	Lipid panel
Diagnostics	X	CXR
	X	12-lead EKG
		ULS of abdomen
		EGD
Medications	X	Nitroglycerin spray
		Acetaminophen
	X	Magnesium hydroxide
		Lisinopril

Rationale: This client's presenting symptoms require further assessment to rule out cardiac conditions. A CBC will rule out anemia, infection, and thrombocytopenia. BMP will evaluate electrolyte imbalances, which can lead to cardiac arrhythmias. Cardiac enzymes will assess for cardiac muscle damage. A lipid panel can indicate increased cholesterol which can cause blockages in coronary arteries and lead to angina pectoris. A CXR will evaluate the chest cavity to rule out pneumonia and cardiac structure abnormalities. An EKG is used to diagnose cardiac rhythm abnormalities and MI. Sublingual nitroglycerin spray can treat angina pectoris and will increase oxygenation to the heart muscle. Giving an antacid can relieve indigestion, which could be another cause of the client's discomfort. All other orders listed would not be initially ordered to rule out cardiac complications and would not be anticipated at this time.

Notes

6 Ingestion, Digestion, Absorption, and Elimination

Gastroesophageal Reflux Disease (GERD)

- A backward flow of stomach acid up into the esophagus.
- Most common upper gastrointestinal (GI) problem seen in adults and can occur in all age groups.
- No one single cause of GERD.
- **Predisposing conditions include:**
  — Incompetent lower esophageal sphincter (LES)
  — Hiatal hernia
  — Decreased esophageal clearance (ability to clear liquids or food from the esophagus into the stomach) resulting from impaired esophageal motility
  — Decreased gastric emptying
- **Symptoms**
  — Heartburn (pyrosis) after eating
  — Eructation
  — Fullness and discomfort after eating
  — Nocturnal coughing and wheezing
  — Ask the client what foods seem to aggravate symptoms
  — Positive diagnosis from barium swallow or fluoroscopy (hiatal hernia)
- **Laboratory Testing**
  — Upper GI endoscopy
  — Esophagram (barium swallow)
  — pH monitoring
  — Motility (manometry) testing
- **Nursing and Collaborative Management**
  — Lifestyle modifications
    - Encourage smoking cessation
    - Weight management
    - Encourage small, frequent meals
    - Sit up while eating and remain upright for 1 hour after eating
    - Stop eating 3 hours before bedtime
    - Elevate head of bed 4 to 6 inches
  — Take proton pump inhibitors (PPIs) to ↓ acid production and H2
  — Take sucralfate, metoclopramide
  — Procedures to strengthen LES
  — Monitor for Barrett's esophagus
- **GERD Medications**
  — Antacids
    - Neutralize/reduce stomach acidity
  — H2-receptor antagonists
    - Decrease acid secretions by blocking histamine receptors
  — PPIs
    - Inhibit gastrin secretion
  — Mucosal healing agents
  — Promotility agents

Peptic Ulcer Disease

- Ulcerations of the mucous membrane or other layers of the GI tract, most commonly occurring in the stomach and duodenum. Most common between ages of 55 and 65 years.
- Significant gastric ulcers are caused by *Helicobacter pylori* bacteria.
- **Risk factors include:**
  — Drugs: nonsteroidal anti-inflammatory drugs (NSAIDs), corticosteroids, aspirin
  — Alcohol, coffee
  — Cigarette smoking
  — Stress
- **Symptoms**
  — Left epigastric pain, may radiate to back
    - Nausea, weight loss, eructation, distention
  — Symptoms occur 1 to 2 hours after meals
  — Epigastric pain relieved with food; if penetrating, then food increases discomfort
  — Laboratory testing:
    - Barium swallow
    - Upper endoscopy
    - *H. pylori* testing
- **Nursing and Collaborative Management**
  — Onset of symptoms
  — What relieves symptoms
  — Monitor stools for color, consistency, occult blood
  — Drug therapy includes:
    - H2 blockers
    - PPIs

Notes

- Antacids
- Antibiotic therapy for *H. pylori*

— Surgery may be needed for complications.
- Perforation
- Hemorrhage
- Penetration
- Gastric outlet obstruction

■ **Complications**

— Dumping syndrome—postoperative complication
- Symptoms include nausea, vomiting, diaphoresis, explosive diarrhea, and changes in blood glucose levels
- Management: eating six small meals daily that are high in protein and fat and low in carbohydrates; eating slowly, and avoiding fluids during meals; anticholinergics to decrease stomach motility

■ **Lifestyle Modifications**

— Small, frequent meals

— High-fat, high-protein, low-CHO diet

— Avoid liquids with meals

■ **Client Teaching**

— Avoid medications such as:
- Salicylates
- NSAIDs

— Inform the health care provider (HCP) of history of peptic ulcer disease.

— Symptoms of GI bleeding:
- Dark, tarry stools
- Coffee-ground emesis
- Bright red rectal bleeding

Dumping Syndrome

■ **Complication after Gastric Surgery**

— Rapid gastric emptying of hypertonic food from the stomach to the small intestine, drawing fluid into the bowel lumen, resulting in distention of the duodenum or jejunum, occurs in one-third to one-half of clients following surgery.

■ **Symptoms**: nausea, vomiting, diaphoresis, explosive diarrhea, and changes in blood glucose levels

■ **Nursing and Collaborative Management**

— Six small meals high in protein and fat and low in carbohydrates

— Eat slowly; avoid fluids during meals

— Anticholinergic agents decrease stomach motility

— Recline for 1 hour after eating

— Symptoms disappear a year postop

Study Break Box

1. While the RN is obtaining the health history of a client and reviewing the medical records, which data would alert the RN that the client has an increased risk of developing peptic ulcer disease (PUD)? (Select all that apply.)

1. Excess of gastric acid or a decrease in the natural ability of the GI mucosa to protect itself from acid and pepsin.
2. Invasion of the stomach and/or duodenum by *H. pylori.*
3. Viral infection, allergies to certain foods, immunological factors, and psychosomatic factors.
4. Taking certain drugs, including corticosteroids and anti-inflammatory medications.
5. Having allergies to foods containing gluten in their ingredients.

Correct Answer(s): 1, 2, 4

Rationale

Excess gastric acid production, decreased ability of the GI mucosa to protect itself from acid and pepsin, and invasion of the GI tract with *H. pylori* are all risk factors for developing PUD. Medications such as corticosteroids and NSAIDs (e.g., aspirin, ibuprofen [Advil], and naproxen [Aleve]) also lead to PUD. Viral infection, food allergies, immunologic factors, and psychosomatic factors do not lead to PUD.

2. A client is admitted with PUD and GI bleeding. Which risk factor would the RN identify in the client's history?

1. Eats heavily seasoned foods.
2. Uses NSAIDs daily.
3. Consumes alcohol every day.
4. Follows an acid-ash diet.

Correct Answer: 2

Rationale

A side effect of frequent use of NSAIDs is gastric irritation and potential for ulceration. Eating heavily seasoned foods does not lead to ulceration. Excessive alcohol consumption can lead to PUD, but a glass of beer/wine a day will not. An acid-ash diet encourages meats, eggs, and cheese, and discourages milk products, fruits and vegetables; it is used to acidify urine and is not a risk factor for gastric ulcer disease.

Notes

Celiac Disease

- **Causes**
  - — Autoimmune disease characterized by damage to the small intestinal mucosa from ingesting wheat, barley, and rye
- **Risk factors**
  - — genetic predisposition, gluten ingestion, and immune-mediated response
- **Symptoms**
  - — steatorrhea, abdominal distention, and malnutrition
- **Possible complications**
  - — decreased bone density, dental enamel hypoplasia, iron and folate deficiency, peripheral neuropathy, vesicular skin lesions (dermatitis herpetiformis)
- **Laboratory testing**
  - — serology testing and small intestine biopsy (early diagnosis and treatment is important to prevent complications)
- **Nursing and collaborative management**
  - — gluten-free diet

Crohn Disease and Ulcerative Colitis

- **Crohn (Regional Enteritis)**
  - — Causes
    - Autoimmune, genetic, and environmental factors
  - — **Location**
    - Affects small and large intestines tract (most common site is terminal ileum and proximal cecum), all layers of the intestine
    - Inflammation can be continuous or intermittent; extends through all layers of the intestine
    - Affected areas have cobblestone appearance
  - — **Symptoms**
    - Right lower quadrant abdominal pain, nausea, vomiting, weight loss, fever, dehydration, steatorrhea (three to four stools per day), and unexplained anemia
    - Onset occurs in early adolescence; second peak occurs in sixth decade
  - — **Possible complications**
    - bowel obstruction, fistulas, fissures, colonic dilation (toxic megacolon), and abscesses
  - — **Diagnostic**
    - Barium enema with small bowel follow through
    - Diagnosis (DX) with barium enema, capsule endoscopy
  - — **Treatment**
    - Sedatives, tranquilizers, antidiarrheals, sulfasalazine, corticosteroids, immunosuppressives, antimicrobials Surgery for complications
    - Complication: fistula
  - — **Nutrition**
    - Total parenteral nutrition (TPN), nothing by mouth (NPO), bland diet, no milk, vitamin and mineral supplementation
  - — **Pharmacology**
    - Anti-inflammatory agents, multivitamins, and B_{12} injections
  - — **Nursing and Collaborative Management**
    - Goal is to achieve remission with first-line drugs
    - Monitor weight
    - Encourage at least 2–3 L of fluid/day
    - Instruct client in low-residue, high-protein, high-calorie diet (limited dairy)
    - Provide emotional support
- **Ulcerative Colitis**
  - — **Location**
    - Large bowel and rectum
    - DX with sigmoidoscopy
  - — Symptoms
    - Diarrhea, abdominal pain, 10 to 20 loose stools/day, electrolyte imbalances, anemia
    - Fever, tachycardia, weight loss, abdominal cramping, pain, anemia
    - Complications: bleeding, rupture, and abdominal bloating; toxic megacolon
  - — **Treatment**
    - Corticosteroids, antidiarrheals, sulfasalazine, mesalamine, infliximab, or other biological treatments
  - — **Nutrition**
    - Low-residue, low-fat, high-protein diet; no dairy; calorie count; I&O

Diverticular Diseases

- **Diverticulosis**: presence of pouch-like herniation of colon

Notes

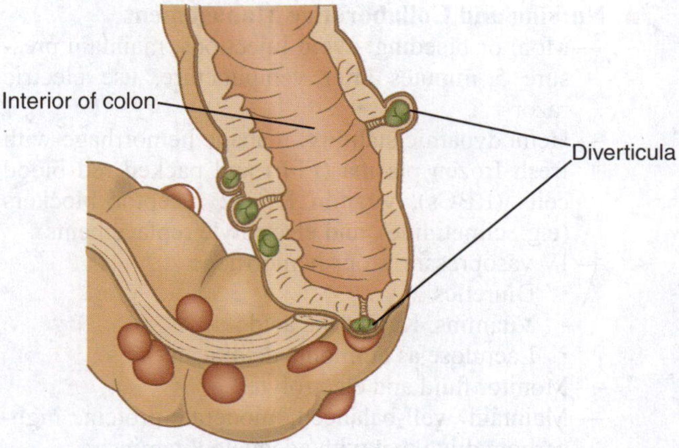

Diverticula are outpouchings of the colon. When they become inflamed, the condition is diverticulitis. The inflammatory process can spread to the surrounding area in the intestine. (Reprinted with permission from Harding, M., Kwong, J., Roberts, D., Hagler, D., & Reinisch, C. [2020]. *Lewis's medical-surgical nursing: Assessment and management of clinical problems* [11th ed.]. Elsevier.)

- **Diverticulitis**: inflammation of one or more of the diverticular sacs
- **Inflammation**: can lead to perforation, abscess, hemorrhage, obstruction, peritonitis.
- **Risk factors**: age >40, lack of exercise, obesity, smoking
- **Symptoms**
  — Left lower quadrant pain, fever, elevated white blood cell (WBC) and erythrocyte sedimentation rate (ESR)
  — S/S of intestinal obstruction
  — Abdominal distention
  — Constipation/diarrhea
- **Diagnostic**
  — Ultrasound, computed tomography (CT) scan, + barium enema/colonoscopy
- **Nursing and Collaborative Management**
  — Sufficient fiber in diet (avoid foods containing seeds)
  — High-fiber diet unless inflammation is present
  — If inflammation present:
    - NPO
    - Then low-residue, bland diet
    - Bulk-forming laxatives
    - Avoid heavy lifting, tight clothing, and straining

Intestinal Obstruction

- **Mechanical Causes**
  — Adhesions most common
  — Strangulated hernia
  — Tumors
- **Neurogenic Causes**
  — Paralytic ileus
  — Spinal cord lesion
- **Vascular Cause**
  — Mesenteric artery occlusion
- **Symptoms**
  — Sudden abdominal pain
  — History of obstruction
  — High-pitched bowel sounds with early mechanical obstruction
  — Bowel sounds diminished or absent with neurogenic or late mechanical obstruction
- **Nursing and Collaborative Management**
  — NPO
  — IV fluids
  — Nasogastric (NG) tube to intermittent suction

Cirrhosis

- **Chronic progressive disease**
  — Lobes of liver covered with scar tissue; liver degenerates and lobes are infiltrated with fat
  — Forms of cirrhosis:
    - Alcohol and/or drug related
    - Post necrotic
    - Biliary
    - Cardiac
  — History
    - Alcohol and/or drug abuse
    - Exposure to hepatotoxins
- **Symptoms**
  — Early signs: right upper quadrant (RUQ) pain, fatigue
  — Jaundice
  — Fruity or musty breath
  — Asterixis
  — Palmar erythema
  — Ascites

Notes

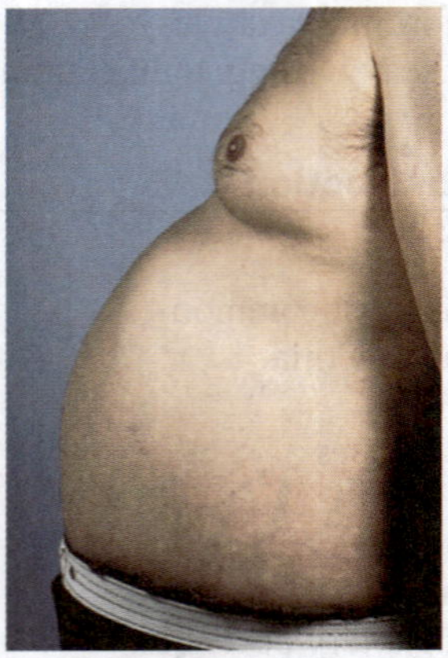

Client with abdominal ascites in late-stage cirrhosis. (Reprinted with permission from Leonard PC. [2020]. *Quick & easy medical terminology* [9th ed.]. St.Louis: Elsevier.)

— Weight loss

- **Esophageal varices may rupture and cause hemorrhage.**
  - — Lab testing: elevated serum bilirubin, aspartate aminotransferase (AST), alanine aminotransferase (ALT), Lactic De-Hydrogenase (LDH), and glucose tolerance test (GTT)
  - — Endoscopic retrograde cholangiopancreatography (ERCP) to detect common bile duct obstruction
- **Treatment**
  - — Esophagogastric balloon
  - — Vitamin K
  - — Blood products
  - — Coagulation factors
- **Dietary Teaching**
  - — Protein may have to be restricted.
  - — Low sodium
  - — Low potassium
  - — Low fat
  - — High carbohydrate
- **Laboratory Testing**
  - — Liver function tests (LFTs)
    - bilirubin, AST, ALT, LDH
- **Nursing and Collaborative Management**
  - — Hemodynamic stability: manage hemorrhage
  - — Avoid injections
  - — Maintain pressure for 5 minutes after venipunctures
  - — Monitor fluid and electrolytes.
  - — Vitamins K and C, folic acid
- **Nursing and Collaborative Management**
  - — Monitor bleeding, avoid injections, maintain pressure 5 minutes after venipuncture, use electric razor
  - — Hemodynamic stability: manage hemorrhage with fresh frozen plasma (FFP) and packed red blood cells (RBCs), vitamin K, H2 receptor blockers (e.g., cimetidine), and electrolyte replacements
  - — IV vasopressin: stops hemorrhage
    - Diuretics
    - Vitamins: K, C, folic acid
    - Lactulose as ammonia detoxicant
  - — Monitor fluid and electrolytes
  - — Maintain well-balanced, moderate-protein, high-carbohydrate diet with adequate vitamins
  - — Limit protein if the client is diagnosed with hepatic encephalopathy
  - — Instruct in skin care: avoid soap, perfumed lotions, and rubbing alcohol; use mild lotions; diphenhydramine may be used for pruritus
  - — Monitor fluids and electrolytes, accurate I&O, weigh daily, restrict fluids (<1500 mL/day), measure abdominal girth, plan for possible paracentesis and peritoneovenous (LeVeen continuous peritoneal jugular shunt)

Study Break Box

1. A client diagnosed with advanced cirrhosis of the liver has an acute exacerbation of hepatic encephalopathy. Which type of food would the RN teach the client to limit? (Select all that apply.)

1. Fruits.
2. Vegetables.
3. Red meat.
4. Bread.
5. White meat.
6. Black beans.

Correct Answer(s): 3, 5, 6

Rationale

Encourage a well-balanced, moderate-protein (limit protein in hepatic encephalopathy), high-carbohydrate diet with adequate vitamins. This client would need to avoid red meat, white meat, and black beans. Fruits, vegetables, and grains are allowed in the client's diet.

Notes

Esophageal Varices

- **Causes**
  - — Complication of cirrhosis associated with portal hypertension
  - — *Rupture is a medical emergency!*
- **Symptoms**
  - — Bloody vomit
  - — Black, tarry, bloody stools
  - — Light-headedness
  - — Loss of consciousness
  - — Jaundice
  - — Easy bleeding, bruising
  - — Ascites
- **Laboratory testing**: endoscopic exam, CT, Doppler ultrasound, capsule endoscopy
- **Nursing and Collaborative Management**
  - — If rupture occurs, this is a medical emergency
  - — Interventions to manage hemorrhage
    - Hemodynamic stability: FFP and packed RBCs, vitamin K, histamine (H2) receptor blockers such as cimetidine, and electrolyte replacements
    - Preventive propranolol is used to reduce the likelihood of rupture
    - Vasopressin administered intravenously or directly into the superior vena cava is used to decrease or stop the hemorrhaging (sometimes used concurrently with nitroglycerin)
    - Balloon tamponade
    - Octreotide is sometimes used in combination with band ligation

Hepatitis

- Widespread inflammation of liver cells, usually caused by a virus
- **Viral Hepatitis**
  - — **Hepatitis A**
    - Most common, transmitted through fecal contamination, vaccine
  - — **Hepatitis B**
    - Long-term incubation, transmitted by contaminated blood, perinatal, sexual contact, vaccine
  - — **Hepatitis C**
    - Contaminated blood, sexual contact
  - — **Hepatitis D**
    - Hepatitis with a coinfection with hepatitis B
  - — **Hepatitis E**
    - Transmitted through fecal contamination, rare in United States
  - — **Hepatitis G**
    - Found in blood donors and can be transmitted by transfusion
- Hepatitis viruses are the most common cause of hepatitis in the world, but other infections, toxic substances (e.g., alcohol, certain drugs), and autoimmune diseases may also cause hepatitis
- **Risk groups**
  - — Men who have sex with men
  - — IV drug users (disease transmitted by contaminated needles)
  - — Tattoo/body piercing with contaminated needles
  - — Living in crowded conditions
  - — Health care workers employed in high-risk areas
  - — Fatigue, weakness, jaundice
  - — Anorexia, dark urine
  - — Joint pain, muscle aches
- **Symptoms**
  - — Fatigue, weakness, anorexia, nausea, jaundice, dark urine, joint pain, muscle aches
  - — Risk Groups
  - — Homosexual males
  - — IV drug users (needles)
  - — Tattoo/body piercing with contaminated needles
  - — Living in crowded conditions
  - — Health care workers employed in high-risk areas
- **Laboratory testing**
  - — ↑ Direct bilirubin, gamma-glutamyl transferase (GGT), AST, ALT, LDH, and alkaline phosphatase levels; leukopenia; hypoglycemia; antigens
- **Nursing and Collaborative Management**
  - — Frequent rest periods
  - — Provide high-calorie, high-carbohydrate diet with moderate fats and proteins
  - — Administer antiemetic as needed
  - — Avoid alcohol intake and drugs detoxified by the liver

Pancreatitis

- **Acute pancreatitis**: autodigestion of the pancreas; alcohol ingestion and biliary tract disease are major causes.
  - — Symptoms
    - Nausea and vomiting
    - Low-grade fever
    - Leukocytosis
    - Jaundice
    - Abdominal tenderness with muscle guarding

Notes

- Areas of ecchymoses, Grey Turner's spots or sign, a bluish flank discoloration, and Cullen's sign, a bluish periumbilical discoloration
- Hypotension
- Tachycardia
- Hypovolemia (massive fluid shift into the retroperitoneal space)
- Shock (hemorrhage into the pancreas)
- Toxemia (activated pancreatic enzymes)
- The lungs are frequently involved (crackles)
- Bowel sounds may be decreased or absent, and ileus may occur

- **Chronic pancreatitis**: progressive, destructive disease; long-term alcohol use is major factor in disease
  - — Symptoms
  - — Steatorrhea
    - Diarrhea
    - Jaundice
    - Ascites
    - Weight loss
- **Nursing and Collaborative Management**
  - **— Acute Management**
    - NPO
    - NG tube to suction
    - Antispasmodic agents
    - Morphine or hydromorphone for pain management
    - Sitting up or leaning forward may reduce pain
    - Monitor blood sugar
    - Teach foods and fluids to avoid
  - **— Chronic Management**
    - Pain management
      - □ Morphine
    - Pancreatic enzymes
      - □ Mix powdered forms with fruit juice or applesauce; avoid mixing with proteins
    - Histamine blocker agents
    - Teach foods and fluids to avoid
    - Support efforts to abstain from alcohol

Study Break Box

1. **A client is receiving pancreatic enzyme replacement therapy for chronic pancreatitis. Which statement by the client indicates a need for more effective teaching?**

   1. "I will need to mix the enzyme with a protein food."
   2. "I will take the enzymes with each meal."
   3. "My stools will decrease in number and frequency."
   4. "My abdominal pain may lessen."

Correct Answer: 1

Rationale

The powder should be mixed with fruit juice or applesauce; avoid mixing with protein foods. Enzymes should be taken with each meal which will decrease the number and frequency of stools and lessen abdominal pain.

Cholecystitis and Cholelithiasis

- **Cholecystitis:** acute inflammation of the gallbladder.
- **Cholelithiasis:** formation or presence of gallstones.

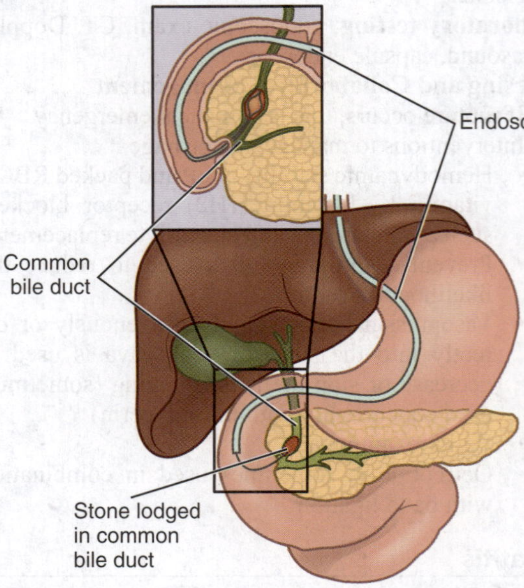

During endoscopic sphincterotomy, an endoscope is advanced through the mouth and stomach until its tip sits in the duodenum opposite the common bile duct. Inset, After widening the duct mouth by incising the sphincter muscle, the HCP advances a basket attachment into the duct and snags the stone. (Reprinted with permission from Harding, M., Kwong, J., Roberts, D., Hagler, D., & Reinisch, C. [2020]. *Lewis's medical-surgical nursing: Assessment and management of clinical problems* [11th ed.]. Elsevier.)

- **Symptoms**
  - — Pain
  - — Fever
  - — Elevated WBCs
  - — Abdominal tenderness
  - — Jaundice

Notes

- **Nursing and Collaborative Management**
  - — Analgesics for pain
  - — NPO
  - — NG to suction
  - — IV antibiotics
  - — Low-fat diet
  - — Cholelithiasis
    - Nonsurgical removal
      - ERCP
      - Lithotripsy
    - Surgical approach
      - Cholecystectomy, laparoscopic, or open

Study Break Box

1. A client who is diagnosed with an obstruction of the common bile duct caused by cholelithiasis passes clay-colored stools containing streaks of fat. Which action would the RN take?

1. Auscultate for diminished bowel sounds.
2. Send a stool specimen to the lab.
3. Document the assessment in the chart.
4. Notify the HCP.

Correct Answer: 3

Rationale

Clay-colored stools streaked with fat in the presence of cholelithiasis is an expected finding in blockage of bile duct (stool contains bilirubin). The finding should be documented in the Client chart. The other interventions are not necessary for this client.

Urinary Tract Infections

- **Causes**: *Escherichia coli*, sexual intercourse, urethritis.
- **Symptoms**: urinary urgency, burning sensation when urinating, cloudy urine, hematuria, pelvic pain, urine with strong odor.
- **Nursing and Collaborative Management**
  - — Obtain clean-catch midstream specimen
  - — Administer antibiotics as ordered
    - Take fully prescribed dose
    - Do not skip doses
  - — Encourage fluid intake of 3000 mL/day
  - — Encourage voiding every 2 to 3 hours
  - — Avoid tight clothing and bubble baths

Urinary Tract Obstruction

- Caused by calculi or stones
- Location of pain can help locate stone
  - — Flank pain (stone usually in upper ureter)
  - — Pain radiating to the abdomen (stone likely in ureter or bladder)
- **Laboratory testing**: clean-catch urine specimen, ultrasound, voiding cystourethrogram, renal nuclear scan, cystoscopy
- **Nursing and Collaborative Management**
  - — Administer narcotics
  - — Strain all urine
  - — Encourage high fluid intake
    - 3 to 4 L/day
  - — Strict I&O
  - — May need surgical management

Benign Prostatic Hyperplasia (BPH)

Enlargement of the Prostate

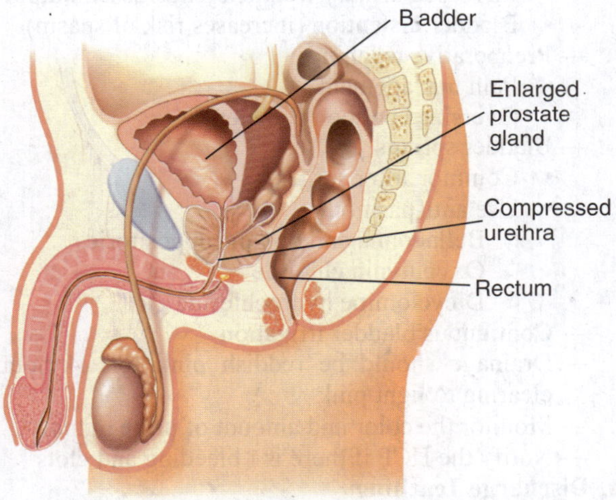

BPH. The enlarged prostate compresses the urethra. (Reprinted with permission from Harding, M., Kwong, J., Roberts, D., Hagler, D., & Reinisch, C. [2020]. *Lewis's medical-surgical nursing: Assessment and management of clinical problems* [11th ed.]. Elsevier.).

Notes

- **Causes**: urinary tract infection, prostatitis, urethral stricture, kidney or bladder stones, nerve damage, cancer of the prostate or bladder, scarring of the bladder neck
- **Laboratory tests**: digital rectal exam, urine analysis, prostate-specific antigen test
- **Symptoms**
  - — Increased urinary frequency
  - — Decreased urinary output
  - — Bladder distention (increases risk of spasm)
- **Nonsurgical Options for Treatment**
  - — Alpha blockers (terazosin, doxazosin, tamsulosin)
  - — 5-alpha reductase inhibitors—finasteride and dutasteride
- **Surgical Options**
  - — Transurethral microwave thermotherapy
  - — Transurethral needle ablation (TUNA)
  - — Photoselective vaporization of the prostate
  - — Most common treatment: transurethral resection of the prostate (TURP)
  - — If prostate is too large, will use suprapubic approach
- **Nursing and Collaborative Management**
  - — Assess for:
    - Increased urinary frequency/decreased output
    - Bladder distention (increases risk of spasm)
  - — Preoperative teaching
    - Pain management
    - Oversized balloon catheter
  - — Bladder spasms
    - Common after surgery
    - Use antispasmodics
      - □ Belladonna and opium suppositories
      - □ Oxybutynin chloride
      - □ Dicyclomine hydrochloride
  - — Continuous bladder irrigation
  - — Drainage should be reddish pink for 24 hours, clearing to light pink
  - — Monitor the color and amount of urine output
  - — Notify the HCP if there is ↑ bleeding and clots
- **Discharge Teaching**
  - — Continue to drink 12 to 14 glasses of water per day
  - — Avoid straining
  - — Avoid strenuous activity, sports, lifting, and intercourse for 3 to 4 weeks
  - — Report large amounts of blood or frank blood

Study Break Box

1. The charge nurse is making assignments on the renal unit. Which client would the registered nurse (RN) assign to a practical nurse (PN) who is new to the unit?

1. An older client who has thick, dark red drainage in a urinary catheter 1 day after a transurethral prostatic resection.
2. A middle-aged client admitted with a diagnosis of acute renal failure secondary to a reaction to IV pyelogram dye.
3. An older client who has end-stage renal disease and complains of nausea after receiving digoxin.
4. A middle-aged client who receives hemodialysis and has been prescribed epoetin alfa subcutaneous daily.

Correct Answer: 4

Rationale
The middle-aged client who receives hemodialysis and has been prescribed epoetin alfa subcutaneous daily can be assigned to the PN. This injection can be administered by the PN. All other clients listed require more advanced assessment by the RN.

2. A client is in the oliguric phase of acute kidney injury. Which finding would the RN expect to assess in the client? (Select all that apply.)

1. 390 mL urine output in 24 hours.
2. Potassium of 6.2 mEq/L.
3. Sodium (serum) 155 mEq/L.
4. Metabolic alkalosis.
5. Weight gain.

Correct Answer(s): 1, 2, 5

Rationale
390 mL urine output in 24 hours is a low output. A high potassium level and weight gain are indicative of the oliguric phase of acute kidney injury. Serum sodium of 155 mEq/L and metabolic alkalosis are not expected in this client.

Acute Kidney Injury

- A reversible syndrome if symptoms are caught early.
- **Remember:**
  - — Kidneys use 25% of normal cardiac output to maintain function
  - — Kidneys excrete 1 to 2 L of urine per 24 hours for adults

Notes

- **Prerenal Failure**
  - — Hemorrhage/hypovolemia
  - — ↓ Cardiac output
  - — ↓ Renal perfusion
- **Intrarenal Failure**
  - — May develop secondary to prerenal failure
  - — Nephrotoxins, infections
  - — Renal injury
  - — Vascular lesions
- **Postrenal Failure**
  - — Obstruction, calculi, BPH
  - — Tumors, strictures
- **Nursing Assessment**
  - — ↓ Urine output
  - — Weight gain
  - — Edema
  - — **Diagnostic test results: Oliguric phase**
    - ↓ Urine output
    - ↑ Blood urea nitrogen (BUN) and creatinine
    - ↑ Potassium
    - ↓ Sodium (serum)
    - ↓ pH
    - Metabolic acidosis
      - □ ↑ Urine sodium
      - □ Fixed at 1.010 specific gravity
  - — **Diagnostic test results: Diuretic phase**
    - ↑ Urine output
    - ↓ Fluid volume
    - ↓ Potassium
    - ↓ Sodium
    - ↓ Urine specific gravity
    - ↓ Urine sodium
  - — **Recovery phase:** Glomerular Filtration Rate (GFR) slowly increases; full recovery may take a year
- **Nursing and Collaborative Management**
  - — **Oliguric phase**: Give only enough fluids to replace losses, + 400 to 500 mL/24 hours
  - — Strict I&O
  - — Monitor lab values closely
  - — Watch for electrocardiogram (ECG) changes
  - — Monitor weight daily

Study Break Box

1. A client who has acute renal failure is admitted to the hospital. The client's potassium level is 6.4 mEq/L. Which snack would the RN offer?

1. An orange.
2. A milkshake.
3. Dried fruit and nuts.
4. A gelatin dessert.

Correct Answer: 4

Rationale

The normal potassium level for an adult is 3.5 to 5 mEq/L. Therefore, gelatin, which contains no potassium, could be offered. A potassium level of 6.4 mEq/L (hyperkalemia) is life threatening. Milk, oranges, and dried fruits and nuts are potassium-rich foods and should not be offered to the client.

Chronic Kidney Disease (CKD)

- End-stage renal disease.
- Progressive irreversible damage to the nephrons and glomeruli.
- **Causes**
  - — Diabetic nephropathy
  - — Hypertensive nephrosclerosis
  - — Glomerulonephritis
  - — Polycystic kidney disease
- **Symptoms**
  - — Early stage
    - Polyuria
    - Renal insufficiency
  - — Late stage
    - Oliguria
    - Hematuria
    - Proteinuria
    - Edema
    - ↑ Blood pressure (BP)
    - Muscle wasting, secondary to negative nitrogen balance
    - Ammonia taste in mouth
    - ↑ Creatinine, ↑ PO_4, ↑ K
  - — End stage
    - Anuria (<100 mL/24 hours)

Notes

- **Nursing and Collaborative Management**
  - — Monitor serum electrolytes
  - — Weigh daily
  - — Strict I&O
  - — Renal diet
    - Low protein
    - Low sodium
    - Low potassium
    - Low phosphate
- **Medications**
  - — Drugs are used to manage the associated complications
    - Aluminum hydroxide to bind phosphates
    - Epoetin to treat anemia
    - Antihypertensive therapy
    - Calcium supplements and vitamin D
    - Antihyperlipidemics
    - Statins to lower low-density lipoprotein (LDL)
    - Fibrates to lower triglycerides
  - — CAUTION: As kidney function decreases, medication doses require adjustment
- **Renal Dialysis**
  - — Hemodialysis
    - AV fistula
  - — Ø Venipunctures, Ø IVs, Ø BP in arteriovenous (AV) shunt arm
  - — Withhold medications that would affect hemodynamic stability before dialysis
- **Peritoneal dialysis**

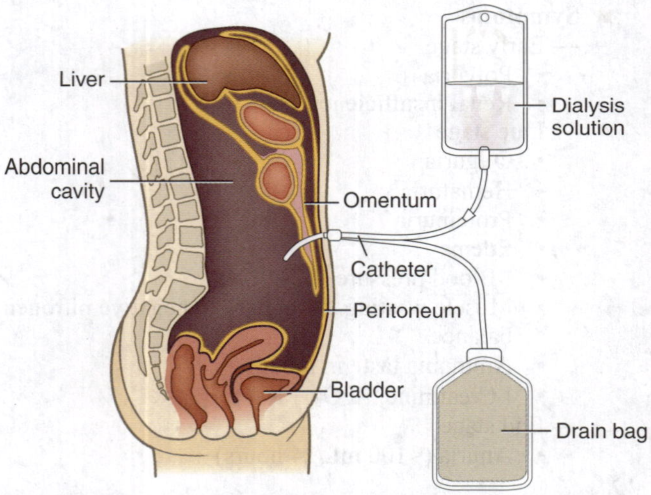

Peritoneal dialysis showing peritoneal catheter inserted into peritoneal cavity. (Reprinted with permission from Harding, M., Kwong, J., Roberts, D., Hagler, D., & Reinisch, C. [2020]. *Lewis's medical-surgical nursing: Assessment and management of clinical problems* [11th ed.]. Elsevier.)

  - — Monitor indwell and outflow times closely
  - — Monitor I&O
- **Postoperative Care: Kidney Surgery**
  - — Auscultate to detect "wet" sounds
  - — Demonstrate splinting method
  - — Monitor for signs and symptoms of shock
  - — Monitor the surgical site for bleeding
  - — Administer narcotic analgesics as needed
  - — Assess urinary output and drainage from all tubes
  - — Strict I&O

Study Break Box

1. After hemodialysis, the RN is evaluating the blood results for a client who has end-stage renal disease. Which value should the RN verify with the laboratory?

1. Elevated serum potassium.
2. Increase in serum calcium.
3. Low hemoglobin.
4. Reduction in serum sodium.

Correct Answer: 1

Rationale

The client with end-stage renal disease going through hemodialysis should not experience hyperkalemia. The RN should verify with the laboratory the values that reflect an elevated serum potassium. It is normal for calcium levels to increase during hemodialysis. Anemia is a normal finding in hemodialysis. A drop in serum sodium is normal in hemodialysis.

2. A client with a 20-year history of type 1 diabetes mellitus is having renal function tests because of recent fatigue, weakness, BUN of 8.5 mmol/L (24 mg/dL), and a serum creatine of 146 mmol/L (1.6 mg/dL). Which additional early symptom of renal insufficiency would the RN expect?

1. Dyspnea.
2. Nocturia.
3. Confusion.
4. Stomatitis.

Notes

Study Break Box—cont'd

Correct Answer: 2

Rationale

Changes in urine frequency, amount, and nocturia are early symptoms of renal insufficiency. Dyspnea and confusion are late signs of renal dysfunction. Stomatitis is not a symptom of renal insufficiency.

Test-Taking Strategy

A helpful method for decreasing test anxiety is to practice self-affirmation. After you have adequately studied and really understand the material, look in the mirror and say to yourself out loud, "I know this material, and I will do well on the test." After several times of watching and hearing yourself reaffirm your knowledge, you will gain inner confidence and be able to perform much better during the NCLEX.

Next-Generation NCLEX® Examination (NGN)–Style Question

Multiple Response: Select N

Scenario: The RN is admitting a client to the medical unit. The client is a 77-year-old with a 3-day history of non-localized abdominal discomfort. Assessment findings: Most current VSs: BP: 116/64, P: 85, R: 21, T: 99.4°F, pain: 4/10. A&O to person only. Incontinence, new-onset mental confusion, and loose stools. The post-void catheterization yielded 150 mL of dark, cloudy urine that had a strong odor. Lungs are clear to auscultation (CTA), no cough present. No peripheral edema. Pulses palpable. Skin is pink, clammy.

Select four assessment findings that require immediate follow-up.	
	1. Vital signs
	2. Lung sounds
	3. Mental status
	4. Skin temperature and moisture
	5. Urine character
	6. Loose stools
	7. Pain

Answer: 3, 5, 6, 7.

Rationale: The client's new onset of mental confusion is of high concern and needs immediate evaluation. This, along with the urine character, loose stools, and pain, could be indicative of a urinary tract infection (UTI), which could be very concerning in a client of this age. These findings indicate need for further follow-up. The vital signs are WNL at this time, lungs are clear, and skin is clammy. These are normal findings and can be monitored routinely.

Notes

7 Regulatory, Reproductive, and Urinary

Obesity, Metabolic Syndrome, Prediabetes, and Diabetes

- Calorie intake exceeds the body's metabolic needs.
- Assessed using body mass index (BMI)
  - **Normal weight**: BMI of 18.5 to 24.9 kg/m^2
  - **Overweight**: BMI of 25 to 29.9 kg/m^2
  - **Obese**: BMI ≥30 kg/m^2
  - **Morbidly obese**: BMI >40 kg/m^2
- Abdominal and visceral fat have been linked to metabolic syndrome.
- Disproportionally represented in minority populations.
- **Nursing Assessment**
  - Risk factor screening
  - Cardiovascular disease
  - Hypertension
  - Sleep apnea
  - Type 2 diabetes
- **Lifestyle Management**
  - Medical/nutritional therapy
  - Physical activity
  - Behavior modification
- **Pharmacological Therapy**
  - Orlistat blocks fat breakdown in the gastrointestinal (GI) track
- **Bariatric Surgery**
  - Criteria for bariatric surgery:
  - BMI ≥40 or ≥35 kg/m^2 with one or more severe, obesity-related complications
  - Gastric bypass, gastric banding, Roux-en-Y
- **Metabolic Syndrome**
  - A collection of risk factors that ↑ an individual's chance of developing cardiovascular disease and diabetes mellitus
  - Meets three or more criteria:
    - **Waist circumference** ≥40 inches (102 cm) in men or ≥35 inches (88 cm) in women
    - **Triglycerides (TG)** >1.7 mmol/L (>150 mg/dL) or drug treatment for elevated TG
    - **High-density lipoprotein (HDL) cholesterol** <0.9 mmol/L (<40 mg/dL) in men or 1.1 mmol/L (<50 mg/dL) in women or drug treatment for ↓ HDL
    - **Blood pressure (BP)** ≥130 mm Hg systolic or ≥85 mm Hg diastolic or drug treatment for hypertension
    - **Fasting blood glucose level** ≥10 mmol/L (100 mg/dL) or drug treatment for elevated glucose

Prediabetes

- ↑ Risk for developing diabetes.
  - Individuals are increased risk of developing diabetes. Blood glucose is elevated but not elevated enough to meet the diagnostic criteria for diabetes
- **Assessment**
  - Fasting blood glucose level of 100 to 125 mg/dL
  - 2-hour oral glucose tolerance test (OGTT) values of 140 to 199 mg/dL
  - Hemoglobin A1c
    - Range: 5.7% to 6.4%

Diabetes Mellitus

- Chronic multisystem disease related to abnormal insulin production, impaired insulin use, or both.
- **Type 1**
  - Immune-related disease
  - Absolute insulin deficiency
  - T cells destroy ß cells
  - Abrupt onset of polyuria, polydipsia, and polyphagia
  - Weight loss may occur as the body cannot get glucose
  - Weakness and fatigue
  - Ketoacidosis may occur
  - Nausea, vomiting, dehydration, abdominal pain, Kussmaul's respirations, acetone odor to breath
  - Onset typically in childhood or adolescence but can occur at any age
  - **Laboratory tests:**
    - Serum glucose ≥250 mg/dL
    - Ketonuria in large amounts
    - Arterial pH of <7.30 and HCO_3 <15 mmol/L (mEq/L)
    - Serum bicarbonate <15 mmol/L (mEq/dL)

Notes

- **Type 2**
  - — Insulin resistance
  - — Relative insulin deficiency
  - — Insulin production
  - — Excessive or unregulated glucose production from liver
- **Other Types**
  - — Cystic fibrosis related
  - — Transplant related
  - — Gestational
  - — Steroid induced
  - — Hospital-related hyperglycemia
- **Diagnosis**
  - — A1c%: ≥6.5%
  - — Fasting plasma glucose: ≥126 mg/dL
  - — OGTT: ≥200 mg/dL
- **Type 2**
  - — Risk Factors
    - Age ≥45 years
    - Overweight (BMI >25)
    - First-degree relative with diabetes
    - Sedentary lifestyle
    - Ethnic at-risk group
    - Gestational diabetes or a baby >9 lb
    - Cardiovascular disease (CVD) and/or hypertension
    - Abnormal lipids (low HDL, high TG)
    - Prediabetes
    - Polycystic ovary syndrome (PCOS)
    - Signs of insulin resistance (acanthosis nigricans)
    - History of CVD
  - — Insidious onset with the following:
    - 3 Ps (polyuria, polyphagia, polydipsia) + fatigue + weight loss
    - Recurrent infections
    - Prolonged wound healing
    - Visual changes
    - Impotence
    - Rare: ketoacidosis; more likely Hyperglycemic hyperosmolar nonketotic syndrome (HHNKS) with Blood sugar (BS) >33.3 mmol/L (600 mg/dL)
    - Dehydration, plasma hyperosmolality, altered mental state, and absent ketone bodies
- **Complications**
  - — Stroke, hypertension
  - — Dermopathy
  - — Atherosclerosis
  - — Nephropathy
  - — Retinopathy, cataracts, glaucoma, blindness
  - — Coronary artery disease
  - — Gastroparesis
  - — Islet cell loss
  - — Peripheral vascular atherosclerosis
  - — Gangrene
  - — Erectile dysfunction (ED)
  - — Peripheral neuropathy
  - — Neurogenic bladder
- **Nursing Assessment**
  - — Integument: skin breakdown
  - — Eyes: retinal problems, cataracts
  - — Kidneys: edema, urinary retention
  - — Periphery: cool skin
  - — Ulcerations on extremities and thick nails
  - — Cardiopulmonary angina and dyspnea
- **Nursing and Collaborative Management**
  - — Medical Nutrition Therapy
    - Type 1: Integrate insulin with eating and exercise
    - Type 2: Heart-healthy diet and moderate weight loss of 10% to 20%
  - — Monitoring
    - Detects extremes and targets
    - Educate client in techniques, calibration, and record keeping
  - — Regular Activity
    - Moderate-intensity aerobic physical activity 150 min/week; resistance training 3 days/week
  - — Education
    - Injection techniques if injectable prescribed
    - Refrigerate unopened insulin
    - Monitor for S/S of hypoglycemia/hyperglycemia
    - Foot care
    - Manage sick days
    - Keep taking insulin
    - Check blood sugar more frequently
    - Watch for S/S of hyperglycemia

Study Break Box

1. The registered nurse (RN) assigns the practical nurse (PN) a client diagnosed with diabetes. Which finding would the RN instruct the PN to report immediately? (Select all that apply.)

1. Fingerstick blood sugar of 247 mg/dL.
2. Cold, clammy skin.
3. Crackles at the end of inspiration.
4. Numbness in the fingertips and toes.
5. Unsteady gait, slurred speech.

Notes

Study Break Box—cont'd

Correct Answer(s): 2, 5

Rationale

Cold, clammy skin, unsteady gait, and slurred speech are concerning findings and need to be reported immediately to the RN. These indicate a serious change in condition that needs further assessment. The other findings can be expected for a client with this condition or do not require immediate assessment by the RN.

- **Pharmacological Interventions**
  - **Sulfonylureas:** increase insulin production from the pancreas
  - **Meglitinides:** increase insulin production from the pancreas
  - **Biguanides:** reduce glucose production by the liver
  - **a-Glucosidase inhibitors:** reduce absorption of carbohydrates
  - Thiazolidinediones: insulin sensitizers
  - **Dipeptidyl peptidase-4 inhibitor:** slows the inactivation of incretin hormones
  - **Incretin mimetic:** simulates one of the incretin hormones
  - **Amylin analog:** a synthetic analog of human amylin
- **Insulin Pharmacokinetics after SC Injection**
  - glulisine (Apidra)
    - Instructions: Given within 15 minutes of meal
    - Onset: 15 minutes
    - Peak: 1 hour
    - Duration: 2 to 3 hours
  - lispro (Humalog)
    - Instructions: Given within 15 minutes of meal
    - Onset: 15 minutes
    - Peak: 1 hour
    - Duration: 4 hours
  - aspart (NovoLog)
    - Instructions: Given within 15 minutes of meal
    - Onset: 30 minutes
    - Peak: 1 to 3 hours
    - Duration: 3 to 5 hours
  - regular (Humulin R)
    - Instructions: Given within 30 minutes of meal
    - Onset: 30 minutes–1 hour
    - Peak: 2 to 4 hours
    - Duration: 5 to 7 hours
  - humulin N (NPH)
    - Instructions: Can be mixed with rapid-acting insulins
    - Onset: 1 to 2 hours
    - Peak: 4 to 10 hours
    - Duration: 10 to 16 hours
  - glargine (Lantus)
    - Instructions: Usually given once a day in the morning
    - Onset: 1 to 5 hours
    - Peak: Plateau
    - Duration: 24 hours
  - detemir (Levemir)
    - Instructions: Acts as basal insulin
    - Onset: 3 to 4 hours
    - Peak: Peakless
    - Duration: 24 hours
- **Long-Acting Insulin:** glargine (Lantus) and detemir (Levemir)
  - Cannot be mixed with any other type of insulin
  - Usually given once daily in the morning
  - Administer 4 hours either before or after contrast x-ray
  - Do NOT shake solutions
  - CAUTION: Clear colored; do not confuse with regular insulin
- **Combination Insulins (Premix Insulins)**
  - Regular insulin 30% and insulin isophane (Humulin N) 70%
    - Onset: 30 min to 1 hours
    - Peak: 1.5 to 12 hours
    - Duration: up to 24 hours
  - Lispro protamine 75% and insulin lispro 25%
    - Onset: 15 to 30 minutes
    - Peak: > or = 2 hours
    - Duration: 22 hours
  - Lispro protamine 50% and insulin lispro 50%
    - Onset: 15 to 30 minutes
    - Peak: 30 to 90 minutes
    - Duration: 22 hours
  - Soluble aspart 30% and 70% aspart protamine crystals
    - Onset: 10 to 20 minutes
    - Peak: 1 to 4 hours
    - Duration: up to 24 hours

Notes

Study Break Box

1. The RN is reviewing the current medication list of a client, newly diagnosed with type 1 diabetes, who will be prescribed insulin. Which medication would the RN discuss with the health care provider? (Select all that apply.)

1. Prednisone
2. Atenolol
3. Clarithromycin
4. Acetaminophen
5. Ibuprofen
6. Pantoprazole sodium

Correct Answer(s): 1, 2, 6

Rationale
Prednisone and pantoprazole sodium can increase blood sugar levels leading to hyperglycemia. Atenolol can mask signs of hypoglycemia. The other medications listed do not have an effect on blood sugar levels.

2. A client who was recently prescribed metformin hydrochloride calls the clinic to discuss symptoms of bloating, nausea, cramping, and diarrhea. Which instruction would the RN provide the client? (Select all that apply.)

1. Discontinue the medication immediately.
2. Increase fiber and fluids in the diet.
3. Monitor the symptoms.
4. Continue to take the metformin as prescribed.
5. Seek immediate emergency medical care.

Correct Answer(s): 3, 4

Rationale
The RN would instruct the client to monitor their symptoms but continue taking the medication as prescribed. These are normal side effects of the medication and should decrease with time. All other instructions are inappropriate.

Thyroid Gland Feedback Loop

- Hypothalamus
  — TRH (+)
    - Anterior Pituitary
  — T3 and T4 (−) TSH (+)
    - Thyroid Gland

Hyperthyroidism

- **Nursing Assessment**
  — Enlarged thyroid gland
  — Exophthalmos
  — Weight loss
  — T3 elevated
  — T4 elevated
  — Diarrhea
  — Tachycardia
  — Bruit over thyroid
- **Nursing and Collaborative Management**
  — Diet: high protein, high calorie, low caffeine, low fiber
  — Treatment may trigger hypothyroidism, may need hormone replacement
  — Propylthiouracil (PTU) therapy to block the synthesis of T3 and T4
  — Iodine (^{131}I) therapy to destroy thyroid cells
- **Surgical Management**
  — Thyroidectomy
    - Position in high Fowler's
    - Assess behind neck for drainage
    - Support neck when moving client
    - Assess for laryngeal edema
    - Have tracheotomy set, oxygen, and suction equipment at bedside
    - Have calcium gluconate at bedside

Hypothyroidism

- **Nursing Assessment**
  — Fatigue
  — Bradycardia
  — Weight gain
  — Constipation
  — Periorbital edema
  — Cold intolerance
  — Low T3 (<70 ng/dL)
  — Low T4 (<5 ng/dL)
- **Medications**
  — Levothyroxine (Synthroid)
    - Take prior to food in a.m. (on an empty stomach)
    - Monitor heart rate
    - Hold for pulse >100 beats/min
  — Liothyronine (Cytomel)
    - Increase metabolic rate
    - Act as synthetic T3

Notes

- Check hormone levels regularly
- Avoid food containing iodine

— Levothyroxine (T4) + liothyronine (T3) (Liotrix)

- Fast onset

■ **Nursing and Collaborative Treatment**

— Myxedema coma: an acute exacerbation of hypothyroidism; maintain airway
— Reinforce medication regimen
— Monitor for side effects of medications
— Monitor bowel program for signs/symptoms of constipation

Study Break Box

1. Which client would the RN assess first?

1. The client diagnosed with hyperthyroidism who is exhibiting exophthalmos.
2. The client diagnosed with type 1 diabetes who has an inflamed foot ulcer.
3. The client with Cushing syndrome exhibiting moon face.
4. The client with Addison disease showing tremors and diaphoresis.

Correct Answer: 4

Rationale
The client with Addison disease showing tremors and diaphoresis needs to be assessed first. These can be signs of Addisonian (adrenal) crisis, which can be a potentially fatal condition. All other findings are expected and are not life-threatening.

2. Which adaptation of the environment is most important for the RN to include in the plan of care for a client diagnosed with myxedema?

1. Reduce environmental stimuli.
2. Prevent direct sunlight from entering the room.
3. Maintain a warm room temperature.
4. Minimize exposure to visitors.

Correct Answer: 3

Rationale
The RN would maintain a warm room temperature for a client with myxedema because clients may experience cold intolerance, which can lead to myxedema crisis. The other environmental adaptations are not necessary for this client.

Study Break Box—cont'd

3. The RN suspects a postoperative thyroidectomy client may have had an inadvertent removal of the parathyroid when the client begins to experience which symptoms? (Select all that apply.)

1. Hematoma formation.
2. Harsh, vibratory sounds on inspiration.
3. Tingling of lips, hands, and toes.
4. Positive Chvostek's sign.
5. Sensation of fullness at the incision site.

Correct Answer(s): 2, 3, 4

Rationale
Removal of the parathyroid during a thyroidectomy can lead to a decrease in serum calcium. Laryngeal stridor may be related to tetany when parathyroid glands are damaged or removed, leading to hypocalcemia. Tingling of toes, fingers, and lips, along with muscular twitching, is a sign of tetany. A positive Chvostek's sign is noted with hypocalcemia. Hematoma formation and sensation of fullness at the incision site are not signs of dysfunctional parathyroid.

Addison Disease

■ **Etiology**

— Sudden withdrawal from corticosteroids
— Hypofunction of adrenal cortex
— Lack of pituitary Adrenocorticotropic hormone (ACTH)

■ **Signs and Symptoms**

— Weight loss, N/V, anorexia
— Hypovolemia, hypoglycemia
— Hyponatremia, hyperkalemia
— Loss of body hair
— Postural hypotension
— Hyperpigmentation

■ **Nursing Collaborative Management**

— Frequent vital signs
— Daily weights
— Monitor serum electrolytes and glucose
— Diet: high sodium, low potassium, high carbohydrates
— At least 3 L of fluid per day
— Wear medic alert bracelet
— Monitor for symptoms of overdosage/underdosage of corticosteroid and mineralocorticoid therapy
— Carry emergency kit with 100 mg IM corticosteroid

Notes

Study Break Box

1. A client is admitted with a diagnosis of Addison's crisis. Which prescription provided by the health care provider (HCP) would the RN question?

1. IV D5NS at 300 mL/hr for 3 hours.
2. Hydrocortisone sodium succinate 100 mg IV push.
3. Potassium 20 mEq in 100 mL saline IV over 60 minutes.
4. 50% dextrose intravenous push.

Correct Answer(s): 3

Rationale

Addison's crisis leads to high potassium levels; therefore, the RN would question an order for IV administration of potassium. Administration of dextrose fluids and solutions can help to maintain glucose levels during Addison's crisis. Hydrocortisone must be administered immediately during Addison's crisis.

Cushing Syndrome: Nursing Assessment

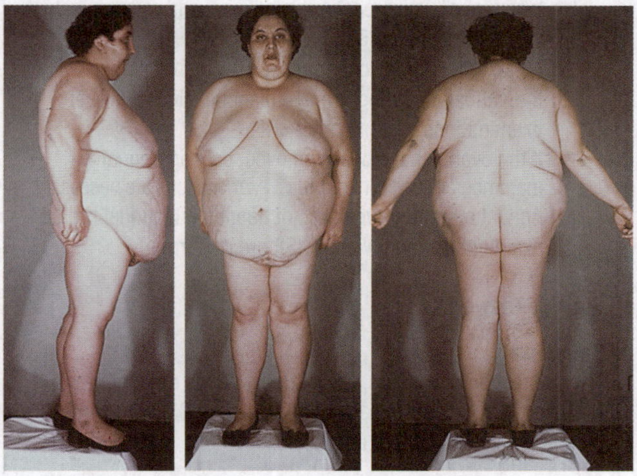

Typical appearance of a client with Cushing disease or syndrome. (Reprinted with permission from Wenig, B.M., Heffess, C.S., & Adair, C.F. [1997]. *Atlas of endocrine pathology.* Philadelphia: Saunders.)

- Excess adrenal corticoid activity caused by adrenal, pituitary, or hypothalamus tumors
- Moon face
- Edema of lower extremities
- Flat affect, irritability, anxiety, depression, psychosis
- Obesity
- Abdominal striae
- Buffalo hump (fat deposits)
- Muscle atrophy, weakness
- Thin, dry, pale skin
- Hypertension
- Osteoporosis
- Immunosuppressed
- Hypervolemia
- Hirsutism
- **Lab results**
  - — Hyperglycemia
  - — Hypernatremia
  - — Hypocalcemia
  - — Hypokalemia
  - — Increased plasma cortisol levels
- **Nursing and Collaborative Management**
  - — Monitor for S/S of infection
    - Fever
    - Skin lesions
    - Elevated white blood cells (WBCs)
  - — Wear a medic alert bracelet
  - — Avoid extreme temperatures, infections, emotional disturbances
  - — Diet:
    - Low sodium; low carbohydrate

Study Break Box

1. The RN provides teaching to a client who is prescribed prednisone 10 mg orally daily. Which statement by the client indicates that further teaching is necessary?

1. "I can take aspirin if I need it for pain."
2. "I need to take medication at the same time daily."
3. "I need to check for bruising on my skin."
4. "If I gain more than 5 lb a week, I will call the HCP."

Correct Answer: 1

Rationale

Clients prescribed prednisone need to be aware that using aspirin with steroids can cause bleeding. Clients are expected to gain 1–2 lb, but if a client were to gain 5 lb in a week, the HCP should be notified. The other client statements do not require further teaching.

Notes

Sexually Transmitted Infections (STIs)

- Symptoms and treatment vary by disease.
- **Teach safer sex:**
  - — Limit number of partners
  - — Abstinence, mutual monogamy
  - — Use latex condoms
  - — Lifestyle risks: drugs and alcohol
- Report the incidence of STIs to appropriate health agencies.
- **Syphilis**
  - — Primary (local, chancre is a highly contagious red painless lesion);
  - — Secondary (occurs 6 weeks to 6 months after exposure; generalized rash that affects palms of hands and soles of feet);
  - — Tertiary (occurs 10 to 30 years postexposure resulting in cardiac and neurologic destruction)
  - — Diagnosis with Venereal disease research laboratory (VDRL) or fluorescent treponemal antibody test absorption test (FTA-ABS)
  - — Treatment: Penicillin G IM (2.4 million units) if allergic to penicillin, use tetracycline
- **Gonorrhea**
  - — Diagnosis via cultures or smears
  - — Females are usually asymptomatic; males experience dysuria, yellowish-green urethral discharge, and urinary frequency
  - — Treat with azithromycin
- **Chlamydia**
  - — Usually asymptomatic in females but may have dysuria, vaginal discharge elevated temperature, uterine or adnexal tenderness;
  - — Diagnosis via culture
- **Trichomonas**
- **Candidiasis**
- **Herpes: Herpes simplex virus 2**
  - — Vesicles in clusters rupture and leave painful erosions that makes urination painful
  - — Treat with acyclovir—it partially controls symptoms: use viscous lidocaine topically to provide palliative care to relieve pain
- **Human papillomavirus (HPV)**
  - — 70 strains implicated in cervical cancer—increasing in adolescent population
  - — Lesions are either small, wart like, clustered, or flat or raised; routine vaccine before onset of sexual activity
  - — Treat with topical podophyllum (contraindicated in pregnancy); laser, cryotherapy
- **HIV/AIDS: Human Immunodeficiency Virus**

Benign Uterine Tumors

- Arise from uterine muscle tissue
  - — Fertility issues
  - — Menorrhagia
  - — Uterine enlargement
  - — Dysmenorrhea
  - — Anemia
  - — Low back and pelvic pain
  - — Tend to disappear after menopause
- Nonsurgical option: magnetic resonance-guided focused ultrasound
- Surgical options: myomectomy, hysterectomy; fertility concerns

Study Break Box

1. A client who had an abdominal hysterectomy for cervical adenocarcinoma in situ is preparing for discharge. Which recommendation about women's health screening examinations should the RN offer?

1. Continue the annual Pap smear and mammogram, biannual clinical breast examinations, and monthly breast self-examination (BSE).
2. A Pap smear is no longer necessary, but continue the annual mammogram and biannual clinical breast examinations, plus monthly BSE.
3. If the ovaries have been removed, only an annual mammogram and clinical breast examinations are necessary.
4. Annual mammograms are not needed if biannual breast examinations and weekly BSE are performed.

Correct Answer: 1

Rationale

The client should continue annual Pap smears, mammogram, and clinical breast examinations and monthly BSE. The other recommendations are not necessary.

2. A client with menopause reports that since she stopped hormone replacement therapy (HRT), she has been experiencing increased vaginal discomfort during intercourse. What action would the RN take?

1. Suggest that the client use a vaginal cream or lubricant.
2. Recommend that the client abstain from sexual intercourse.
3. Teach the client Kegel exercises to perform daily.
4. Instruct the client to resume HRT.

Notes

Study Break Box—cont'd

Correct Answer: 1

Rationale

Lack of estrogen results in vaginal dryness, causing discomfort. Use of a vaginal cream or lubrication will help ease the client's discomfort. The other nursing interventions are not necessary for this client situation.

Pelvic Organ Prolapse (POP): Uterine Prolapse, Cystocele, and Rectocele

- **Preventive measures**
  - — Postpartum perineal exercises (Kegel)
  - — Spaced pregnancy
  - — Weight control
- **Surgical Intervention**
  - — Hysterectomy
  - — Anterior and posterior vaginal repair
- **Nursing and Collaborative Management**
  - — Manage postoperative pain
  - — Monitor postoperative urinary output
  - — Observe for S/S of bleeding and infection postoperative

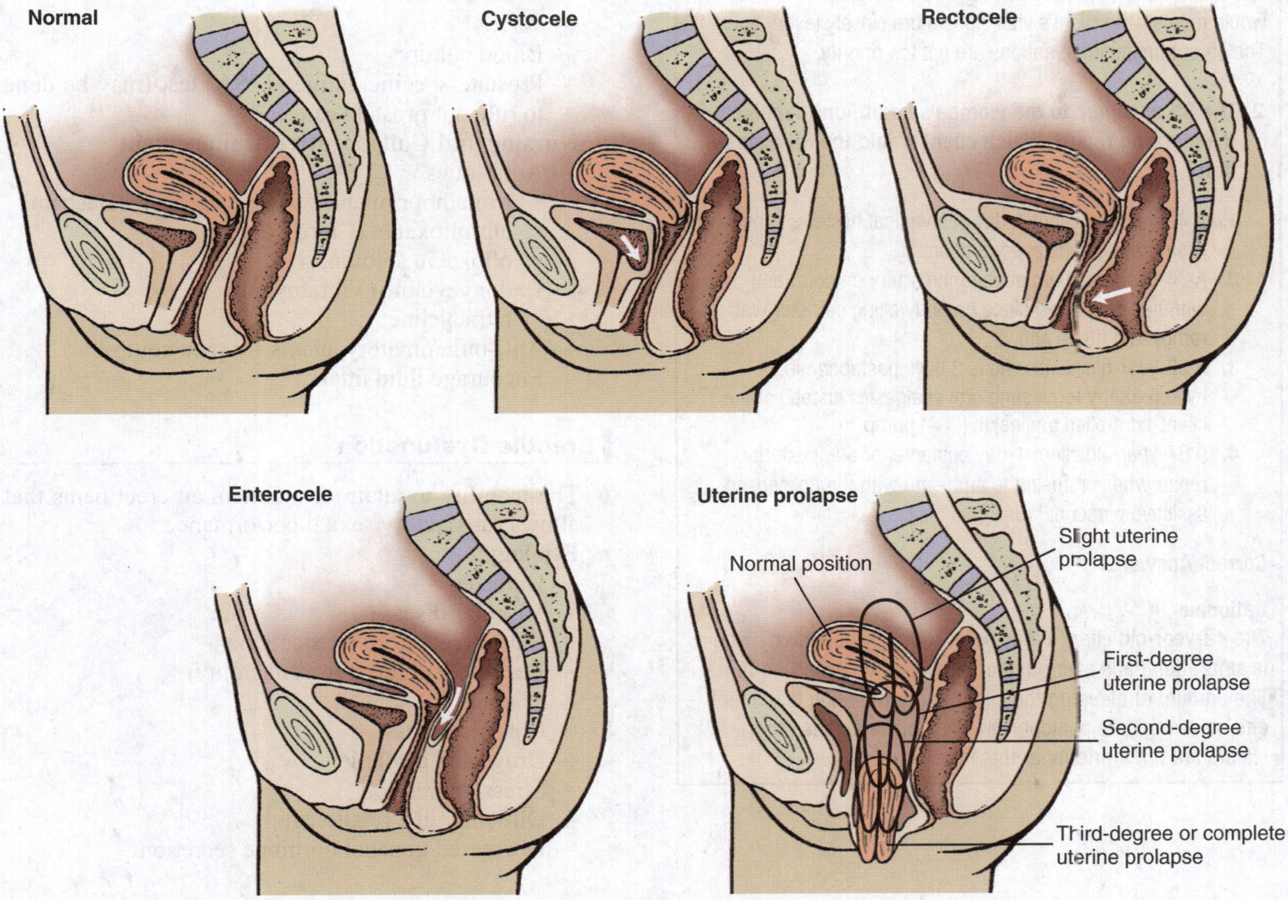

Types of genital prolapse. (Reprinted with permission from Monahan, F.D., Drake, D.T., & Neighbors, M. [eds.]. [1998]. *Medical-surgical nursing: Foundations for clinical practice* [2nd ed.]. Philadelphia: Saunders.)

Notes

Study Break Box

1. A client who had a vaginal hysterectomy the previous day is saturating perineal pads with blood that require frequent changes during the night. Which priority action would the RN take?

1. Provide iron-rich foods on each dietary tray.
2. Monitor the client's vital signs every hour.
3. Administer IV fluids at the prescribed rate.
4. Encourage postoperative leg exercises.

Correct Answer: 2

Rationale

The client has experienced excessive bleeding, and the RN would monitor the client's vital signs more closely (every hour). The other nursing interventions are not the priority.

2. The RN assigned to the women's health unit received the morning report. Which client would the RN assess first?

1. A 49-year-old client 1-day postvaginal hysterectomy who is saturating pads every 3 hours.
2. A 34-year-old client postuterine artery embolization who has not voided since her indwelling catheter was removed 4 hours ago.
3. A 52-year-old client who is 2 days postabdominal hysterectomy requesting oral analgesics instead of the client-controlled analgesia (PCA) pump.
4. A 67-year-old client 1-day postanterior and posterior repair who is refusing to ambulate with the unlicensed assistive personnel (UAP).

Correct Answer: 1

Rationale

The 49-year-old client 1-day postvaginal hysterectomy who is saturating pads every 3 hours needs to be assessed first. The amount of bleeding the client is experiencing is too high and could indicate postoperative hemorrhage. The other clients are not a priority at this time.

Male Reproductive Conditions: Prostatitis

- Prostatitis is one of the most common urologic disorders.
- **Common manifestations of acute bacterial prostatitis include the following:**
  - — Fever
  - — Chills
  - — Back pain
  - — Perineal pain
  - — Dysuria
  - — Urinary frequency
  - — Urgency
  - — Cloudy urine
- **Diagnostic Studies**
  - — Urinalysis (UA)
  - — Urine culture
  - — WBCs
  - — Blood cultures
  - — Prostate-specific antigen (PSA) test (may be done to rule out prostate cancer)
- **Nursing and Collaborative Management**
  - — Antibiotics
    - trimethoprim and sulfamethoxazole (Bactrim)
    - ciprofloxacin (Cipro)
    - ofloxacin (Floxin)
    - doxycycline (Vibramycin)
    - tetracycline
  - — Anti-inflammatory agents for pain control
  - — Encourage fluid intake

Erectile Dysfunction

- The inability to attain or maintain an erect penis that allows satisfactory sexual performance.
- **Etiology**
  - — Diabetes
  - — Vascular disease
  - — Side effects from medications
  - — Result of surgery (prostatectomy)
  - — Trauma
  - — Chronic illness
  - — Drugs and alcohol
  - — Stress/depression
  - — Difficulty in a relationship
  - — Decreased gonadal hormone secretion

Notes

- **Oral Drug Therapy**
  - — The treatment for ED is based on the underlying cause
  - — sildenafil citrate
    - Dosage: 25 to 100 mg PO, one dose per day, 1 hour before sexual activity
    - May potentiate the hypotensive effect of nitrates
    - They are contraindicated for individuals taking nitrates (e.g., nitroglycerin) or riociguat
    - Reinforce to clients to seek medical attention for an erection lasting longer than 4 hours (priapism)
    - Use with caution in elderly because drugs are slow to metabolize and be excreted

Test-Taking Strategy

Read the entire scenario and question before focusing on the answer options. Candidates who do not thoroughly read the questions may miss keywords/phrases within the scenario or misinterpret the question's focus. When you are preparing for or actually taking the NCLEX exam, make sure you understand what the question is *really* asking.

Next-Generation NCLEX® Examination (NGN)–Style Question

Drop Down Table Box

Scenario: The RN is assessing a 25-year-old female complaining of severe left flank and abdominal pain, nausea, and vomiting. Skin is warm and clammy. She is bending over at the waist and clutching her abdomen and appears very tired. She reports that pain started last night and has steadily increased throughout the morning. She states she works outside but has limited break times to drink water. Assessment: her abdomen is soft and non-tender, but her left flank is extremely tender to touch. VSs: BP: 178/97, P: 110, R: 24, T: 99°F (37.2°C), pain: 8/10.

Complete the following table by choosing the anticipated order for each area of care.	
Radiology	(1)
Laboratory	(2)
Medication	(3)

Drop-Down Options #1	Drop-Down Options #2	Drop-Down Options #3
Abdominal x-ray	BNP	Ketorolac
MRI of abdomen	Midstream U/A	Ceftriaxone
CT of abdomen	Blood cultures ×2	Desmopressin
Pelvic ULS	Urea breath test	Nitrofurantoin

Answer: The scenario indicates that this client may be experiencing a kidney stone. Computed tomography (CT) of abdomen is the most accurate radiological procedure to diagnose renal calculi. A midstream U/A can also be effective for diagnosing urinary complications. Ketorolac can help with pain and relax the ureter to facilitate stone passage. The other orders are not indicated for this client at this time.

Notes

8 Movement, Coordination, and Sensory Input

Level of Consciousness

- **Glasgow Coma Scale**
  - — Used to assess level of consciousness (LOC)
  - — Maximum score 15, minimum 3
  - — Score of >8 = good prognosis
  - — Score of <7 = coma
  - — Score of 3 to 4 = high mortality rate

GLASGOW COMA SCALE*	
Eye Opening	
Spontaneous	4
To sound	3
To pain	2
Never	1
Motor Response	
Obeys commands	6
Localizes pain	5
Normal flexion (withdrawal)	4
Abnormal flexion	3
Extension	2
None	1
Verbal Response	
Oriented	5
Confused conversation	4
Inappropriate words	3
Incomprehensible sounds	2
None	1

* The highest possible score is 15.

The Glasgow Coma Scale. (Reprinted with permission from Ignatavicius, D. D., Workman, M. L., Rebar, C. R., & Heimgartner, N. M. [2021]. Medical-Surgical Nursing: Concepts for Interprofessional Collaborative Care [10th ed.]. Elsevier.)

- A decrease in LOC may be the earliest sign of increasing intracranial pressure (ICP).
- **Neurological vital signs (VSs)**
  - — Pupil size
  - — Limb movement
  - — VSs
- **Nursing Assessment**
  - — Assess for early signs/symptoms of changes in LOC, which is the most sensitive and reliable indicator
  - — Early signs
    - ↓ LOC
    - Change in orientation
  - — Late signs
    - Cushing's triad
      - Widening pulse pressure
      - Slowing heart rate with full bounding pulse
      - Slowing and irregular respirations
    - Change in size, response of pupils, dilated on side of injury initially
    - Elevated temperature
    - Posturing
    - Assess for change in respiratory status
      - Cheyne-Stokes respiration
- **Nursing and Collaborative Management**
  - — Maintain airway and provide adequate oxygenation
  - — ↓ LOC will need mechanical ventilation
    - Hyperventilate before suctioning
    - Limit suctioning to 15 seconds
    - Keep airway free of secretions
    - Prevent aspiration; turn head to side
    - Elevate head of bed (HOB) to 30 degrees to enhance respiration
  - — Prevent complications r/t sustained ↑ ICP
    - ICP monitoring target: 5–15 mm Hg
    - Elevate HOB 30 to 45 degrees to promote venous return
    - Place the neck in a neutral position (not flexed or extended) to promote venous drainage
    - Position the client to avoid flexion of the hips, waist, and neck, especially to the right
    - Implement measures to help client avoid Valsalva maneuver

Notes

- — ICP monitoring
  - Goal ICP: <20 mm Hg
- — Controlled hyperventilation
- — Mild hypothermia
- — Cerebrospinal fluid (CSF) drainage
- — Infection is a serious complication, and systemic antibiotics are often ordered prophylactically
- — **Medications**
  - Hyperosmotic agents: 20% mannitol
  - Steroids (associated with ↑ risk of infection)
    - Dexamethasone
    - Methylprednisolone
  - Barbiturates
  - Prophylactic phenytoin sodium
  - Diuretics: alternate with mannitol
  - Avoid narcotics!

Study Break Box

1. **The RN is caring for several clients. Which client would the RN assess first?**
   1. A 20-year-old client whose Glasgow Coma Scale is 8 and unchanged from the last assessment.
   2. A 45-year-old client with a left-sided cerebrovascular accident (CVA) who refuses his morning care.
   3. A 38-year-old client who is increasingly stuporous after an aneurysm repair.
   4. A 29-year-old client post motor vehicle accident (MVA) whose Glasgow Coma Scale was 9 one hour ago and is now 10.

Correct Answer: 3

Rationale

The 38-year-old client who is increasingly stuporous after an aneurysm repair is of highest priority and needs to be assessed first. Changes in LOC may be the earliest sign of increasing ICP. The other clients are not as high of a priority.

2. **Which change in the status of a client being treated for increased ICP warrants immediate action by the RN?**
   1. Urinary output changes from 20 to 50 mL/hr.
   2. Arterial PCO_2 changes from 40 to 30 mm Hg.
   3. Glasgow Coma Scale score changes from 5 to 7.
   4. Pulse decreases from 88 to 68 beats/min.

Study Break Box—cont'd

Correct Answer: 4

Rationale

A client's pulse that drops from 88 to 68 beats/min is a component of sign of Cushing's triad, which indicates incrəased ICP.

Head Injury

- **Symptoms**
  - — Changes in LOC
  - — Signs of increased ICP
    - Changes in VS
    - Headache, amnesia
    - Vomiting
    - Pupillary changes (unequal/dilated)
    - Seizure
    - Ataxia
    - Abnormal posturing (decorticate [A] or decerebrate [B])

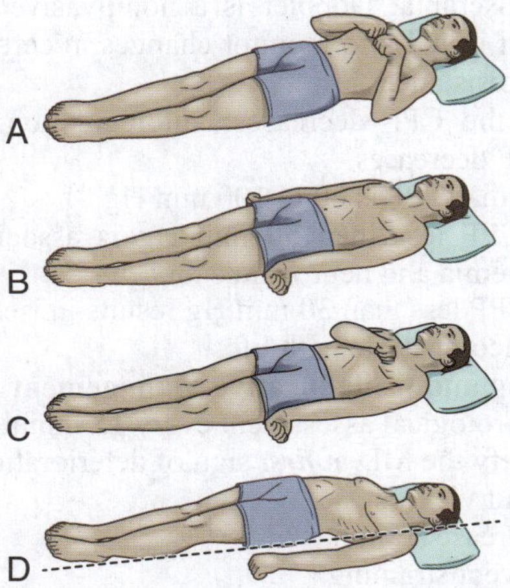

Decorticate and decerebrate posturing. A, Decorticate response. Flexion of arms, wrists, and fingers with adduction in upper extremities. Extension, internal rotation, and plantar flexion in lower extremities. B, Decerebrate response. All 4 extremities in rigid extension, with hyperpronation of forearms and plantar flexion of feet. C, Decorticate response on right side of body and decerebrate response on left side of body. D, Opisthotonic posturing. (Reprinted with permission from Harding, M., Kwong, J., Roberts, D., Hagler, D., & Reinisch, C. [2020]. *Lewis's medical-surgical nursing: Assessment and management of clinical problems* [11th ed.]. Elsevier.)

Notes

- Extremity motor strength and use: depressed or hyperactive
- Check for lacerations, bruises, skull depression, confusion, combativeness, personality changes

CSF Leakage

- Risk for meningitis with leakage
- Usual signs of ↑ ICP may not be seen with leakage of CSF
- Drainage may come from nose (rhinorrhea) or ears (otorrhea)
- Mean arterial pressure (MAP) – ICP = CPP (cerebral perfusion pressure)
- CPP > 70 mm Hg
  - The cerebral perfusion pressure (CPP) is the pressure needed to ensure blood flow to the brain.
  - CPP is equal to the MAP minus the ICP (CPP = MAP – ICP)
  - When cerebral vascular resistance is high, blood flow to brain tissue is impaired.
  - Transcranial Doppler is a noninvasive technique used in ICUs to monitor changes in cerebrovascular resistance.
  - As the CPP decreases, autoregulation fails and CBF decreases.
  - Normal CPP is 60 to 100 mm Hg.
  - A CPP less than 50 mm Hg is associated with ischemia and neuronal death.
  - A CPP less than 30 mm Hg results in ischemia and is incompatible with life.*
- **Nursing and Collaborative Management**
  - Neurological assessment every 15 minutes
  - Notify the MD at ***first*** sign of deterioration
  - Limit visitors
  - Decrease stimuli
  - Prevent straining
  - Keep HOB at 30 to 45 degrees
  - Avoid neck flexion
  - Monitor I&O

*Harding, M., Kwong, J., Roberts, D., Hagler, D., & Reinisch, C. (2020). *Lewis's medical-surgical nursing: Assessment and management of clinical problems* (11th ed.). Elsevier.

Study Break Box

1. Which assessment finding would the RN recognize as a late sign of increased ICP in a client diagnosed with a CVA or stroke? (Select all that apply.)

1. Alteration in the ability to respond to questions.
2. Irregular breathing with periods of apnea.
3. Consensual response of pupils.
4. Heart rate 50, blood pressure (BP) 192/60.
5. Drooping of the mouth on one side.

Correct Answer(s): 2, 4

Rationale

Irregular breathing with periods of apnea is a late sign of increased ICP. A heart rate of 50 beats/min and a BP of 192/60 mm Hg are late signs of increased ICP. The other findings are not late signs of increased ICP.

Strokes/Cerebrovascular Accident (CVA)

- **Causes**: a disruption in the blood supply to part of the brain. A medical emergency, strokes are classified as ischemic or hemorrhagic.
  - Transient ischemic attack (TIA): a transient episode of neurological dysfunction caused by focal brain, spinal cord, or retinal ischemia but without acute infarction of the brain. Clinical symptoms typically last less than 1 hour. Most fully resolve.
  - Ischemic stroke: a clot may be thromboembolic or embolic, causing minimal or absent blood flow to the neurons.
  - Hemorrhagic stroke: may be a subarachnoid hemorrhage (SAH; bleeding into the subarachnoid space) or an intracranial hemorrhage (direct bleeding into the brain tissue)

Notes

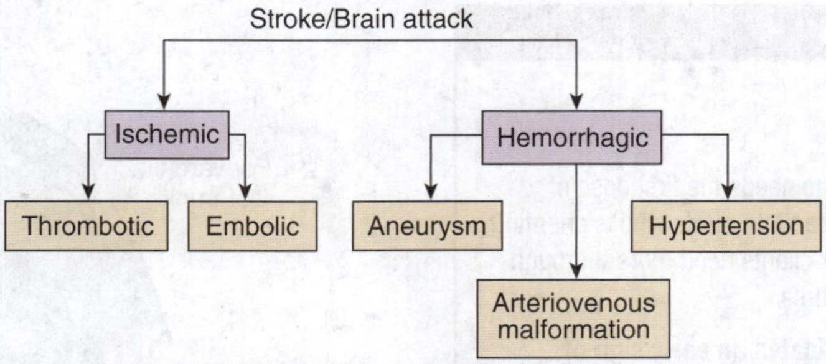

Types of stroke or brain attack. (Reprinted with permission from Ignatavicius, D. D., Workman, M. L., Rebar, C. R., & Heimgartner, N. M. [2021]. Medical-Surgical Nursing: Concepts for Interprofessional Collaborative Care [10th ed.]. Elsevier.)

- **Risk factors**
  - Cardiovascular disease (CVD), hypertension (HTN), history of TIA
  - Diabetes
  - Advanced age, males, African American
  - History of a-fib or flutter
  - Birth control pills (BCPs), hormone replacement, antihistamine drugs
  - Smoking, alcohol, substance abuse
- **Symptoms**
  - Hemiparesis, hemiplegia
  - Dysarthria, dysphasia, aphasia, apraxia
  - Sensory disturbances
  - Impaired mental capacity/psychological loss
  - Bladder dysfunction
  - Face, arms, speech, time (FAST)

Nursing and Collaborative Management

- Time lost is brain lost
- Hemorrhagic or ischemic
- Computed tomography (CT) scan or magnetic resonance imaging (MRI)
- Prepare for thrombolytic therapy (limited therapeutic window)
- Assess for signs and symptoms of increased ICP
- Assess verbal ability and plan care appropriate to the client's ability to communicate
- Assess swallowing to prevent aspiration
- Assess for bowel and bladder control
- Assess functional abilities
  - Mobility, activities of daily living (ADLs), elimination

Study Break Box

1. The RN is planning a class on stroke prevention for clients with HTN. Which information reflects accurate prevention measures that the clients can undertake? (Select all that apply.)

1. Limit salt intake to 1500 mg/day or less.
2. Eliminate tobacco products.
3. Initiate a program of walking 1 mile per day.
4. Achieve a body mass index (BMI) of 26.2.
5. Schedule routine health assessments biannually.

Correct Answer(s): 1, 2, 3

Rationale

Limiting salt intake, eliminating tobacco products, and initiating a program of walking every day can help reduce the risk of stroke for at risk clients. A BMI of 26.2 is considered overweight; therefore, the client should attempt to achieve a BMI of less than 25. Clients with HTN should follow up with their care providers more frequently until BP is well controlled.

2. Which client would be assigned to a graduate nurse orienting to the neurological unit?

1. A client with a head injury who has a Glasgow Coma Scale of 6.
2. A client who developed autonomic dysreflexia after a T6 spinal cord injury.
3. A client with multiple sclerosis who needs the first dose of interferon.
4. A client diagnosed with Guillain-Barré syndrome.

Notes

Study Break Box—cont'd

Correct Answer: 3

Rationale

A client with multiple sclerosis who needs the first dose of interferon can be assigned to a graduate nurse who is orienting to the neurological unit. The other clients need more thorough assessment by an experienced nurse.

3. **Which finding by the RN indicates an early sign of increased ICP in a client newly diagnosed with a cerebral vascular accident? (Select all that apply.)**

   1. Alteration in the ability to respond to questions.
   2. Alteration in the ability to respond to verbal stimuli.
   3. Consensual response of pupils.
   4. Heart rate 50, BP 192/60.
   5. Drooping of the mouth on one side.

Correct Answer(s): 1, 2

Rationale

Confusion and difficulty speaking are early signs of increased ICP. Alteration in the ability to respond to questions and a change in the ability to respond to verbal stimuli are included in these symptoms. Consensual pupil response is a normal reaction. Widening pulse pressure and bradycardia are two components of Cushing's triad, which is a late sign of increased ICP and indicate a life-threatening condition. Drooping of the mouth on one side can indicate a CVA.

Parkinson's Disease

- **Symptoms**
  - — Rigidity
  - — Masklike face
  - — Akinesia
    - Difficulty initiating and continuing movement
    - Bradykinesia
  - — Tremors
    - Resting
    - Pill rolling
  - — Postural instability

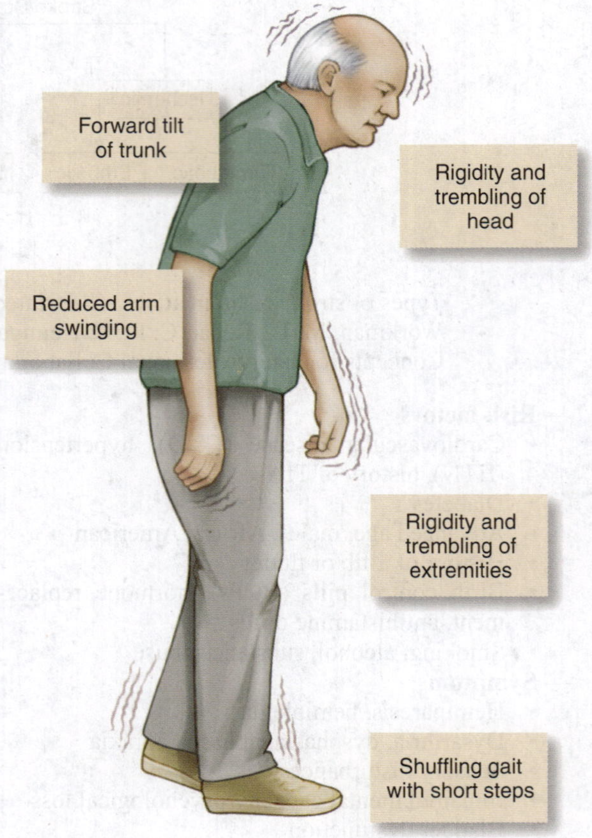

Characteristic appearance of a client with Parkinson's disease. (Reprinted with permission from Patton, K.T., & Thibodeau, G.A. [2018]. *The human body in health & disease* [7th ed.]. St. Louis: Mosby.)

- **Nursing and Collaborative Management**
  - — Safety is always a priority!
  - — Take medications with meals
  - — Administer as prescribed
  - — Change positions slowly to decrease postural hypotension
  - — Thicken liquids
  - — Provide soft, ground foods
  - — Encourage activity and exercise

Notes

- **Medications**
  - — Dopaminergics
    - Levodopa
      - Blocks breakdown of levodopa to allow more levodopa to cross the blood-brain barrier
      - Avoid foods high in vitamin B6 and protein
    - Levodopa-carbidopa oral
      - Allows for less use of levodopa and assists with decreasing side effects
  - — Dopaminergic Agonists
    - Help with motor fluctuations
    - Rotigotine, pramipexole, ropinirole, amantadine, apomorphine
  - — Anticholinergics
    - Treat tremors
    - Trihexyphenidyl
    - Benztropine mesylate
    - Procyclidine hydrochloride
  - — Antihistamine
    - Diphenhydramine
  - — Monoamine Oxidase Inhibitors
    - Selegiline
  - — Catechol-*O*-methyl transferase (COMT) inhibitors
    - Entacapone

Study Break Box

1. **A client diagnosed with Parkinson's disease is prescribed carbidopa-levodopa. Which observation by the RN indicates that the desired effect of the medication is being achieved?**

   1. Decreased BP.
   2. Steady gait.
   3. Increased salivation.
   4. Increased attention span.

Correct Answer: 2

Rationale

Carbidopa-levodopa has a dramatic effect on controlling the symptoms of unsteady or ataxic gait. The other findings do not indicate effective medication therapy with carbidopa-levodopa.

Guillain-Barré Syndrome

- **Causes**
  - — Involves peripheral and cranial nerves in acute inflammatory demyelination process
  - — Usually occurs after an upper respiratory infection
- **Nursing Assessment**
  - — Ascending paralysis
  - — Rapid demyelination of the nerves
  - — Paralysis of respiratory system may occur quickly
    - Prepare to intubate
  - — Tingling in fingers and toes
  - — Muscle weakness
  - — Severe lower back pain
  - — Facial paralysis
  - — Some clients experience a prolonged recovery time
- **Nursing and Collaborative Management**
  - — Plasmapheresis over 10 to 15 days
  - — IV high-dose immunoglobulin (Sandoglobulin) is effective as plasma exchange and has the advantage of immediate availability and greater safety
    - Immunoglobulin client must be well hydrated and have adequate renal function
  - — Maintain patent airway. Position with the head to the side
  - — Reposition every 2 hours and PRN
  - — Impaired swallowing may need:
    - Thickened liquids
    - Small, frequent feedings
    - TPN
    - NPO if gag reflex is absent
  - — Provide psychological support

Study Break Box

1. **The RN is caring for a client with Guillain-Barré syndrome. Which information would the RN report to the primary health care provider (HCP) immediately?**

   1. Ascending numbness from the feet to the knees.
   2. A decrease in cognitive status.
   3. Blurred vision and sensation changes
   4. A persistent unilateral headache.

Correct Answer: 2

Rationale

Decrease in cognitive status is the most concerning sign because it indicates decreased oxygenation of the brain, which occurs as the respiratory muscles are affected with ascending paralysis. The other findings do not need to be reported to the HCP immediately.

Notes

Multiple Sclerosis

- Demyelination of the central nervous system (CNS)

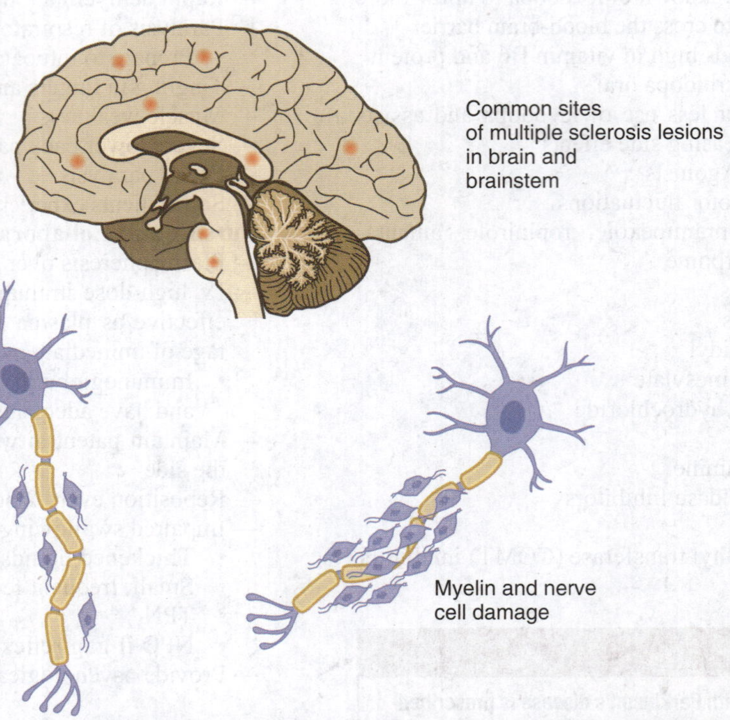

The lesions in multiple sclerosis: location and effects. (Reprinted with permission from Hopper, T. [2013]. *Mosby's pharmacy technician* [3rd ed.]. St. Louis: Saunders.)

- **Symptoms**
  — Messages garbled, short-circuited from brain to CNS
  — Clients experience periods of remissions and exacerbations
  — Changes in visual field, diplopia
  — Weaknesses in extremities
  — Numbness, tremors
  — Visual or swallowing difficulties
  — Severe fatigue/emotional problems
  — Gait disturbances
- **Nursing and Collaborative Management**
  — Encourage self-care, rest periods
  — Initiate fall prevention
  — Implement voiding schedule, bowel regimen
  — Refer to home care
  — Administer steroids, chemotherapeutic drugs
  — Avoid abrupt changes in room lighting
  — Provide assistive devices to meet client's specific deficits
  — Thicken liquids
- **Pharmacological Therapy**
  — Corticosteroids
  - Prednisone
  - Methylprednisone

  — Immunomodulators
  - Interfereron-beta
  - Glatiramer acetate

  — Immunosuppressants
  - Mitoxantrone HCL

  Cholinergics
  - Bethanechol
  - Neostigmine

Notes

- Anticholinergics
  - Propantheline bromide
  - Ocybutynin
- Muscle Relaxants
  - Diazepam
  - Baclofen
  - Dantrolene sodium
  - Tizanidine
- CNS Stimulants
  - Methyphenidate HCL
  - Modafinil
  - Pemoline
- Antiviral/Antiparkinsonian drugs
  - Amantadine

Myasthenia Gravis

- A chronic neuromuscular autoimmune disease.
- **Causes**
  - Fluctuating muscle weakness and abnormal fatigue of voluntary muscles that increase throughout the day
- **Symptoms**
  - Ocular muscle weakness
  - Bulbar muscle weakness
  - Skeletal muscle weakness
- **Diagnosis**
  - Based on clinical presentation
    - Muscle weakness
  - Tensilon test: 2 mg IV given in small doses
    - Confirmed by improved response to anticholinesterase drugs
- **Nursing and Collaborative Management**
  - Anticholinesterase agents
    - Try to achieve maximum strength and endurance
    - Block action of cholinesterase
    - Increase levels of ACH at junctions
    - Common medications: mestinon, prostigmin
    - Start with minimal doses
      - Onset 30 minutes
      - Duration 3 to 4 hours
      - Must take on time!
  - Corticosteroid: prednisone
  - Immunosuppressive agents: azathioprine, cyclophosphamide
- **Types of Crises**
  - **Myasthenic Crisis**
    - **MEDICAL EMERGENCY!**
    - Neostigmine may be administered
    - Caused by undermedication or infection
    - Positive Tensilon test
    - Changes in VS, cyanosis, loss of cough and gag reflex, incontinence
    - May require intubation
  - **Cholinergic Crisis**
    - Atropine may be administered
    - Results from overmedication
    - Toxic levels of anticholinesterase medications
    - Negative Tensilon test
    - Symptoms: abdominal cramps, diarrhea, excessive pulmonary secretions, n/v, blurred vision, pallor
- **Nursing and Collaborative Management**
  - Coughing and deep-breathing exercises
  - Suction equipment
  - Sit upright when eating and for 1 hour afterward
  - Keep chin downward when swallowing
  - Plan activities and rest carefully; weakness worsens at end of the day

Notes

Spinal Cord Injury

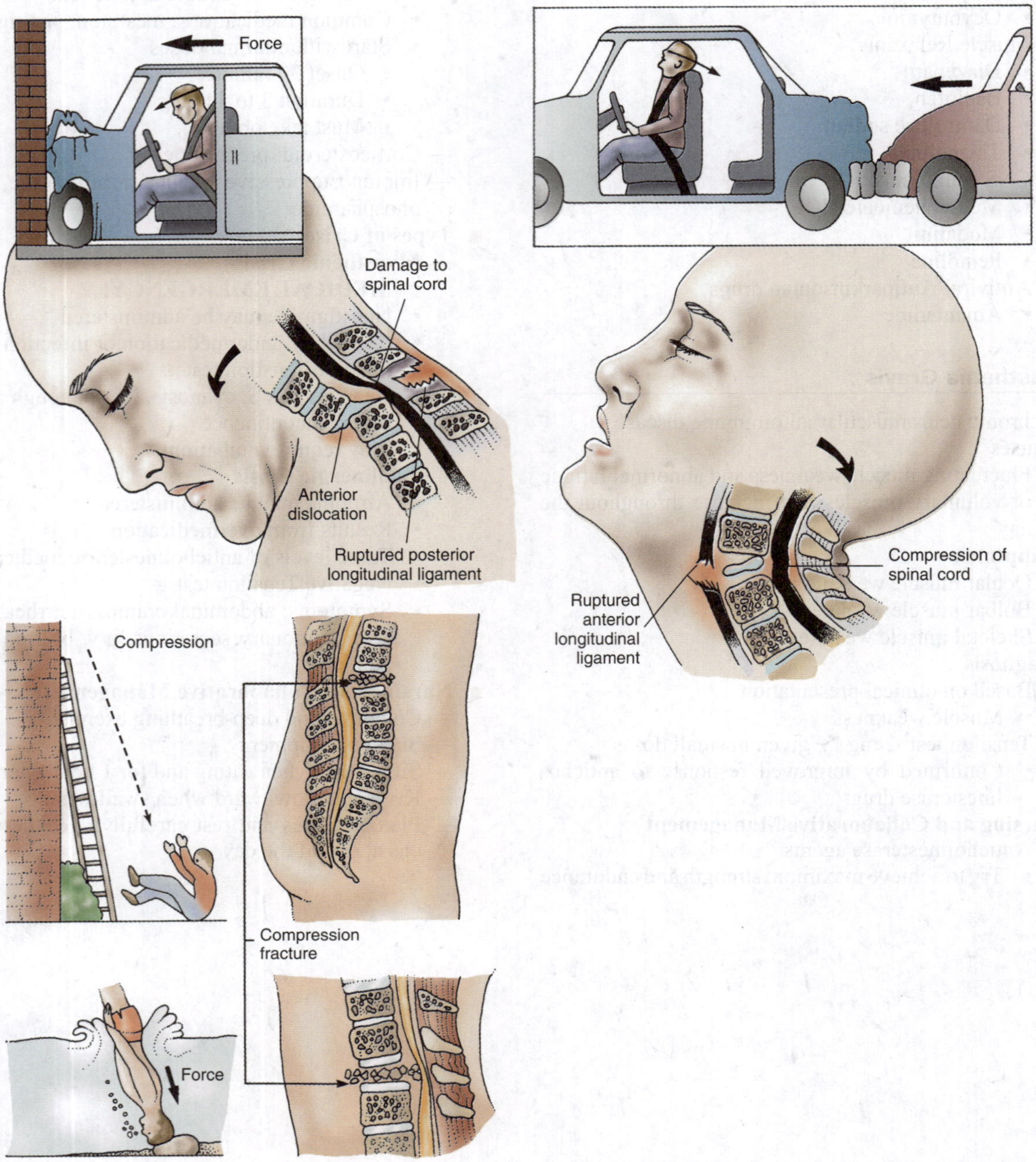

Mechanisms of spinal cord injury. (Reprinted with permission from Ignatavicius, D. D., Workman, M. L., Rebar, C. R., & Heimgartner, N. M. [2021]. Medical-Surgical Nursing: Concepts for Interprofessional Collaborative Care [10th ed.]. Elsevier.)

Notes

- **Classification**
  - — Extent of injury (complete, incomplete)
  - — Level of injury (skeletal, neurological)
  - — Mechanism of injury (i.e., flexion)
    - Transection/partial transection
- **Rule of thumb**
  - — Above C8 = quadriplegic
  - — Below C8 = paraplegic
- **Nursing and Collaborative Management**
  - — Start with the ABCs: Priority nursing assessment!
  - — Determine quality of respiratory rate
  - — Assess neurological status
  - — Assess VSs
  - — Hypotension and bradycardia occur in injuries above T6
  - — Immobilize and stabilize
  - — Keep neck and body in anatomical alignment
  - — Maintain patent airway
  - — Spinal shock: temporary loss of sensation and reflexes
  - — **Flaccid paralysis/neurogenic shock**
    - Complete loss of reflexes
    - Hypotension
    - Bradycardia
    - Bowel and bladder distention
    - Reverse as quickly as possible
  - — **Autonomic Dysreflexia**
    - Medical emergency with injuries at or above T6
      - Notify the HCP immediately
    - Exaggerated autonomic reflex response
    - Usually triggered by bowel or bladder distention
    - S/S: severe headache, ↑ BP, bradycardia, flushing, and profuse sweating
    - Elevate HOB (while maintaining correct alignment)
    - Administer nitrates, hydralazine
- **Post Spinal Shock**
  - — Rehabilitation
  - — Monitor for paralytic ileus
    - Assess bowel sounds
  - — Kinetic bed to promote blood flow, range of motion (ROM) exercises
  - — Anti-embolism stockings, sequential compression devices
  - — Protect from skin breakdown
  - — Psychosocial assessment
  - — Bowel and bladder training
    - Keep bladder empty and urine dilute and acidic to prevent urinary tract infection

Notes

Fractures: Nursing Assessment

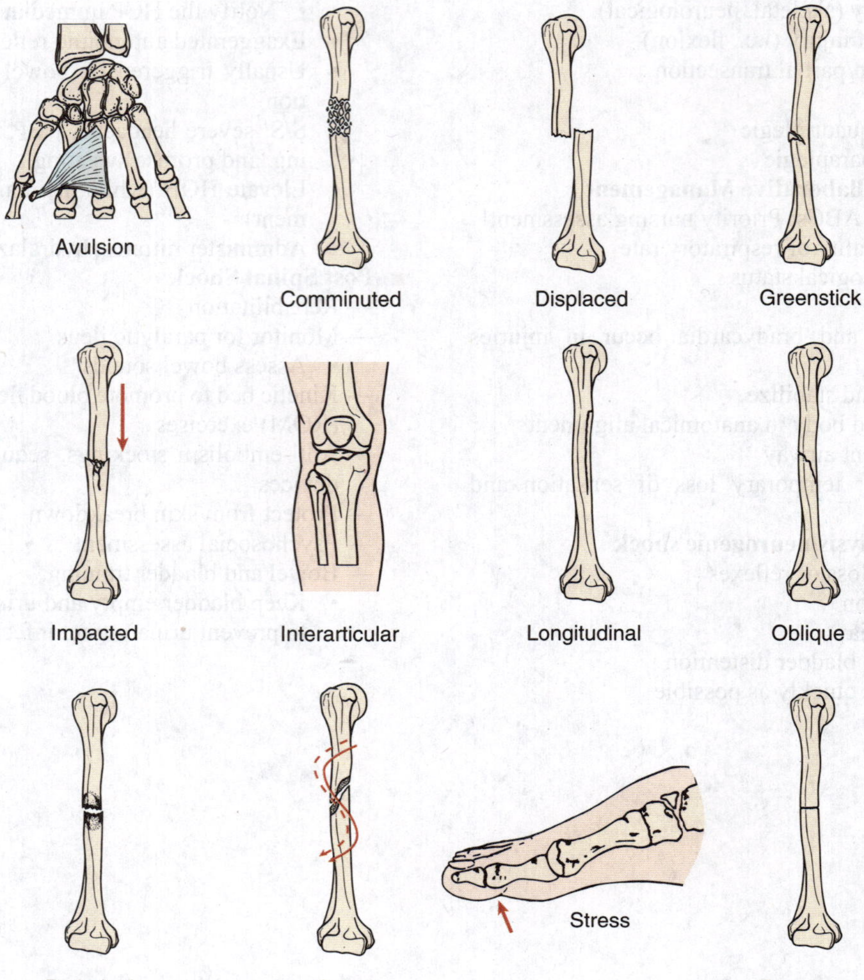

Common types of fractures. (Reprinted with permission from Lewis, S., Dirksen, S., Heitkemper, M., Bucher, L., O'Brien, P. [2007]. *Medical-surgical nursing* [7th ed.]. St. Louis: Mosby.)

- **Symptoms and Assessment**
  - — Swelling, deformity of the extremity
  - — Discoloration, loss of functional ability
  - — Fracture evident on x-ray
  - — Assess for 5 Ps of neurovascular functioning.
    - **P**ain, **P**aresthesia, **P**ulse, **P**allor, and **P**aralysis
  - — Assess neurovascular area distal to injury
    - Skin color, temperature, sensation, capillary refill, mobility, pain, pulses, compartment syndrome
- **Nursing and Collaborative Management**
  - — Instruct the client on proper use of assistive devices
  - — Closed or open reduction
  - — Postreduction
    - Cast
    - Traction

Notes

- External fixation
- Splints
- Orthoses (braces)

Study Break Box

1. The RN is assessing a client who is scheduled for surgical fixation of a compound fracture of the right ulna. Which finding would the RN report to the HCP?

1. Ecchymosis around the fracture site.
2. Crepitus at the fracture site.
3. Paresthesia distal to the fracture site.
4. Diminished ROM of the right arm.

Correct Answer: 3

Rationale

Paresthesia distal to the fracture site could be an early sign of compartment syndrome, which is a medical emergency that could result in loss of the limb if not treated immediately. All other findings are expected with this type of injury.

Joint Replacement

- **Post–Operative Care**
  - — Assess circulation, sensation, and movement of extremity distal to replacement area
  - — Keep body in proper alignment
  - — Encourage fluid intake
  - — Use of bedpan, commode chair
  - — Coordinate rehabilitation process
- **Instructions for Discharge Home**
  - — Safety
  - — Accessibility
- **Drugs**
  - — Anticoagulants
  - — Analgesics
  - — Parenteral antibiotics

Amputation

- **Postoperative Care**
  - — Monitor surgical dressing for drainage
  - — Proper body alignment
    - *Elevate* the residual limb (stump) in the first 24 hours
    - Do **NOT** elevate after *48 hours*
  - — Provide passive ROM
  - — Encourage prone position periodically to decrease risk of contracture
  - — Proper stump bandaging to prepare for prosthesis
  - — Coordinate of care with occupational therapist (OT), physical therapist (PT), and social worker
  - — Assess and address grieving
  - — Administer analgesics and antibiotics
  - — REMEMBER: Phantom limb pain is real and requires pharmacological interventions; be sure to assess and address client grief

Osteoporosis

- **Risk Factors**
  - — Small-boned postmenopausal females, Caucasian, Asian, pregnancy, breastfeeding, family history
  - — Diet low in calcium
  - — Excessive alcohol, tobacco, and caffeine
  - — Sedentary lifestyle
  - — Low testosterone level in men
  - — Diabetes, cirrhosis, corticosteroids, loop diuretics
- **Symptoms**
  - — Dowager's hump (outward curvature of the upper spine)
  - — Kyphosis of the dorsal spine
  - — Loss of height
  - — Pathological fractures
  - — Compression fracture of the spine can occur
- **Nursing and Collaborative Management**
  - — Keep the bed in low position
  - — Provide adequate lighting
  - — Avoid using throw rugs
  - — Provide assistance with ambulation
  - — Follow regular exercise program
  - — Encourage diet high in vitamin D, protein, and calcium
  - — Encourage 20 minutes of UV exposure a day
  - — Routine dual-energy x-ray absorptiometry (DEXA) screening begins at 60
- **Drug Therapy**
  - — Bisphosphonates
    - Alendronate, etidronate, zoledronic acid, ibandronate, pamidronate, risedronate
  - — Selective Estrogen Receptor Modulators
    - Raloxifene HCL
    - Teriparatide
  - — Recombinant Parathyroid Hormone
    - Teriparatide

Notes

Study Break Box

1. A postmenopausal client with a BMI of 19 has come to the clinic for an annual examination. Which information is most important for the RN to prepare for this high-risk client?

1. Osteoporosis.
2. Obesity.
3. Anorexia.
4. Breast cancer.

Correct Answer: 1

Rationale

The RN would prepare a teaching plan for this client who is at high risk for osteoporosis due to her postmenopausal status and a low BMI, indicating she is underweight relative to height. The other information is not priority information that the RN needs to share.

2. The RN is conducting an osteoporosis screening clinic at a health fair. Which information would the RN provide to individuals who are at risk for osteoporosis? (Select all that apply.)

1. Limit alcohol and stop smoking.
2. Suggest supplementing the diet with vitamin E.
3. Promote regular weight-bearing exercise.
4. Implement a home safety plan to prevent falls.
5. Propose a regular sleep pattern of 8 hours nightly.

Correct Answer(s): 1, 3, 4

Rationale

The RN would advise at risk individuals to limit consumption of alcohol and tobacco, increase weight-bearing exercise, and instruct on home safety with fall precautions. A diet high in vitamin D (not E) will help with calcium absorption. Regular sleep patterns will not decrease the risk for osteoporosis.

Rheumatoid Arthritis

- Chronic, systemic, progressive deterioration of the connective tissue.
- Etiology: unknown, believed to be autoimmune.
- Young to middle age; more females than males.

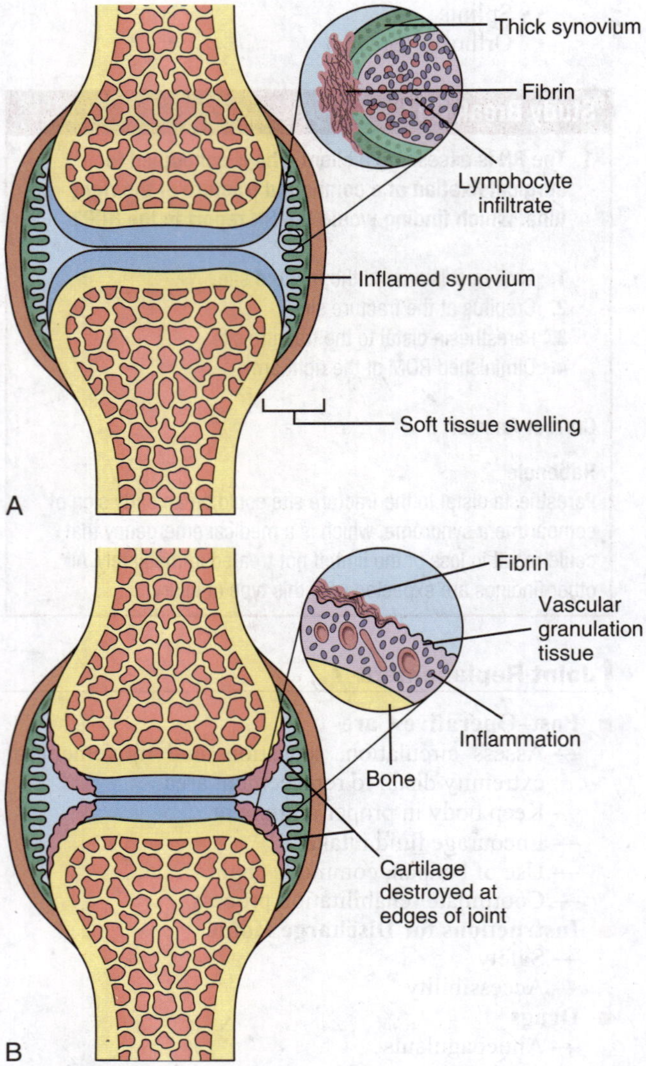

Phases in the progression of rheumatoid arthritis (RA). (A) Early phase: leukocytes increase in inflamed synovium. (B) Pannus grows over the cartilage; bone edges erode; destruction of articular tissue.

(Cont'd)

Notes

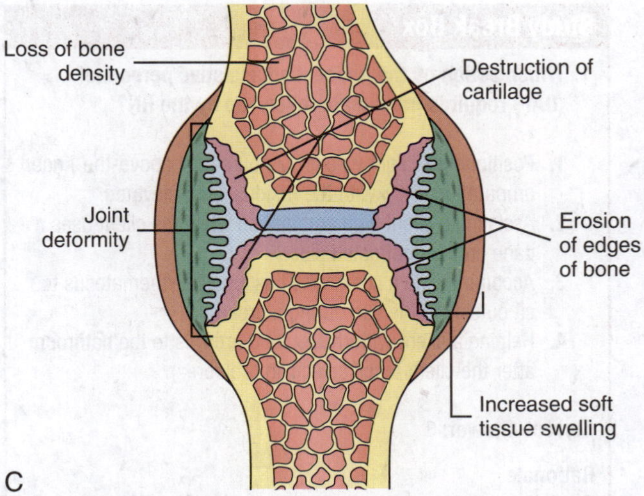

(C) Destruction of bone. (Reprinted with permission from Stevens, A., & Lowe, J. [2000]. Pathology: *Illustrated review in color* [2nd ed.]. London: Mosby.

- **Symptoms**
  - — Systemic with exacerbations and remissions
  - — Small joints first, then spreads
  - — Joint pain, stiffness (may decrease with use)
  - — Decreased ROM
  - — Elevated erythrocyte sedimentation rate (ESR)
  - — Positive rheumatoid factor (RF) in 80% of clients
  - — Narrowed joint space

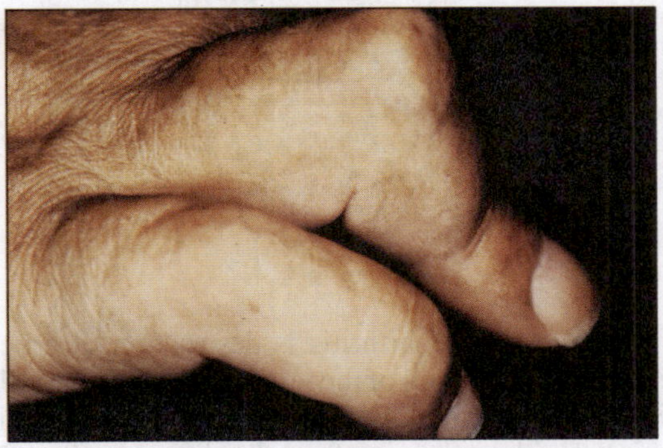

Boutonniere deformity. (Reprinted with permission from Hochberg, M. C., Gravallese, E. M., Silman, A. J., et al. [2019]. *Rheumatology* [7th ed.]. Philadelphia: Elsevier.)

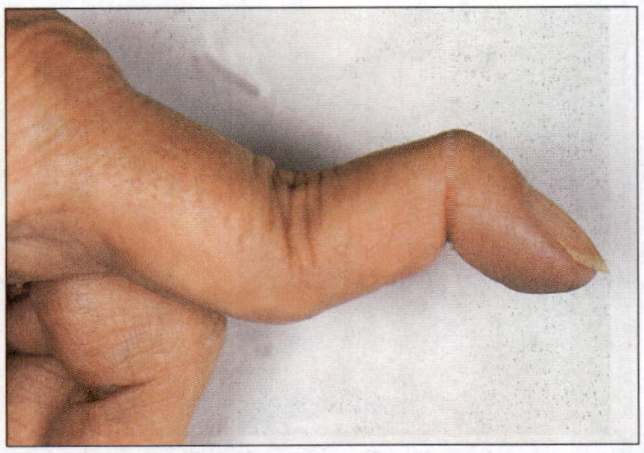

Swan neck deformity. (Reprinted with permission from Hochberg, M. C., Gravallese, E. M., Silman, A. J., et al. [2019]. *Rheumatology* [7th ed.]. Philadelphia: Elsevier.)

- **Nursing and Collaborative Management**
  - — **Drug Therapy**
    - High-dose aspirin (ASA) or nonsteroidal antiinflammatory drugs (NSAIDs)
    - Systemic corticosteroids
    - Disease-modifying antirheumatic drugs (DMARDs)
      - Methotrexate
      - Sulfasalazine
      - Hydroxychloroquine
      - Leflunomide
      - Adalimumab
  - — **Collaborative Management**
    - Heat and cold applications
    - Weight management
    - Rest and joint protection to maintain function
    - Use assistive devices
  - — Shower chair
  - — Canes, walkers
  - — Straight-back chairs, elevated seats

Lupus Erythematosus

- **Two Classifications**
  - — Discoid lupus erythematosus (DLE): affects the skin only. The characteristic "butterfly" rash of systemic lupus erythematosus (SLE)

Notes

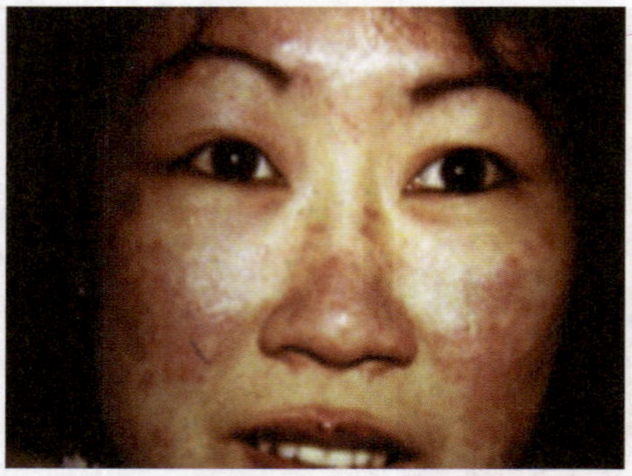

Butterfly rash of SLE. (Reprinted with permission from Firestein, G.S., Budd, R.C., Gabriel, S.E., McInnes, I.B. [2012]. *Kelley's textbook of rheumatology* [9th ed.]. Philadelphia: Saunders.)

- — SLE: more prevalent than DLE
- **Major Trigger Factors**
  - — Sunlight
  - — Infectious agents
  - — Stress
  - — Drugs
  - — Pregnancy
- **Nursing and Collaborative Management**
  - — **Nursing Assessment**
  - — DLE: scaly rash and/or butterfly rash on bridge of nose
    - SLE: joint pain, fever, nephritis, and pericarditis
    - Photosensitivity
  - — **Collaborative Management**
    - Teaching
      - Drugs
      - Pain management
      - Disease process
      - Conservation of energy
      - Avoid exposure to ultraviolet rays
      - Avoid/reduce stress.
      - Use mild soaps, creams for skin care
      - Use steroids for joint inflammation
    - Therapeutic exercise and heat therapy
    - Pregnancy counseling

Degenerative Joint Disease (Osteoarthritis)

- Joint pain increases with activity
- Morning stiffness
- Crepitus
- Limited movement
- Joint enlargements

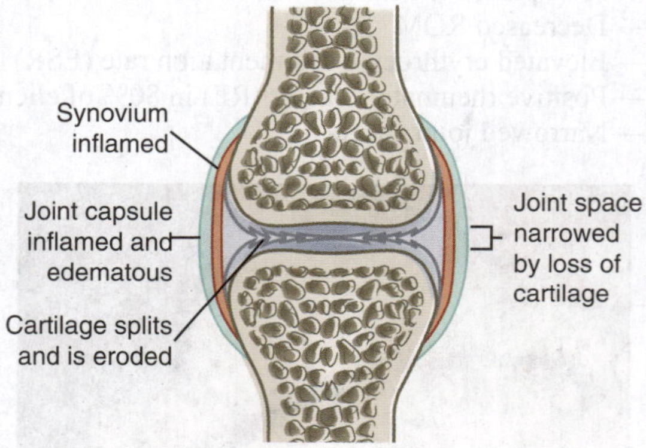

Early change in osteoarthritis is destruction of articular cartilage and narrowing of the joint space. There is inflammation and thickening of the joint capsule and synovium. (Reprinted with permission from Harding, M., Kwong, J., Roberts, D., Hagler, D., & Reinisch, C. [2020]. *Lewis's medical-surgical nursing: Assessment and management of clinical problems* [11th ed.]. Elsevier.) Reprinted with permission from Ignatavicius: *Medical-Surgical Nursing, 10th Edition*.

Study Break Box

1. Which action by the unlicensed assistive personnel (UAP) requires immediate follow-up by the RN?

1. Positioning a client who is 12 hours post above-the-knee amputation (AKA) with the residual limb elevated.
2. Assisting a client with ambulation while the client uses a cane on the unaffected side.
3. Accompanying a client who has lupus erythematosus to sit outside in the sun during a break.
4. Helping a client with rheumatoid arthritis to the bathroom after the client takes celecoxib (Celebrex).

Correct Answer: 3

Rationale

Sunlight may trigger lupus and should be avoided. The RN needs to instruct both the client and the UAP. The other clients do not require immediate follow-up.

Notes

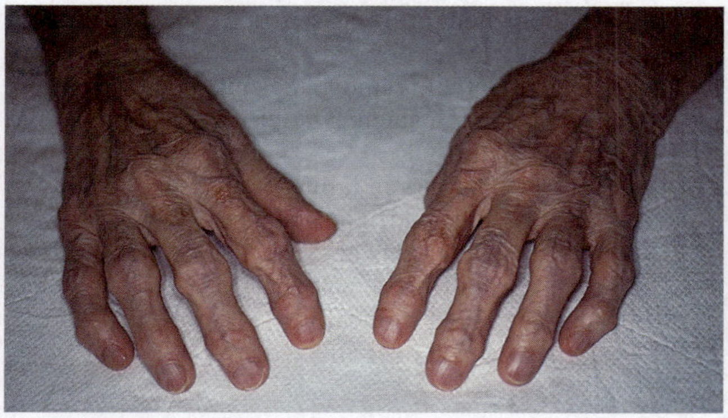

Osteoarthritis (degenerative joint disease): Heberden nodes at the distal interphalangeal joints and Bouchard nodes at the proximal interphalangeal joints. (Reprinted with permission from Swartz, M. [2009]. *Textbook of physical diagnosis: History and examination* [6th ed.]. Philadelphia: Saunders.)

- **Nursing and Collaborative Management**
  - — Follow weight-reduction diet
  - — Excessive use of the involved joint may accelerate degeneration
  - — Use proper body mechanics
  - — Keep the joints in a functional position
  - — Apply heat and cold applications for pain and stiffness
  - — Administer NSAIDs, opioid analgesics, and intra-articular corticosteroids

Glaucoma

- **Primary Open Angle**
  - — Drainage channels become clogged
  - — Aqueous humor flow is reduced in the trabecular meshwork
- **Primary Closure Angle**
  - — Bulging lens disrupts flow
  - — Silent thief of vision
  - — Sudden, excruciating pain in or around the eye
    - Normally painless until later stages
  - — Loss of peripheral vision
  - — May see halos around lights
  - — Diagnosed with tonometer to measure intraocular pressure
- **Keys to Treatment**
  - — ↓ Intraocular pressure
  - — ↓ Aqueous humor production
  - — ↑ Drainage of aqueous humor
  - — Teach the client and family proper eye drop instillation and how to avoid activities that can increase intraocular pressure
- **Acute Care for Closure Angle**
  - — Topical cholinergic agent
  - — Hyperosmotic agent
  - — Laser peripheral iridotomy
  - — Surgical iridectomy
- **Ambulatory/Home Care**
  - — Drug Therapy
    - β-Adrenergic blockers
    - α-Adrenergic agonists
    - Cholinergic agents (miotics)
    - Carbonic anhydrase inhibitors
  - — Surgical options
    - Argon Laser Trabeculoplasty (ALT)
    - Trabeculectomy

Study Break Box

1. The RN observes an older client with glaucoma administer eye drops by tilting back the head, instilling each drop close to the inner canthus, and keeping the eye closed for 15 seconds. Which action would the RN take first?

1. Ask the client whether another family member is available to administer the drops.
2. Review the correct steps of the procedure with the client.
3. Administer the eye drops correctly in the other eye to demonstrate the technique.
4. Discuss the importance of correct eye drop administration for persons with glaucoma.

Correct Answer: 2

Rationale

Immediate feedback and reteaching by reviewing the correct steps of the procedure are the best nursing action at this time. The other answer choices do not indicate the best teaching strategies.

Cataracts

- Clouding or opacity of the lens due to trauma, aging, or genetic defect

Notes

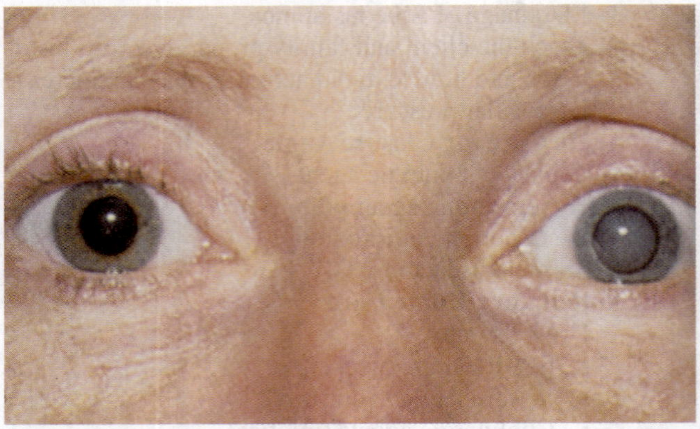

Appearance of an eye with a mature cataract. (Reprinted with permission from Patton, K. T., & Thibodeau, G. A. [2016]. Anatomy and physiology [9th ed.]. St. Louis: Mosby.)

- **Early Signs**
  - — Blurred vision
  - — Decreased color perception
- **Late Signs**
  - — Double vision
  - — Clouded pupil
- **Nursing and Collaborative Management**
  - — Preoperative
    - Assess current medications
    - Stop anticoagulants before surgery
    - Teach technique to instill eye drops
  - — Postoperative
    - Wear eye shield while sleeping
    - Avoid lifting >10 lb
    - Avoid lying on operative side
    - Report signs of ↑ Intraocular pressure (IOP)
      - Loss of peripheral vision
      - Visual field defects
    - Acute pain is an abnormal finding

Eye Trauma/Injury

- **Trauma**
  - — Determine type of injury
  - — Early notification of HCP
  - — Position client in sitting position to reduce intraocular pressure
  - — Never attempt to remove the embedded object
  - — Irrigate eye if a chemical injury has occurred
- **Detached Retina**
  - — Described as curtain falling over visual field
  - — Painless with sudden loss of vision
  - — May see black spots or floaters (indicates bleeding has occurred with detachment)
  - — Retina repaired surgically
  - — Keep eye patch over affected area

Hearing Loss

- **Conductive Hearing Loss**
  - Sounds do not travel to the inner ear
  - — May benefit from hearing aid
  - — Cerumen buildup
- **Sensorineural Hearing Loss**
  - — Sound distorted by a defect in the inner ear
  - — Common Causes:
    - Infections
    - Ototoxic drugs
      - Gentamicin
      - Vancomycin
      - Lasix
    - Trauma
    - Aging process
- **Symptoms**
  - — Inability to hear a whisper from 1 to 2 feet
  - — Shouting in conversations
  - — Turning the head to favor one ear
  - — Loud volume on TV
- **Nursing and Collaborative Management**
  - — Face the client directly when speaking
  - — Ensure the client is wearing hearing aids and eyeglasses, if appropriate
  - — Speak at a normal tone being sure to enunciate words
  - — Rephrase questions instead of repeating them
  - — Do not cover mouth with hand when speaking

Notes

Study Break Box

1. The RN is teaching an 86-year-old client who has glaucoma and bilateral hearing loss. Which intervention would the RN implement?

1. Maintain constant eye contact.
2. Stand on the side unaffected by glaucoma.
3. Speak in a lower tone of voice.
4. Keep the environment dimly lit.

Correct Answer: 3

Rationale

The RN should speak in a lower tone of voice because older adults with hearing impairment have a hard time with high-pitch noises. The other interventions will not help the RN communicate effectively with this client.

Test-Taking Strategy

Take the NCLEX as soon as possible after graduation to ensure that everything you've learned in your nursing program is still in your long-term and short-term memory. Small details of complex concepts will become vague in your memory over time. Taking your NCLEX is a personal decision; however, we strongly recommend that you prepare well for your NCLEX and take the exam as soon as possible after graduation. Knowing that a given Authorization to Test (ATT) is valid for 90 days, you must take the exam within that time frame once your ATT is obtained.

Next-Generation NCLEX® Examination (NGN)–Style Question

Trend

Scenario: The RN is assessing a 17-year-old male who was brought to the emergency room. The client was at a baseball game when a ball hit by the batter struck the client on the left side of his head. The client was playing first base and, therefore, he was not wearing a helmet.

Neurological Exam:

Assessment findings	Admission	1 hour after arrival	2 hours after arrival
BP:	132/76	144/62	168/58
Pulse:	98	78	54 (bounding)
Respirations:	22	17	13 (irregular)
Temp:	97.9°F	99.8°F	100.7°F
Pupils:	Equal 3 mm	R = 3 mm, L = 5 mm	R = 4 mm, L = 8 mm
GCS:	15	12	8

Drop-Down Rationale: Complete the statement by choosing the appropriate option from the list.

The client is most likely experiencing ______(1)______ as evidenced by the presence of ______(2)______.

Drop-Down Option #1	Drop-Down Option #2
CSF leakage	Cushing's triad
increased ICP	narrowing pulse pressure
spinal cord injury	scalp hematoma
skull fracture	improving GCS

Answer: #1 = Increased ICP, #2 = Cushing's triad

Rationale: The evidence listed in the table chronicled from admission to 2 hours after client arrival reveal the presence of Cushing's triad, which is a late indicator of increased ICP in a client with a head injury. Cushing's triad includes widening pulse pressure, slowing heart rate with full bounding pulse, and slowing and irregular respirations.

Notes

9 Pediatric Nursing

Growth and Development

- Five major developmental periods:
  - — Infancy
  - — Toddler
  - — Preschool
  - — School age
  - — Adolescence
- Developmental theories most widely used in explaining child growth and development:
  - — Freud's psychosexual stages
  - — Erikson's stages of psychosocial development
  - — Piaget's stages of cognitive development
  - — Kohlberg's stages of moral development

Study Break Box

1. The RN directs the unlicensed assistive personnel (UAP) to play with a 4-year-old child on bed rest. Which activities would the RN recommend? (Select all that apply.)

1. Monopoly board game.
2. Checkers.
3. 100-piece puzzle.
4. Hand puppets.
5. Coloring book.

Correct Answer: 2, 4, 5

Rationale
Checkers, hand puppets, and a coloring book are appropriate activities for this age group. Board games and a 100-piece puzzle are too advanced for preschoolers.

2. While receiving IV antibiotics for sepsis, a 2-month-old infant is crying inconsolably, despite the parent's presence. The RN recognizes that the infant is exhibiting symptoms related to which likely condition?

1. Allergic reaction to antibiotics.
2. Pain related to IV infiltration.
3. Separation anxiety from parent.
4. Hunger and thirst.

Study Break Box—cont'd

Correct Answer: 2

Rationale
Alterations in an infant's behavior, such as a 2-month-old crying inconsolably, may signify pain related to IV infiltration. The infant's behavior is not related to allergies, separation anxiety, or hunger and thirst.

Normal Growth and Development

- **Infant (birth to 1 year)**
  - — Birth weight doubles by 6 months, triples by 12 months
  - — Social smile occurs at 2 months
  - — Plays "peek-a-boo" by 6 months
  - — Sits upright without support by 8 months
  - — Develops separation/stranger anxiety at 6 months
  - — Crawls at 9 months
  - — Fine pincer grasp by 10 to 12 months (can pick up pieces of cereal)
  - — Walking with support: 11 to 12 months
  - — Says a few words in addition to "mama" or "dada" at 12 months
- **Toddler (1 to 3 years)**
  - — Two- to three-word sentences at 2 years
  - — Toilet training starts around 2 years
  - — Ritualistic
  - — No concept of time
  - — Frequent tantrums
  - — Magical thinker
- **Preschool (3 to 5 years)**
  - — Favorite word: *Why?*
  - — Sentences of five to eight words
- **School age (6 to 12 years)**
  - — Each year gains 4 to 6 lb, grows 2 inches
  - — Learns to tell time
  - — Socialization with peers very important

Notes

- **Adolescence (12 to 19 years)**
  - — Rapid growth, second only to the first year of life
  - — Secondary sex characteristics develop
  - — Development of identity

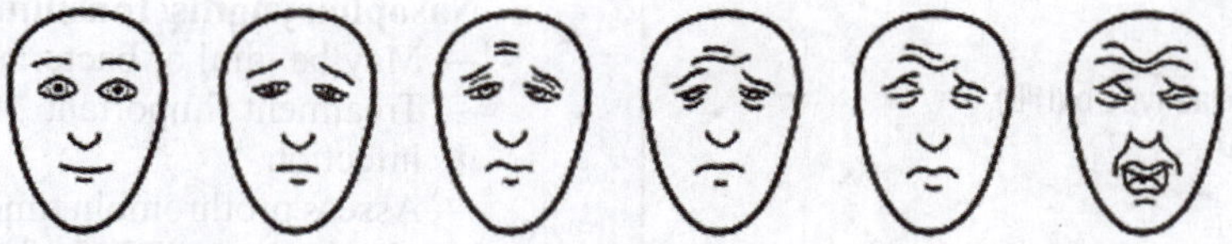

Faces Pain Scale. (Modified from Baird, M. [2015]. *Manual of critical care nursing: Nursing interventions and collaborative management* [2nd ed.]. St. Louis: Elsevier.)

- Safety is a major priority for administering medication.
- Make sure dose is safe for age and weight.
- **Nonpharmacological Interventions**
  - — Infants may respond best to pacifiers, holding, and rocking
  - — Toddlers and preschoolers may respond best to distraction
  - — School-age children and adolescents may use guided imagery
- **Pharmacological Interventions**
  - — Verify that the prescribed dose is safe based on weight
  - — Monitor the child's vital signs after administration of opioids
  - — Children as young as 5 years of age may be taught to use a client-controlled analgesia (PCA) pump

Poisonings

- Frequent cause of childhood injury—teach poison-proofing methods for the home.
- Children <6 years with peak at 2 years of age.
- Gastrointestinal (GI) disturbance is a common symptom.
- Burns of mouth and pharynx with caustic poisonings.
- Identify poisonous agent immediately.
- Assess ABCs.
- Teach parents NOT to make the child vomit because it may cause more damage.
- Call Poison Control Center or 911, based on how the child is acting.

Pain Assessment and Management

- Assessment is based on verbal and nonverbal cues from child and includes parents' information.
- Be aware of developmental responses.
- Use appropriate pain scale.

Immunizations

- Common cold ***does not*** contraindicate immunization unless the fever is >37.2°C (99°F).
- A fever <38.9°C (<102°F) and redness and soreness at the injection site are normal for 2 to 3 days after vaccination.
- Call the health care provider (HCP) if the child has high-pitched crying, seizures, or high fever.
- Use acetaminophen orally, before and every 4 to 6 hours after for 24 hours.
- Hold measles, mumps, and rubella (MMR) vaccine if anaphylactic reaction to neomycin/eggs.

Study Break Box

1. A parent is preparing a 5-year-old child for kindergarten. The child has not received any immunizations. Which vaccine would be given to this child? (Select all that apply.)

1. Diphtheria, Tetanus, and Pertussis (DTaP).
2. Inactivated polio virus (IPV).
3. Varicella.
4. Pneumococcal conjugate vaccine (PCV).
5. Trivalent inactivated influenza vaccine (TIV).

Correct Answer(s): 1, 2, 3

Rationale

The immunizations required for kindergarten are DTaP, IPV, and varicella. PCV and TIV are not required. Centers for Disease Control and Prevention (CDC) guidelines for immunizations: http://www.cdc.gov/vaccines/schedules/hcp/imz/catchup.html.

Notes

Study Break Box—cont'd

2. Which vaccine would the RN expect to be prescribed for a 2-month-old brought into the pediatrician's office for a well-baby checkup? (Select all that apply.)

1. DTaP.
2. Hep B.
3. Hep C.
4. Haemophilus influenzae type b (HIB).
5. IPV.
6. PCV.

Correct Answer(s): 1, 2, 4, 5, 6

Rationale

The immunizations required for a 2-month-old are DTaP, hepatitis B, HIB, IPV, and PCV. Hepatitis C is not required for this age group. CDC guidelines for immunizations: http://www.cdc.gov/vaccines/schedules/hcp/imz/catchup.html

Communicable Diseases

- The incidence of common childhood communicable diseases has declined greatly since the advent of immunizations, but they do occur, and nurses should be able to identify the infection.
  - Measles
  - Rubeola
  - Rubella
  - Roseola
  - Mumps
  - Pertussis
  - Diphtheria
  - Varicella
  - Erythema infectiosum (fifth disease)
- Treat fever from infection with acetaminophen, not ASA (acetylsalicylic acid, aspirin).
- Isolation is required during the infectious phase of the infection.
- Teaching is the primary intervention for prevention of spread.
- Hand washing.
- Supportive measures are given while the disease runs its course.

Respiratory Disorders

- Be familiar with normal values for respiratory and pulse rates for children.
- **Cardinal signs of respiratory distress:**
  - Restlessness
  - Increased respiratory rate
  - Increased pulse rate
  - Diaphoresis
- Respiratory failure usually occurs before cardiac failure.
- **Nasopharyngitis/Tonsillitis**
  - May be viral or bacterial
  - Treatment important if related to streptococcal infection
  - Assess prothrombin time (PT) and partial thromboplastin time (PTT) before surgery
  - Monitor for bleeding
  - The highest risk for bleeding is during the first 24 hours and 5 to 10 days postoperative
- **Otitis media**
  - Fever, pulling at ear, discharge
  - Administer antibiotics if prescribed
  - Position on the affected side
  - Reduce temperature to prevent seizures
- **Bronchitis**
  - Inflammation of trachea and bronchi
  - Rhinitis and cough
  - Crackles and rhonchi
  - Symptomatic treatment

Study Break Box

1. The RN is caring for a child who had a tonsillectomy 2 hours ago. Which sign or symptom most likely relates to a complication?

1. Apical rate 90 beats/min.
2. Blood pressure (BP) 96/50.
3. Frequent swallowing.
4. Nasal congestion.

Correct Answer: 3

Rationale

Postoperative hemorrhage may occur after a tonsillectomy, and it is prudent to inspect the throat directly for evidence of bleeding. Other signs are frequent swallowing and vomiting of bright red blood. The other symptoms are not indicative of postoperative hemorrhage due to tonsillectomy.

Notes

- **Respiratory syncytial virus bronchiolitis (RSV)**
  - — Isolate the child (contact isolation)
  - — Monitor respiratory status
  - — Maintain patent airway
  - — Antiviral agent (ribavirin aerosols)
  - — RSV prophylaxis with monoclonal antibody palivizumab (Synagis) in high-risk children <2 years of age
- **Epiglottitis**
  - — Major cause is Hib
  - — Fever, sore throat, muffled voice, drooling
  - — IV antibiotics
  - — Do NOT examine the throat.
  - — Prepare for tracheostomy.
- **Croup**
  - — Primarily viral infection
  - — Hoarseness, brassy or barky cough; respiratory distress; worse at night
  - — Supportive measures
    - Cool mist humidity
    - Increased oral intake
    - Oral dexamethasone

Study Break Box

1. A 4-year-old is brought to the clinic with a fever of 103°F, sore throat, and moderate respiratory distress caused by a suspected bacterial infection. Which medical diagnosis is a contraindication to obtaining a throat culture in the child?

1. Tonsillitis.
2. Streptococcal infection.
3. Bronchiolitis.
4. Epiglottitis.

Correct Answer: 4

Rationale

To avoid airway compromise in epiglottitis, the RN should not culture the child's throat. It is safe to culture the child's throat in tonsillitis, streptococcal infection, and bronchiolitis.

Study Break Box—cont'd

2. The RN is caring for a 2-year-old child suspected of having croup. Which early sign of respiratory distress requires the RN's immediate attention?

1. Cyanosis.
2. Restlessness.
3. Crying.
4. Barking cough.

Correct Answer: 2

Rationale

Restlessness is an early symptom of croup that should be immediately assessed. Cyanosis, barking cough, and crying are later symptoms that should also be assessed but do not require immediate attention.

- **Asthma**
  - — The leading cause of chronic illness in children
  - — Allergies influence persistence and severity of the illness
  - — Complex disorder involving biochemical, immunologic, infections, endocrine, and psychological factors
  - — **Nursing and Collaborative Management**
    - S/S: tight cough, expiratory wheezing, decreased peak flow levels
    - Monitor for respiratory distress, need for O_2 nebulizer therapy
    - Rescue versus maintenance medications
    - Evaluate the effects of β-adrenergic agonists, such as albuterol and levalbuterol, as well as corticosteroids

Study Break Box

1. The RN is reinforcing teaching for a school-age child and the child's parent regarding the administration of inhaled beclomethasone dipropionate and albuterol for the treatment of asthma. Which statement by the parent indicates that teaching has been effective?

1. "My child knows which refrigerator shelf the inhalers are kept."
2. "My child only needs to use inhalers when the peak flow numbers are in the red."
3. "My child will take the bronchodilator first, then the corticosteroid."
4. "My child will take the corticosteroid first, wait a few minutes, and then take the bronchodilator."

Notes

Study Break Box—cont'd

Correct Answer: 3

Rationale

A bronchodilator (albuterol) is used to open up and relax constricted airways, making it easier to breathe. After the airways have been opened up and are more relaxed, the corticosteroid can penetrate the lungs more effectively. The parent statement indicates an understanding of the teaching. The other parent statements do not reflect an understanding of the teaching.

- **Cystic fibrosis (CF)**
  - — The most frequently occurring inherited disease of Caucasian children
  - — Transmitted by an autosomal recessive gene
  - — Chronic multisystem disorder

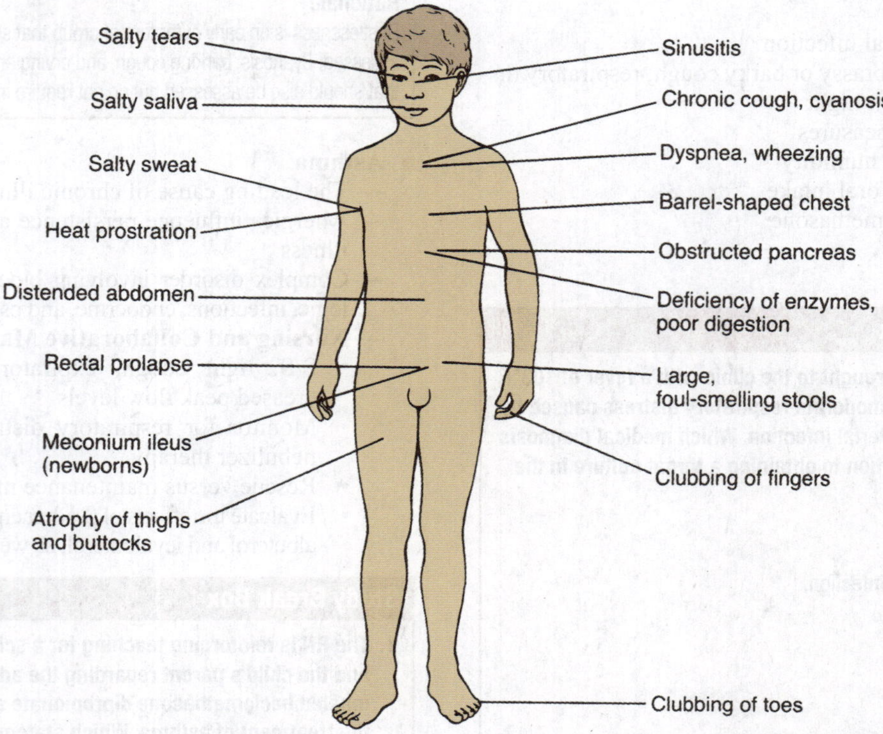

Manifestations of cystic fibrosis. (Reprinted with permission from Leifer, G. [2015]. Introduction to maternity and pediatric nursing [7th ed.]. Elsevier Saunders.)

- — Abnormally thick mucus
- — Primarily lung and pancreatic involvement
- — + Newborn screening test
- — First sign may be meconium ileus at birth.
- — High sweat chloride concentration (pilocarpine test or sweat test)
- — Delayed growth, poor weight gain
- — Pancreatic enzymes with each meal and snacks, fat-soluble vitamins
- — Teach the family percussion and postural drainage techniques

Notes

Study Break Box

1. The RN is reinforcing discharge teaching for parents of a 4-year-old with Cystic Fibrosis (CF). Which statement by the parents demonstrates understanding of the teaching presented?

1. "We will discourage our child from playing outdoors."
2. "We will use pancreatic enzymes only if needed."
3. "We will wash our child's hands after toileting."
4. "We will schedule a physical therapist evaluation."

Correct Answer: 3

Rationale

Children with CF are at an increased risk of developing infection. Hand washing is the number one prevention against transmission of microbes. This parent statement indicates an understanding of the teaching. The other parent statements do not reflect an understanding of the teaching.

Cardiovascular Disorders: Congenital Heart Disorders

- May be classified as acyanotic or cyanotic. Most important is the management of the symptoms. For descriptions and illustrations of congenital cardiovascular disorders, see a textbook or NCLEX review manual:
  - Evolve Reach Comprehensive Review for the NCLEX-RN Examination (powered by HESI)
  - HESI's Comprehensive Review of Nursing for the NCLEX-RN Examination
  - Saunders Comprehensive Review for the NCLEX-RN Examination Nursing
- **Heart Failure**
  - Common complication of cardiovascular disorders
  - S/S: pedal edema, neck vein distention, respiratory distress, fatigue, irritability, sudden weight gain
  - Monitor vital signs, elevate head of bed, O_2.
  - Digoxin, diuretics, and angiotensin-converting enzyme (ACE) inhibitors
  - Weigh daily on the same scale at the same time of day
  - Maintain nutritional status; feeding should not last >30 minutes
  - Plan frequent rest periods
- **Managing Digoxin Therapy in Children**
  - Count apical rate when the child is at rest; withhold medication if pulse is <90 beats/min in infants or <70 beats/min in older children
    - Notify the HCP if dose is held
  - Do not skip or try to make up doses
  - Give 1 to 2 hours before meals
  - Watch for S/S of toxicity and teach them to parents: vomiting, anorexia, diarrhea, muscle weakness, drowsiness
  - Provide adequate potassium in the diet

Rheumatic Fever

- Peaks in school-age children.
- Most common cause of acquired heart disease.
- Affects connective tissue.
- S/S: sore throat that appears to be improving, then fever develops along with rash, chorea, elevated erythrocyte sedimentation rate.

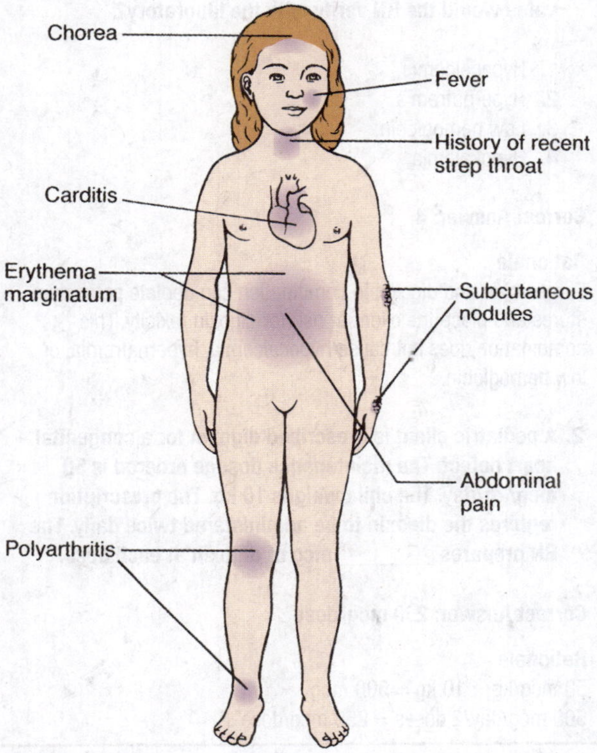

Manifestations of rheumatic fever. (Reprinted with permission from Leifer, G. [2015]. Introduction to maternity and pediatric nursing [7th ed.]. Elsevier Saunders.)

Notes

- Antibiotic prophylaxis for invasive procedures.
- **Nursing and Collaborative Management**
  - — Encourage compliance with drug regimens
  - — Penicillin remains the drug of choice
  - — Salicylates are used to control the inflammatory process and to reduce fever and discomfort
  - — Prednisone may be indicated in some clients with heart failure
  - — Bed rest or at least limited activity during the acute illness
  - — Provide emotional support

Study Break Box

1. A 2-year-old child's blood work is evaluated by the RN. Considering that the child is prescribed furosemide, captopril, and digoxin for congestive heart failure, which value would the RN verify with the laboratory?

1. Hypocalcemia.
2. Hypernatremia.
3. Low hemoglobin.
4. Hypokalemia.

Correct Answer: 4

Rationale

Furosemide and digoxin in combination can deplete potassium stores and place the client at risk for digoxin toxicity. This combination does not cause hypocalcemia, hypernatremia, or low hemoglobin.

2. A pediatric client is prescribed digoxin for a congenital heart defect. The maintenance dosage ordered is 50 mcg/kg/day. The child weighs 10 kg. The prescription requires the digoxin to be administered twice daily. The RN prepares ________ mcg of digoxin at each dose.

Correct Answer: 250 mcg/dose

Rationale

50 mcg/kg × 10 kg = 500 mcg

500 mcg/day/2 doses = 250 mcg/dose

Study Break Box—cont'd

3. The RN reviews the medication record of a 2-month-old and notes that the infant was given a scheduled dose of digoxin with a documented apical pulse of 76 beats/min. Which action would the RN take first?

1. Assess the current apical pulse rate.
2. Assess for the onset of diarrhea.
3. Complete an adverse occurrence report.
4. Determine the serum potassium level.

Correct Answer: 1

Rationale

The RN would first verify the infant's current cardiac function by assessing the apical heart rate. The other nursing interventions are not necessary for this situation.

Kawasaki Disease

- Acute systemic vasculitis.
- Occurs in children <5 years.
- Self-limiting disease.
- 25% of children develop coronary artery dilation or aneurysm if left untreated.
- Symptoms: fever >5 days, erythema of palms and soles, peeling of hands and feet, bilateral conjunctival inflammation without exudate, erythema of lips, oropharynx, strawberry tongue, rash, and cervical lymphadenopathy.

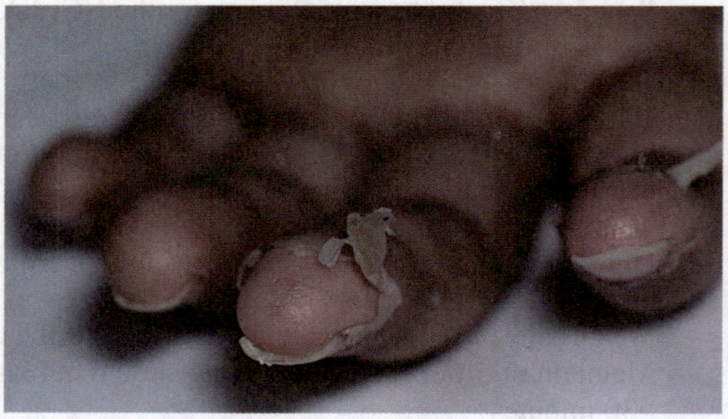

Kawasaki disease. Fingertip peeling in the subacute phase. (Reprinted with permission from Zitelli, B. J., McIntire, S. C., Nowalk, A. J., Garrison, J., & Davis, H. W. [2023]. Zitelli and Davis' Atlas of Pediatric physical diagnosis [8th ed.]. Elsevier.)

Notes

- Nursing and collaborative management
  - Compliance with medication
    - High-dose Intravenous Immunoglobulin (IVIg)
    - Aspirin
    - Possible anticoagulation therapy

Down Syndrome

- **Physical Characteristics:**
  - Flat, broad nasal bridge; upward, outward-slanting eyes.
  - The straight simian crease in the palm of the hand is a typical finding in children with Down syndrome.
  - The short fifth finger is a typical finding in children with Down syndrome. The tip of the fifth finger does not extend to the distal joint of the adjoining finger.

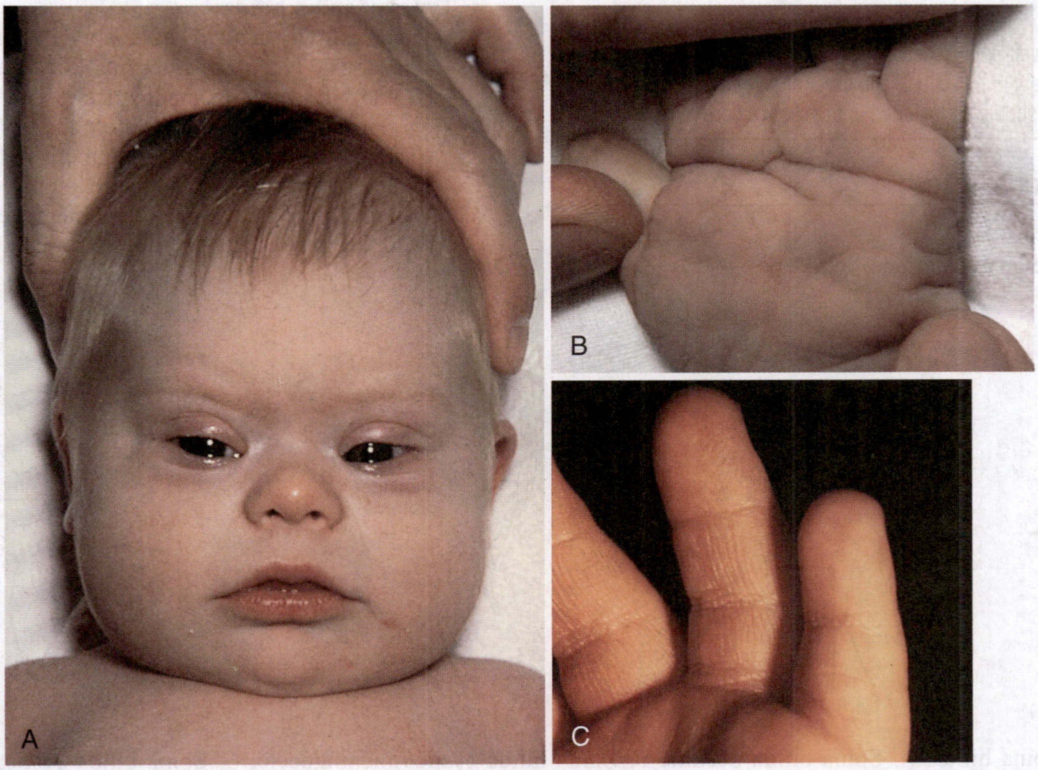

Down syndrome. (Reprinted with permission from Zitelli, B. J., McIntire, S. C., Nowalk, A. J., Garrison, J., & Davis, H. W. [2023]. Zitelli and Davis' Atlas of Pediatric physical diagnosis [8th ed.]. Elsevier.)

- Commonly associated problems
  - Cardiac defects
  - Delayed development
  - Respiratory infections
- Always evaluate functional age.
- Feed to back and side of mouth due to tongue thrust.
- Support child/parent relationship to achieve highest level of functioning.
- Refer family to early intervention program.

Notes

Study Break Box

1. **The RN is caring for a 16-year-old client with Down syndrome who has a mental age of 5. Which priority nursing action would be included in this client's plan of care?**
   1. Monitoring for hearing loss.
   2. Monitoring I&O.
   3. Providing a dependable routine.
   4. Providing small puzzles.

Correct Answer: 3

Rationale
A suitable, well-established, predictable schedule will help reduce anxiety in this client. The other answer choices are not factors that should be included in the client's care plan.

Cerebral Palsy (CP)

- **Diagnosis**
  — Made on evaluation of child
  — Permanent injury to the motor centers of the brain before, during, or after birth
  — Persistent neonatal reflexes after 6 months—no parachute reflex
  — Spasticity, muscle, and motor tone abnormalities
- **Nursing and Collaborative Management**
  — Prevent aspiration with feedings.
  — Medication for seizures, muscle spasticity, muscle pain

Congenital Abnormalities of the Spine

- **Types of spina bifida:**
  — Spina bifida occulta. There is a defect in the bony canal. The meninges and spinal cord are normal.
  — Spina bifida cystica meningocele. The spinal cord is normal, but there is a defect in the bony canal. The meninges protrude through this defect.
  — Spina bifida cystica meningomyelocele. There is a defect in the bony canal. The meninges protrude, and the spinal cord protrudes through the defect.

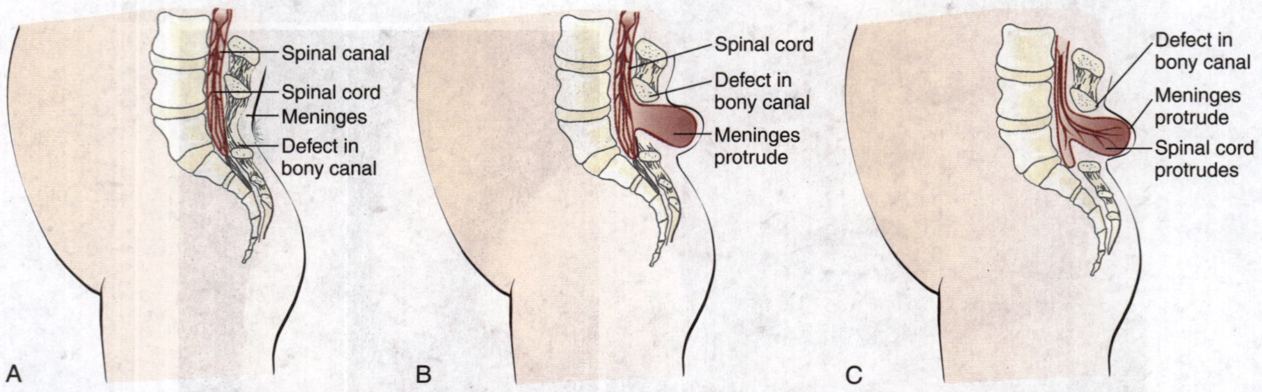

Types of spina bifida. *A,* Spina bifida occulta. *B,* Spina bifida cystica meningocele. *C,* Spina bifida cystica meningomyelocele. (Reprinted with permission from Leifer, G. [2015]. Introduction to maternity and pediatric nursing [7th ed.]. Elsevier Saunders.)

Notes

- **Spina Bifida Occulta**
  - — No sac present
  - — Sacral dimple present
  - — Suspect if tuft of hair at base of spine
- **Meningocele**
  - — Sac contains only meninges and spinal fluid
  - — No nerves are in spinal sac
- **Myelomeningocele**
  - — Sac contains spinal fluid, meninges, and nerves
  - — Will have sensory and motor defects
  - — Preoperative/postoperative care:
    - Monitor urine output
    - Monitor for ↑ ICP
    - Keep sac free of stool/urine
    - Measure head circumference every 8 hours and assess fontanels
    - Be alert for signs of latex allergy

Hydrocephalus

- Abnormal accumulation of cerebrospinal fluid (CSF)

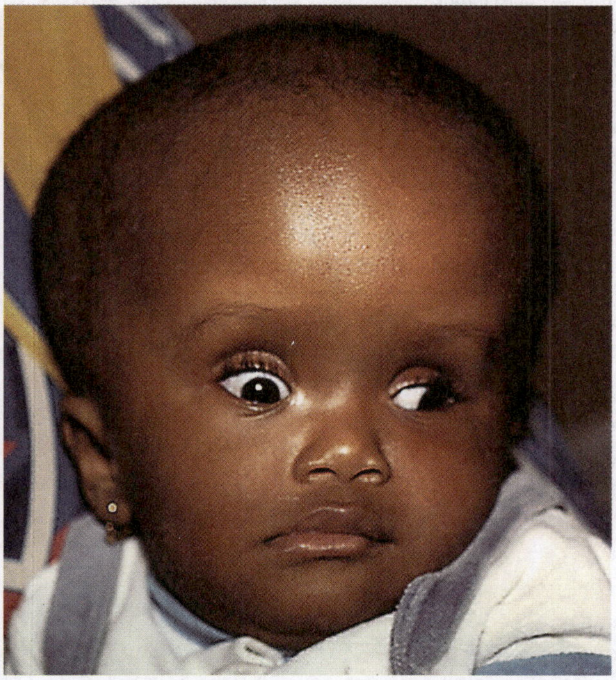

Hydrocephalus. (Reprinted with permission from Lissauer [Ed.], Illustrated textbook of paediatrics. London, Elsevier.)

- **Symptoms**
  - — ↑ Intracranial pressure (ICP)
  - — ↑ BP, ↓ pulse
  - — Changes in LOC
  - — Irritability and vomiting
  - — Shrill, high-pitched cry in infants
- **Nursing and Collaborative Management**
  - — Elevate head of bed
  - — Seizure precautions
  - — Prepare for shunt placement
  - — Assess for shunt malfunctioning
  - — Monitor for S/S of infection
  - — Teaching related to shunt replacement

Study Break Box

1. A child with hydrocephalus is 1 day postoperative for revision of a ventriculoatrial shunt. Which finding is most important for the RN to assess first?

1. Increased BP.
2. Increased temperature.
3. Increased serum glucose.
4. Increased hematocrit.

Correct Answer: 1

Rationale

Increased BP is a sign of increased ICP, so this should be assessed first. The other findings are of lesser priority.

Seizures/Epilepsy

- Uncontrolled neuronal electrical activity.
- More common in children younger than 2 years.
- **Types of Seizures**
  - — **Generalized:** Tonic/clonic (formerly grand mal)
    - Aura
    - Loss of consciousness
    - Tonic phase: stiffness of body
    - Clonic phase: spasms and relaxation
    - Postictal phase: sleepy and disoriented
  - — **Myoclonic**
    - Sudden, brief contraction of muscle, group of muscles
  - — **Partial Seizures**
    - Specific area in the brain; limited symptoms

Notes

— **Absence Seizures (formerly petit mal)**
  - Momentary loss of consciousness, appears to be daydreaming, poor performance in school
  - Lasts 5 to 30 seconds

— **Status Epilepticus**
  - Series of seizures at intervals too brief to allow the child to regain consciousness

— **Nursing and Collaborative Management**
  - Maintain patent airway
  - Side rails up/pad side rails
  - Do not use tongue blade
  - Administer anticonvulsants
  - **Phenobarbital and primidone**
    - ☐ Generalized tonic clonic
    - ☐ Partial
    - ☐ Status epilepticus
  - **Phenytoin**
    - ☐ Generalized tonic clonic
    - ☐ Partial
    - ☐ Status epilepticus
  - **Carbamazepine**
    - ☐ Generalized tonic clonic
    - ☐ Partial
  - **Fosphenytoin (IM, IV)**
    - ☐ Generalized status epilepticus
    - ☐ Treatment of seizures during neurosurgery
    - ☐ Short-term parenteral replacement for oral phenytoin
  - **Valproic acid**
    - ☐ Generalized tonic clonic
    - ☐ Absence
    - ☐ Myoclonic
    - ☐ Partial
  - **Clonazepam**
    - ☐ Absence
    - ☐ Myoclonic
    - ☐ Infantile spasms
    - ☐ Partial

Study Break Box

1. The RN observes an adolescent client experiencing a tonic-clonic seizure. Which action would the RN take first?

1. Restrain the client to protect against injury.
2. Flex the neck to ensure stabilization.
3. Use a tongue blade to open the airway.
4. Turn client on side to aid ventilation.

Correct Answer: 4

Rationale
Turning the client on the side helps aid ventilation and protect from injury during a seizure. The other nursing interventions are not recommended for this client.

2. The HCP prescribes the anticonvulsant phenytoin for an adolescent with a seizure disorder. The RN would instruct the client to notify the HCP if which condition develops?

1. Dry mouth.
2. Abnormal bruising.
3. Sore throat.
4. Gingival hyperplasia.

Correct Answer: 2

Rationale
Phenytoin can cause liver issues that manifest as easily bruising, loss of appetite, or dark urine. The RN would monitor the client taking phenytoin for safety and advise the client to report symptoms to the HCP. Dry mouth, sore throat, and gingival hyperplasia do not need to be reported to the HCP.

Bacterial Meningitis

- Usually caused by *Haemophilus influenzae* type B, *Streptococcus pneumoniae*, and *Neisseria meningitidis*.

Notes

- Diagnostic procedures include lumbar puncture for laboratory analysis.
- **Signs and Symptoms**
  - — Petechial or purpuric rashes, especially when associated with shock-like state
  - — Older children: include S/S of increased ICP, neck stiffness, + Kernig's sign, + Brudzinski's sign
  - — Infants: classic signs absent; poor feeding, vomiting, irritability, bulging fontanels
- **Nursing and Collaborative Management**
  - — Isolate at least 24 hours
    - Droplet precautions
  - — Administer antibiotics
  - — Frequent VS and neurological assessments
  - — Monitor for increased ICP, muscle twitching, and changes in LOC
  - — Measure head circumference daily
  - — SIADH (syndrome of inappropriate antidiuretic hormone) occurs frequently
  - — Fluid restriction may be necessary

Reye Syndrome and Muscular Dystrophy

- **Reye Syndrome**
  - — Etiology often, but *not always*, associated with aspirin use and influenza or varicella
  - — Rapidly progressing encephalopathy; altered hepatic function
  - — S/S: lethargy progressing to coma, vomiting, hypoglycemia
  - — Neurological assessments, maintain airway
  - — Mannitol for ICP control
  - — Early diagnosis is important to improve client outcome
- **Duchenne Muscular Dystrophy (MD)**
  - — Onset ages 2 to 6 years
  - — Most severe and most common MD
  - — X-linked recessive disorder
  - — **Diagnosis**
    - Muscle biopsy
    - Serum creatine phosphokinase (CK)
  - — **Symptoms**
    - Delayed walking and frequent falls
    - Gower sign
    - Easily tires when walking
  - — **Nursing and Collaborative Management**
    - Exercise and assistive devices for ambulation
    - Prevent falls (loss of ambulation at 8 to 12 years of age)

Renal Disorders

- **Urinary Tract Infection (UTI)**
  - — More common with female anatomy
  - — **Symptoms**
    - Poor food intake
    - Strong-smelling urine
    - Fever
    - Pain with urination
  - — **Nursing and Collaborative Management**
    - Obtain urine culture before starting antibiotics
    - Teach home care
      - ☐ Finish all antibiotics
      - ☐ Avoid bubble baths
      - ☐ Increase intake of acidic fluids, such as apple or cranberry juice
- **Acute Glomerulonephritis (AGN)**
  - — **Common Features**
    - Oliguria, hematuria, proteinuria
    - Edema
    - Hypertension
    - Circulatory congestion
  - — **Therapeutic Management**
    - Maintenance of fluid balance
    - Treatment of hypertension
  - — **Nursing Assessment**
    - Recent strep infection
    - Dark "iced tea" urine
    - Irritable and/or lethargic
  - — **Nursing and Collaborative Management**
    - VS every 4 hours
    - Daily weights
    - Low-sodium, low-potassium diet
- **Nephrotic Syndrome**
  - — Characterized by increased glomerular permeability to protein
  - — **Assessment**
    - Frothy urine
    - Massive proteinuria
    - Edema
    - Anorexia
  - — **Nursing and Collaborative Management**
    - Reducing excretion of protein
    - Reducing or preventing fluid retention
    - Preventing infection
    - Skin care
    - Administer medications
      - ☐ Diuretics, corticosteroid therapy, immunosuppressants, antibiotics

Notes

- Small frequent feeding
- Discharge Teaching
  - Daily weights
  - Side effects of meds
  - Prevent infections

Study Break Box

1. **A school-age child with nephrotic syndrome is seen at the clinic 2 days after discharge from the hospital. Which assessment is most important for the RN to perform after discharge?**

   1. Pain.
   2. Capillary refill.
   3. Urine ketones.
   4. Daily weight.

Correct Answer: 4

Rationale

Obtaining the client's weight informs the RN about fluid balance. This is the most important nursing assessment after discharge for the client with nephrotic syndrome. Pain, capillary refill, and urine ketones are not the most important symptoms to assess.

Diarrhea

- Worldwide, leading cause of death in children <5 years of age.
- Classified as acute or chronic.
- Common problem for infants.
- Assessment:
  - Depressed/sunken eyes
  - Weight loss
  - ↓ Urine output
- **Nursing and Collaborative Management**
  - Fluid and electrolyte balance
  - Rehydration
  - Maintenance fluid therapy
  - Reintroduction of adequate diet
  - Do not give antidiarrheal agents

Gastrointestinal Disorders

- **Cleft Lip or Cleft Palate**
  - Malformation of the face or oral cavity
  - Initial closure of cleft lip is performed when infant is approximately 3 months
  - Closure of cleft palate at around 9 to 15 months
  - Promote bonding
  - Breck/Haberman feeder and slow-flow nipple
  - Maintain airway
  - No straws or spoons, only soft foods for cleft palate
- **Pyloric Stenosis**

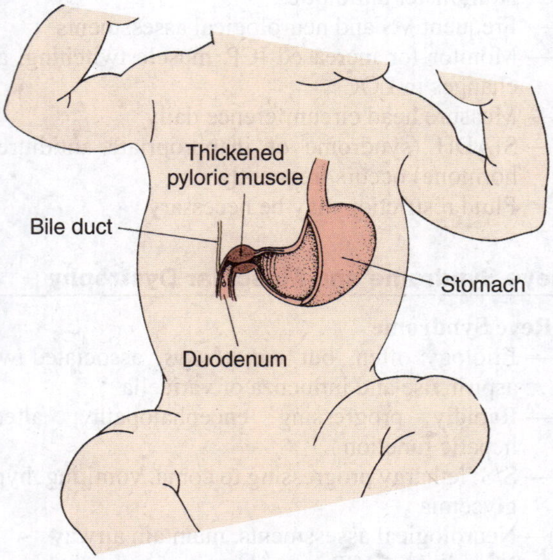

Pyloric stenosis. (Reprinted with permission from Betz, C., Hunsburger, M., & Wright, S. [1994]. Family-centered nursing care of children. [2nd ed.]. Philadelphia: Saunders.)

  - Common in first-born males
  - Vomiting becomes projectile around day 14 after birth
  - Dehydration, weight loss, and failure to thrive

Notes

- **Intussusception**

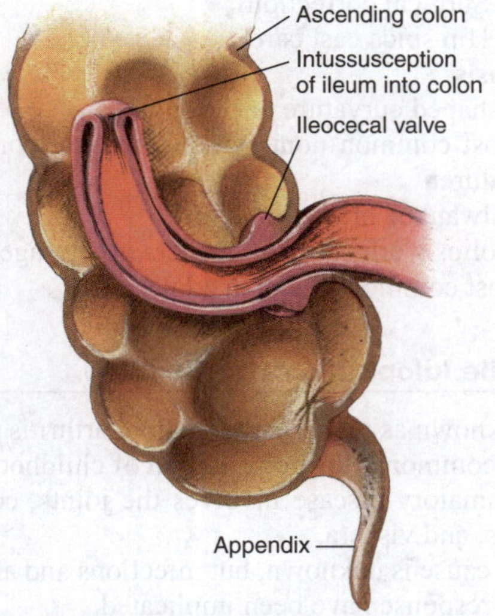

Intussusception. (Reprinted with permission from McKinney, E.S. [2005]. *Nursing care of children: Principles and practice* [2nd ed.]. Philadelphia: Saunders.)

— Telescoping of one part of intestine
— Emergency intervention is needed
— Sudden onset of crampy abdominal pain, inconsolable crying, and drawing knees to chest in otherwise healthy child

> **Study Break Box**
>
> **1. A 3-week-old infant with pyloric stenosis has severe vomiting. Which sign of dehydration would the RN anticipate in the infant? (Select all that apply.)**
>
> 1. Sunken fontanel.
> 2. Increased urine output.
> 3. High serum hematocrit level.
> 4. Cracked lips.
> 5. Thirst.
>
> **Correct Answer(s): 1, 3, 4, 5**
>
> **Rationale**
> Signs and symptoms of dehydration in an infant include sunken fontanels, high hematocrit levels, cracked lips, and thirst. Increased urine output is not a symptom of dehydration.

Hematological Disorders

- **Sickle Cell Anemia**
  — Autosomal recessive disorder
  — Fetal Hgb does not sickle
  — **Maintenance**
    - Keep well hydrated.
    - Do not give supplemental iron
    - Give folic acid orally
    - Penicillin (PCN) prophylactically at 2 months of age
  — **Crisis: Fever and Pain**
    - Bed rest, hydration, and analgesia
    - Improve oxygen utilization
    - Blood replacement and antibiotic therapy
- **Hemophilia**
  — X-linked recessive disorder
  — Factor VIII deficiency
  — **Nursing and Collaborative Management**
    - Administer fresh frozen plasma
    - Apply pressure to even minor bleeds because of increased risk for bleeding

> **Study Break Box**
>
> **1. A child admitted with sickle cell crisis is anemic and has painful joints and a fever of 101° F. Which priority intervention would the RN include in the plan of care for this child?**
>
> 1. Maintain oral fluids for hydration.
> 2. Apply cold packs to painful joints.
> 3. Administer aspirin daily for pain and fever.
> 4. Perform range-of-motion exercises to decrease joint pain.
>
> **Correct Answer: 1**
>
> **Rationale**
> The child with sickle cell should remain well hydrated to promote hemodilution, which will decrease symptoms of pain. Exposure to cold can worsen symptoms and should be avoided. The other nursing interventions are not the priority for this client.

Metabolic and Endocrine Disorders

- **Phenylketonuria (PKU)**
  — Autosomal recessive disorder
  — Newborn screening (after 24 hours of age)

Notes

— Strict adherence to low-phenylalanine diet; prevents mental retardation
  - Special PKU formula
  - Avoid meat, milk, dairy, and aspartame-containing foods
  - Diet: fruits, juices, cereal, bread, and starches

- **Diabetes**
  — Childhood obesity leads to adult obesity with increased risks of Cardiovascular disease (CVD) and type 2 diabetes
  — 19% of 6- to 11-year-olds categorized as overweight or obese
  — Minorities disproportionally at risk
  — Parental obesity is the highest predictor of childhood obesity
  — Body mass index (BMI), dietary, and activity assessments evaluated

Skeletal Disorders

- **Fractures**
  — Visible signs of fractures.
  — Obtain baseline pulses, color, movement, sensation, temperature, swelling, and pain.
  — Report any changes immediately.
- **Traction** (Fractures not easily reduced by casting and for presurgical stabilization)
  — Buck's traction: knee immobilization
  — Russell traction: femur/lower leg fracture
  - 90 degree/90 degree traction
  - Can be skeletal or skin
  - Pinned for desired line of pull and flexion at the hip and knee of 90 degrees
  - Appropriate toys, cast care, prevent cast soilage, monitor Neurovascular (NV) signs
- **Congenital Dislocated Hip (a.k.a. hip dysplasia)**
  — Assessment
  - Positive Ortolani sign
  - Unequal fold of skin on buttocks
  - Limited abduction of hip

  — Nursing and Collaborative Management
  - Pavlik harness (worn 24 hr/day)
  - Surgical correction
  - Hip spica cast care
- **Scoliosis**
  — S-shaped curvature of the spine
  — Most common nontraumatic skeletal condition in children
  — Milwaukee brace
  — Scoliosis affects both genders at any age, but it is most commonly seen in adolescents

Juvenile Idiopathic Arthritis (JIA)

- Also known as juvenile rheumatoid arthritis (JRA).
- Most common arthritic condition of childhood.
- Inflammatory disease involves the joints, connective tissues, and viscera.
- Exact cause is unknown, but infections and an autoimmune response have been implicated.
- Therapy consists of administration of medications, such as nonsteroidal anti-inflammatory drugs (NSAIDs), methotrexate, or aspirin, along with exercise, heat application, and support of joints.

Test-Taking Strategy

As you prepare for NCLEX, avoid negative people and negative thoughts. Limit time with people who make you think negative feelings toward yourself or the NCLEX. Create time to prepare for your NCLEX and care for yourself. Do not see yourself as being selfish. It is important to surround yourself with supportive, optimistic people as you prepare for NCLEX. Allow their positive attitude to build up your confidence. Remember this fact. You have been successful through nursing school; therefore, you can be successful on your NCLEX. Think positive thoughts!

Notes

Next-Generation NCLEX® Examination (NGN)–Style Question

Matrix/Grid – Multiple Response

Scenario: The RN is working in a pediatric clinic and is preparing parent education about the differences in common childhood illnesses. For each symptom listed, click to specify if the symptom is frequently associated with common colds, seasonal allergies, and/or influenza. Each symptom could be found in more than one disease process. (NOTE: Each column and row must have at least one option selected.)

Symptoms	Common Cold	Influenza	Seasonal Allergies
Fever			
Aches and pain			
Extreme exhaustion			
Nasal congestion			
Sneezing			
Cough			
Headache			

Answer:

Symptoms	Common Cold	Influenza	Seasonal Allergies
Fever		X	
Aches and pain		X	
Extreme exhaustion		X	
Nasal congestion	X		X
Sneezing	X		X
Cough	X	X	
Headache		X	X

Rationale: Fever, aches and pain, and exhaustion are usually very high with influenza cases but are not normally seen with colds or allergies. Nasal congestion and sneezing are frequently seen with colds and allergies but are not as common with the flu. Cough commonly occurs in the common cold and influenza but are uncommon with allergies. Headaches are frequent occurrences in clients with influenza and allergies but is less likely to occur with the common cold.

Notes

10

Maternal-Newborn Nursing

Pregnancy

- **Assess for Intimate Partner Violence (IPV)**
  - Battering and emotional or physical abuse often begin with pregnancy
  - Assess for abuse in private
  - The nurse needs to know:
    - Local community resources
    - Where to recommend safety venues or places for the client
- **Gravidity and Parity**
  - Gravida and parity: counts pregnancies, not offspring
  - Gravida: number of times a female has been pregnant, regardless of outcome
  - Para: number of deliveries (not children) occurred after 20 weeks' gestation
  - Multiple births count as one gravidity
  - Pregnancy loss before 20 weeks counted as abortion but add 1 to gravidity
  - Fetal demise after 20 weeks added to parity
- Past and future GTPAL represents obstetric history:
  - **G** = Gravidity (total number of pregnancies)
  - **T** = Term pregnancies (after 37 weeks)
  - **P** = Preterm pregnancies (before 37 weeks)
  - **A** = Abortions (elective or spontaneous): loss before 20 weeks
  - **L** = Living children
- **Gestation**
  - Naegele's rule
  - Count back 3 months from the date of last normal menstrual period
  - Add 1 year and 7 days
- **Fundal Height**
  - 12 to 13 weeks: fundus rises out of symphysis
  - 20 weeks: fundus at umbilicus
  - 24 to about 36 weeks: fundal height (in centimeters) from the symphysis is equal to number of weeks of gestation if this is a single pregnancy
- **Weight gain** (Optimal weight gain depends on maternal and fetal factors.)
  - First-trimester average total weight gain is 1 to 2 kg
  - Approximately 0.5 kg per week for a woman of normal weight during the second and third trimesters
- **Maternal Psychological Changes**
  - Ambivalence
    - Occurs early in pregnancy, even with a planned pregnancy
  - Acceptance
    - Occurs with the woman's readiness for the experience. Prolonged nonacceptance is a warning sign not directly related to nonacceptance of the child
  - Emotional lability
    - Rapid, unpredictable changes in mood
- **Warning Signs of Physical Maternal Changes**
  - Abdominal pain/cramping or pelvic pain
  - Decreased or absent fetal movement
  - Fever or chills
  - Urinary changes, eg. urinary frequency
  - Signs or symptoms of preterm labor
  - Signs of hypertensive disorders
- **Common Diagnostic Tests**
  - **Maternal**
    - Urine screen
    - Glucose tolerance test
    - Uterine activity
  - **Fetal**
    - **Quad screen** includes alpha fetoprotein, human chorionic gonadotropin (hCG), estriol, inhibin A; for high-risk pregnancy, chromosomal abnormalities and neural tube defects
    - **Chorionic villi sampling** (CVS) for genetic and chromosomal disorders at 8 to 12 weeks; full bladder required; Rh-negative mother requires RhoGAM (Rho[D] immune globulin) postprocedure
    - **Amniocentesis** performed at 16 weeks to determine genetic disorders, at 30 weeks to determine lung maturity; bladder emptied if performed after 20 weeks' gestation; Rh-negative mother requires RhoGAM postprocedure
    - **Ultrasound**: multiple purposes; client must have a full bladder
    - **Nonstress test** (NST) via ultrasound transducer records fetal movement and heart rate after 28 weeks; increase in heart rate (reactivity) expected in healthy fetus

Notes

- **Biophysical profile** (via ultrasound): includes NST results, amniotic fluid volume, fetal breathing movements, fetal tone and body movements
- Uterine activity

Study Break Box

1. **A client who is at 36 weeks' gestation is placed in the lithotomy position. She suddenly complains of dyspnea, lighted headedness and shows marked pallor. Which action would the RN take first?**

    1. Turn the client to a lateral position.
    2. Place the client in Trendelenburg position.
    3. Obtain vital signs and pulse oximetry reading.
    4. Initiate distraction techniques.

Correct Answer: 1

Rationale
Supine hypotension occurs when the gravid uterus compresses the vena cava. Turning the client to a lateral position will displace the uterus, which allows adequate blood return to the heart, increases cardiac output, and subsequently improves placental and renal perfusion. The other nursing interventions are not the priority.

2. **A client's suspected pregnancy is confirmed. The client tells the RN that she had three previous pregnancies where she delivered one infant at 39 weeks, twins at 34 weeks, and another infant at 35 weeks. Using the GTPAL notation, how should the RN record the client's gravidity and parity?**

    1. 3-0-3-0-3.
    2. 3-1-1-1-3.
    3. 4-1-2-0-4.
    4. 4-2-1-0-3.

Study Break Box—cont'd

Correct Answer: 3

Rationale
GTPAL for this client would be recorded as 4-1-2-0-4. This occurrence will be her fourth pregnancy, with one full-term delivery, two preterm deliveries (the pregnancy with twins is counted as only one delivery), zero abortions, and three living children. The other notations are incorrect.

Labor

- **True labor**
  — Pain in lower back radiating to the abdomen
  — Regular, rhythmic contractions
  — Increased intensity with ambulation
  — Progressive cervical dilation and effacement
- **False labor**
  — Discomfort localized to the abdomen
  — No lower back pain
  — Contractions often stop with ambulation or position change
- **Stages of Labor**
  — ***First stage***: dilation and effacement with 100% cervical effacement and complete dilation of cervix (10 cm). Duration is from 8 to 20 hours in the primipara and 5 to 14 hours in the multipara. Includes three phases: latent (0 to 3 cm), active (4 to 7 cm), and transition (8 to 10 cm)
  — ***Second stage***: begins with complete cervical dilatation; expulsion ending with birth of the baby. Generally lasts from a few minutes to 2 hours
  — ***Third stage***: placental separation. It begins with the birth of the baby and ends with the expulsion of the placenta. This process can last up to 30 minutes, with an average length of 5 to 10 minutes
  — ***Fourth stage***: defined as the first 1 to 4 hours after delivery of the placenta. Monitor for excessive bleeding and uterine atony

Notes

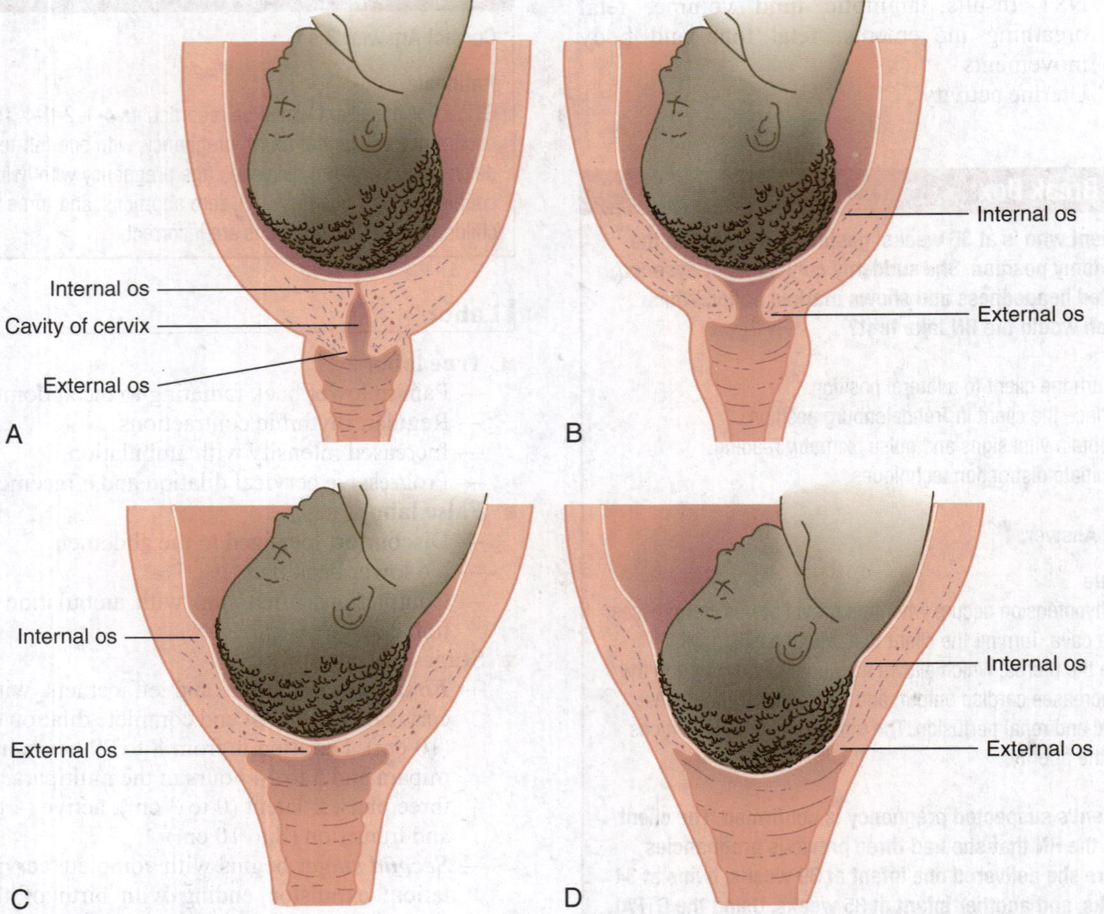

Cervical effacement and dilation. A, No effacement, no dilation. B, Early effacement and dilation. C, Complete effacement, some dilation. D, Complete dilation and effacement. (Reprinted with permission from Matteson, P.S. [2001]. Women's health during the childbearing years: A community-based approach. St. Louis: Mosby.)

Labor Progression

— *Cervical dilation:* stretching of the cervical os to allow passage of the infant (from 0 to 10 cm)

— ***Effacement:*** thinning and shortening of the cervix (0% to 100%)

— ***Station:*** location of the presenting part in relation to the midpelvis or ischial spines, measured in centimeters above and below, using a scale from −5 to + 5 or −3 to + 3

- Station 0 = engaged
- Station + 2 = 2 cm below the level of the ischial spines
- +5 = crowning

— ***Fetal presentation:*** part of the fetus that presents to the inlet

— ***Position:*** relationship of the point of reference (occiput sacrum, acromion) on the fetal presenting part to the mother's pelvis

- Left occiput anterior (LOA): most common position

Notes

- — ***Lie:*** relationship of the long axis (spine) of the fetus to the long axis (spine) of the mother
  - Longitudinal: up and down
  - Transverse: perpendicular
  - Oblique: slanted
- — ***Attitude:*** relationship of fetal parts to one another
  - Flexion: desired attitude, so that smallest diameter of the fetal head is presented
  - Extension can cause dystocia

Nursing and Collaborative Management

- — Assessment
  - Baseline maternal vital signs including pain
  - Medication history
  - Physical assessment
    - Food and fluid intake: hydration and bladder status, need for catheterization, intravenous (IV) therapy
    - Bowel elimination
    - Ambulation and positioning: upright, sitting, squatting (best position)
    - Labs and diagnostic tests
  - Emotional and cultural responses
- — Labor Assessment
  - Onset of labor and progression
  - Vaginal exam (assess dilation, effacement, station, position, and fetal presentation; do not perform in the presence of bleeding, which could indicate placenta previa or abruption)
  - Status of membranes
  - Bloody "show"
  - Fetal heart rate (FHR) pattern
  - Complications: infection, pregnancy-induced hypertension (PIH) or gestational hypertension (GH), bleeding, prolapsed cord, fetal distress
- — Assessment of contractions (uterine activity pattern)
  - Duration: amount of time a contraction lasts, from the beginning to the end
  - Frequency: the time from the beginning of one contraction to the beginning of the next contraction
  - Intensity: internal monitoring from 30 mm Hg (mild) to 70 mm Hg (strong)
  - Resting tone/time: tension of uterine muscle between contractions and time between contractions
- — Fetal Heart Rate
  - Characteristics of the FHR
    - Normal range: 110 to 160 beats/min
    - Tachycardia: >160 beats/min
    - Bradycardia: <110 beats/min
    - Variability: change in the heart rate from beat to beat (short-term) and cyclic changes over time (long term), in three to five cycles per minute; moderate long-term variability is reassuring
  - Changes in FHR
    - Accelerations: FHR increases with movement; reassuring
- — Decelerations:
  - Early decelerations (reassuring) often occur during second stage and indicate head compression.
  - Late decelerations (nonreassuring) (even if not very "deep") indicate placental insufficiency or hypoxia
  - Variable decelerations (nonreassuring): may or may not be associated with contractions, indicate compression of umbilical cord
  - The deceleration pattern indicates an insult to the fetus; the variability indicates how well the fetus is tolerating the insult
- — Fetal Monitoring
  - External fetal monitoring
    - Is noninvasive and is performed with a Toco transducer or Doppler ultrasonic transducer
  - Internal fetal monitoring
    - Is invasive; the fetal membranes (amniotic membranes) must be ruptured and an electrode must be attached to the presenting part of the fetus.

Study Break Box

1. A woman in labor becomes nauseated, starts hiccupping, and tells her partner to leave her alone. The partner asks the RN what the partner did to make this happen. Which response would the RN provide?

1. "In active labor, it is quite common for women to react this way. It's nothing you did."
2. "I don't know what you did, but stop, because she is quite sensitive right now."
3. "I'll come and examine her. This reaction is common during the transition phase of labor."
4. "Early labor can be very frustrating. I'm sure she doesn't mean to take it out on you."

Notes

Study Break Box—cont'd

Correct Answer: 3

Rationale

These symptoms are commonly seen in the transition phase of labor and could indicate progression of labor. The RN should perform a vaginal examination to determine phase of labor, cervical dilation, and station of fetus. Women become irritable and emotional and may reject their partners as the stress of labor progresses quickly during the transition phase. Laboring mothers can often experience gastrointestinal (GI) upset in preparation for delivery of the infant. The other options are not appropriate statements to make to the partner at this time.

- **Nursing and Collaborative Care During Labor**
  - **Assessment**
    - Cultural factors: influence response to labor and coping
    - Emotional response: support and coping
    - Pain and discomfort: medications and nonpharmacological measures
    - Response to medications: epidural and oxytocin
    - Maternal vital signs
    - FHR pattern
    - Uterine activity
    - Fetal position—Leopold's maneuvers and vaginal exam
  - **Assessment of Labor Progression Dilatation, Effacement, and Descent**
    - Status of the membranes: prevent and detect infection
    - Signs of complications: infection, PIH, bleeding, prolapsed cord, fetal distress
- **Types of Regional Blocks Used to Manage Labor Discomfort**
  - Pudendal block
    - Given for episiotomy
    - Has no effect on pain of uterine contractions
  - Peridural (epidural or caudal)
    - Given first or second stage; may prolong second stage
    - Single dose or continuously
    - Fluid bolus to prevent hypotension
  - Intradural (subarachnoid, spinal)
    - Usually only performed for cesarean deliveries
    - Rapid onset
    - Client must remain flat for 6-8 hours after delivery
- **Drugs Used During Labor**
  - Narcotics: inhibit contractions if given before well-established labor; can cause respiratory depression if given too close to birth; antidote is naloxone
    - Fentanyl
    - Morphine sulfate
    - Hydromorphone
  - Mixed agonist/antagonists: use these drugs with caution in substance abusers, as they could cause withdrawal in narcotics users
    - Butorphanol tartrate
    - Nalbuphine

Postpartum Maternal Assessment Memory Tool: BUBBLE HA

- **Breasts**
  - Assess consistency (soft, firm, filling, engorged), nipples (intact, sore, flat, everted or inverted), masses
- **Uterus: Fundal Involution**
  - Immediately after delivery: the fundus is several centimeters below the umbilicus
  - Within 12 hours: the fundus rises to the umbilicus
  - Descends 1 cm (fingerbreadth) a day for 9 to 10 days; then the fundus is below the symphysis pubis
  - Should be midline and firm
- **Bladder**
  - Measure output; assess for distention or retention
- **Bowel**
  - Assess for distention, passing flatus, and bowel sounds
- **Lochia**
  - Endometrial sloughing from rubra (red); serosa (pink); alba (white)
  - Assess color, odor, volume
- **Leg Assessment**
  - Assess for signs of thrombosis
- **Episiotomy**
  - Assess episiotomy or laceration repair for intactness, hematoma, edema, bruising, redness, and drainage
- **Hemorrhoids**
  - Treat with: Sitz bath; Tucks; ointments
- **Attachment**
  - Assess maternal-infant interaction for bonding behaviors
    - Teaching Points

Notes

— Primary focus is on signs of physical and emotional symptoms of potential problems for mother and infant.
  - Change peri pads as needed and with voiding/defecation
  - Wipe perineum front to back
  - Good handwashing technique
  - Ice packs, sitz baths, peri bottle lavage, and topical anesthetic spray and pads
  - Breastfeeding instructions
  - Healthy diet and adequate fluid intake
  - Rest/nap when the baby sleeps
  - Contraceptive use

— Reinforce Teaching Points
  - RhoGAM
    - Administered to Rh-negative women with possible exposure to Rh-positive blood
    - Should have negative indirect Coombs' test
    - Administered IM within 72 hours after delivery
    - Compatibility Assessment performed by two nurses (blood product)
  - Rubella Vaccine
    - Given subcutaneously to the nonimmune client before discharge from hospital
    - May breastfeed
    - Do not administer if the client or family member is immunocompromised
    - Avoid pregnancy for 2 to 3 months (reinforce contraception)

Study Break Box

1. A client who is 72 hours post cesarean section is preparing to go home. She complains to the RN that she can't get the baby's diaper on right. Which action would the RN take?

1. Demonstrate how to diaper the baby correctly.
2. Observe the client diapering the baby while offering praise and hints.
3. Call the social worker for long-term follow-up.
4. Reassure the client that she knows how to take care of her baby.

Correct Answer: 2

Rationale

This client is in the taking-hold phase. Although she may still feel inadequate in her mothering skills, the RN should observe her diapering technique, which will reinforce her confidence when the RN offers praise and teaching hints. The other nursing interventions are not appropriate for this client scenario.

Complications of Childbearing

Chronic Hypertension

— Hypertension and/or proteinuria in pregnant woman:
  - Chronic hypertension before 20 weeks of gestation
  - Persistent after 12 weeks postpartum

Superimposed Preeclampsia or Eclampsia

— Development of preeclampsia or eclampsia in a woman with chronic hypertension before 20 weeks of gestation

Gestational Hypertension

— Hypertension in pregnant women without proteinuria.

— Risk factors: obesity, prior kidney disorders, AMA (advanced maternal age), multiple pregnancies such as twins or triplets

Study Break Box

1. A client at 33 weeks' gestation who has been diagnosed with GH is admitted to the labor and delivery area. The client expresses concern for the health of her baby. Which response would the RN make?

1. "You have the best doctor on the staff so don't worry about a thing."
2. "Your anxiety is contributing to your condition and may be the reason for your admission."
3. "This is a minor problem that is easily controlled, and everything will be all right."
4. "As I assess you and your baby, I will explain the plan for your care and answer your questions."

Correct Answer: 4

Rationale

The RN should provide teaching and reassurance to the woman during the assessment. The RN should also encourage questions. The other responses are not therapeutic.

Preeclampsia/Eclampsia

— Preeclampsia Symptoms
  - Blood pressure (BP)
    - Mild: rise to 30 mm Hg systolic and/or 15 mm Hg diastolic over baseline, or 140/90 or greater
    - Severe: BP of 160/110 mm Hg, when either systolic reaches 160 mm Hg or diastolic reaches 110 mm Hg, or both occur simultaneously. Can be confirmed quickly

Notes

- Proteinuria
  - Mild: ≥1+ (≥0.3 g in a 24-hour specimen)
  - Severe: >2+ (2 g in a 24-hour specimen)
- Edema
  - Mild: Eyes, face, fingers
  - Severe: Generalized edema
- Deep Tendon Reflex (DTR)
  - Mild: May be normal
  - Severe: 3+ or greater and clonus
- Central nervous system (CNS) symptoms
  - Mild: Headache, irritability
  - Severe: Severe headache, visual disturbances
- Other
  - Weight gain > 2 lb/week; oliguria <100 mL/4 hours; epigastric pain, ↑ creatinine, thrombocytopenia, increased serum glutamic-oxaloacetic transaminase (SGOT)

— **Nursing and Collaborative Management: Preeclampsia**
- ↓ Stimulation in room
- Explain procedures
- Maintain IV (16- to 18-g venocatheter)
- Monitor BP every 15 to 30 minutes
- Monitor urine for protein every 1 hour
- The health care provider (HCP) may prescribe magnesium sulfate

— **Nursing and Collaborative Management: Eclampsia (Seizures)**
- Remember that seizures can occur postpartum
- Notify HCP if the client starts having seizures
- Stay with client
- Reposition the client to side
- Administer oxygen
- Have suction available at the bedside

Gestational Diabetes

■ Screening

— 1-hour glucose screen between 24 and 26 weeks
- Blood glucose level is higher than 140 mg/dL (7.8 mmol/L) 1 hour after consuming glucose solution.

— Goal: strict blood glucose control

— Generally, glyburide or insulin is used during pregnancy
- Glyburide is classified as a Category C by the US FDA for use in pregnancy.

— Insulin does not cross the placenta, and glyburide only minimally crosses it

Study Break Box

1. A client with gestational diabetes asks the RN to explain the reason her baby is at risk for macrosomia. Which explanation would the RN offer?

1. The placenta receives decreased maternal blood flow during pregnancy because of vascular constriction.
2. The fetus secretes insulin in response to maternal hyperglycemia, causing weight gain and growth.
3. Infants of diabetic mothers are postmature, which allows the fetus extra time to grow.
4. Rapid fetal growth contributes to congenital anomalies, which are more common in infants of diabetic mothers.

Correct Answer: 2

Rationale

Maternal glucose crosses the placenta, but insulin (either the mother's own or synthetic) does not. As the fetus gets too much glucose, fetal insulin secretion follows and acts as a growth hormone, thus causing the macrosomia. The other explanations are not correct.

Preterm Labor (PTL)

■ **Signs and Symptoms**

— More than five contractions in an hour

— Feels like menstrual-like cramps

— Low, dull backache

— Pelvic pressure

— Increase/change in vaginal discharge

— Leaking or gush of amniotic fluid

■ **Tocolytics**: Administration

— **Terbutaline**
- Side effects
  - Nervousness
  - Tremulousness
  - Headache
  - Nausea and vomiting (N/V), diarrhea
  - Epigastric pain
- Adverse effects
  - Maternal pulse >130 beats/min; arrhythmias
  - BP <90/60 mm Hg
  - Chest pain
  - Pulmonary edema
  - Hypokalemia
  - Hyperglycemia
  - FHR >180 beats/min

Notes

- Nursing interventions
  - Assess hyperglycemia in clients treated with steroids.
  - I&O, daily weight
- Antidote
  - Propranolol
  - Beta-blocker

— **Magnesium sulfate**
- Side effects
  - CNS depression
  - ↓ Respirations
  - ↓ Deep Tendon Reflexes (DTRs)
- Adverse effects
  - ↓ Urine output
  - Pulmonary edema
- Nursing interventions
  - Hold if R <12, urine output <100 mL/4 hours, absent DTRs
  - Monitor magnesium levels.
- Antidote
  - Calcium gluconate

■ **Other Drugs Used to Decrease Contractions**
— Indomethacin, naproxen
— Fenoprofen
— Nifedipine
— Nicardipine

■ **Drug to Enhance Fetal Lung Maturity**
— Betamethasone
— Administered if fetus is <35 weeks' gestation

Spontaneous Abortion

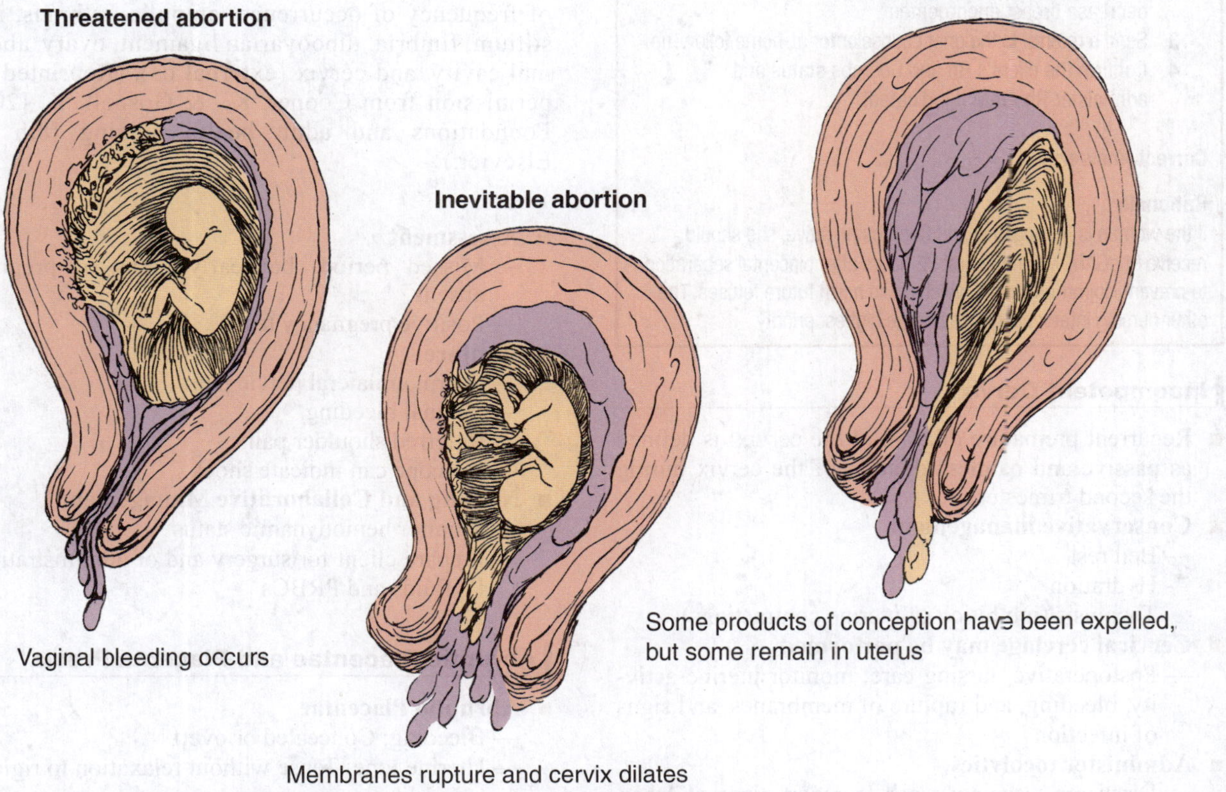

Three types of spontaneous abortion. (Reprinted with permission from Leifer, G. [2015]. Introduction to maternity and pediatric nursing [7th ed.]. Elsevier: Saunders.)

Notes

- **Assessment**
  - — Vaginal bleeding at week 20 or less of gestation
  - — Uterine cramping, backache, and pelvic pressure
  - — May have signs and symptoms of shock
  - — Assess client's and family members' emotional status, needs, and provide support.
- **Nursing and Collaborative Management**
  - — Monitor VS, LOC, and amount of bleeding.
  - — Prepare the client to receive IV fluids and/or PRBCs.
  - — If the client is Rh negative, administer RhoGAM.

Study Break Box

1. **A client at 15 weeks' gestation is admitted for an inevitable abortion. Thirty minutes after returning from surgery, her vital signs are stable. Which intervention has the highest priority?**

   1. Ask the client if she would like to talk about losing her baby.
   2. Place cold cabbage leaves on the client's breasts to decrease breast engorgement.
   3. Send a referral to the grief counselor for at-home follow-up.
   4. Confirm the client's Rh and Coombs status and administer RhoGAM if indicated.

Correct Answer: 4

Rationale

If the woman is Rh negative and Coombs negative, she should receive RhoGAM within the first 72 hours after placental separation to prevent isoimmunization, which could harm future fetuses. The other nursing interventions are not the highest priority.

Incompetent Cervix

- Recurrent premature dilation of the cervix; is defined as passive and painless dilation of the cervix during the second trimester.
- **Conservative management**
  - — Bed rest
  - — Hydration
  - — Tocolysis (inhibition of uterine contractions)
- **Cervical cerclage may be performed**
  - — Postoperative nursing care: monitor uterine activity, bleeding, and rupture of membranes, and signs of infection
- **Administer tocolytics**
  - — Discharge teaching: teach to report signs of labor, bleeding, and infection; decrease activity; pelvic rest.

Ectopic Pregnancy

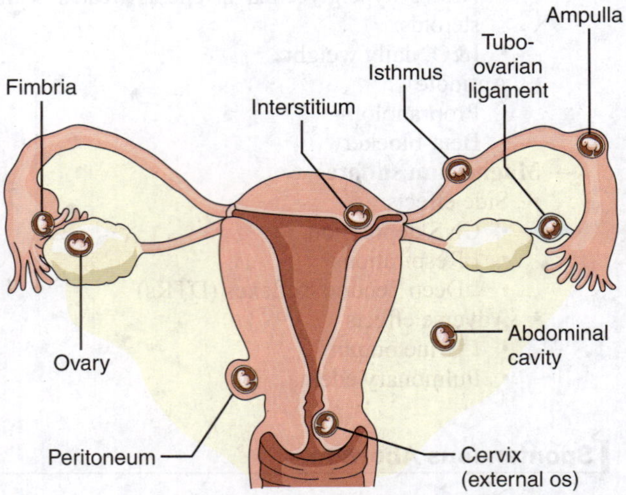

Sites of implantation of ectopic pregnancies in order of frequency of occurrence: ampulla, isthmus, interstitium, fimbria, tuboovarian ligament, ovary, abdominal cavity, and cervix (external os). (Reprinted with permission from Cooper, K., & Gosnell, K. [2019)] Foundations and adult health nursing [8th ed.]. Elsevier.)

- **Assessment**
  - — Missed period, but early signs of pregnancy absent
  - — Positive pregnancy test
- **Rupture**
  - — Sharp, unilateral pelvic pain
  - — Vaginal bleeding
  - — Referred shoulder pain
  - — Syncope can indicate shock
- **Nursing and Collaborative Management**
  - — Monitor hemodynamic status
  - — Prepare client for surgery and or administration of IV fluids and PRBCs

Abruptio Placentae and Placenta Previa

- **Abruptio Placentae**
  - — Bleeding: Concealed or overt
  - — Uterine tone: Tense without relaxation to rigid and board-like
  - — Pain: Persistently painful

Notes

— FHR: Abnormal (complete abruption = absent FHR)

- **Placenta Previa**
  — Bleeding: Bright red vaginal (usually in third trimester)
  — Uterine tone: Soft
  — Pain: Painless
  — FHR: Usually normal unless bleeding is severe and mother becomes hypovolemic

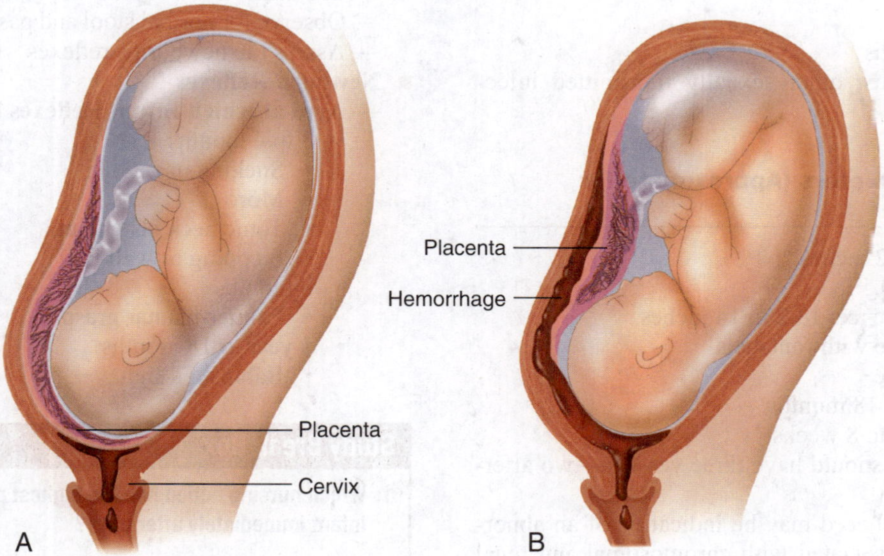

Placenta previa and abruptio placentae. *A*, Placenta previa. The placenta (purple in this illustration) is implanted low in the uterus. Detachment of the placenta from the uterine wall occurs as the cervix dilates, resulting in bleeding. *B*, Abruptio placentae. The placenta (purple) is implanted normally in the uterus but separates from the uterine wall. If the fetal head is engaged, bleeding (red in this illustration) may accumulate in the uterus instead of being expelled externally. (Reprinted with permission from Patton, K. T., & Thibodeau, G. A. [2016]. Anatomy and physiology [9th ed.]. St. Louis: Mosby.)

Disseminated Intravascular Coagulation (DIC)

- **Disseminated Intravascular Coagulation**
  — Risk factors for DIC in pregnancy:
    - Fetal demise
    - Infection/sepsis
    - Gestational Hypertension (GH)
    - Abruptio placentae

Dystocia

- A difficult birth resulting from problems involving the "5 Ps" (powers, passage, passenger, psyche, and/or position). Examples include a lack of progress in cervical dilation, delay in fetal descent, cephalopelvic disproportion, or change in the characteristics of uterine contraction.

Postpartum Complications

- **Hemorrhage**
  — Assess fundal location and consistency
  — Assess vaginal bleeding; saturating one pad/hour indicates hemorrhage
  — Monitor for signs and symptoms of shock
  — Assess for bladder distention: can prevent involution and lead to hemorrhage
- **Venous Thromboembolism**
  — Related to venous stasis and hypercoagulability
  — Can result in superficial venous thrombosis, deep vein thrombosis, or pulmonary embolism
  — Assess legs for pain, tenderness, swelling (Homans' sign not reliable)
  — Treatment: bed rest, anticoagulants, leg elevation, and analgesia

Notes

- **Infection**
  - — Perineal infections
  - — Endometritis
  - — Parametritis
  - — Peritonitis
  - — Mastitis
  - — Cystitis
  - — Pyelonephritis
  - — HIV, hepatitis, other sexually transmitted infections

Newborn Parameters (Approximate for Full Term)

- Length: 18 to 22 inches.
- Weight: 5.5 to 9.5 lb.
- Head circumference: 13.2 to 14 inches.
- Sutures palpable with fontanels.
- Fontanel closure
  - — Anterior: by 18 months
  - — Posterior: 6 to 8 weeks
- Umbilical cord should have three vessels—two arteries and one vein
  - — A two-vessel cord may be indicative of an abnormality or associated with chromosomal and renal defects.
- Extremities should be flexed.
- Major gluteal folds should be even.
- Ortolani's sign and Barlow's sign for developmental dysplasia of the hip.
- Creases should present on soles of feet.
- Pulses should be palpable (radial, brachial, femoral).
- **Nursing and Collaborative Management**
  - — Keep the newborn warm
  - — Suction airway as needed
  - — Assess for respiratory distress
  - — Normal or physiological jaundice appears after the first 24 hours in full-term newborns
  - — Pathological jaundice occurs before this time and may indicate early hemolysis of red blood cells
  - — Assess the hemoglobin and hematocrit (H & H) and blood glucose levels
  - — Weigh daily
  - — Monitor intake and output; weigh diapers if necessary (1 g = 1 mL of urine)
  - — Monitor temperature
  - — Observe for any cracks in skin
  - — Administer eye medication within 1 hour after birth
  - — Provide cord care
  - — Provide circumcision care. Teach client how to care for circumcision site
  - — Supine position ("back to sleep") to prevent Sudden Infant Death Syndrome (SIDs)
  - — Observe for normal stool and passage of meconium
  - — Assess the newborn's reflexes
- **Newborn Reflexes**
  - — **Ages at which Infant Reflexes Disappear**
    - 3 to 4 months
      - Sucking or rooting
      - Moro
      - Tonic neck or fencing
      - Stepping or walking
    - 8 months
      - Palmar-plantar grasp
    - 1 year to 18 months
      - Babinski's sign

Study Break Box

1. Which nursing action has the highest priority for an infant immediately after birth?

1. Place the infant's head in the "sniff" position and give oxygen via face mask.
2. Perform a bedside glucose test and feed the infant glucose water as needed.
3. Assess the heart rate and perform chest compressions if rate is below 60 beats/min.
4. Dry the infant and place him or her under a radiant warmer or skin-to-skin with the mother.

Correct Answer: 4

Rationale

Cold stress is a major cause of metabolic problems in the newborn, including hypoglycemia. The neonatal resuscitation protocol is T-A-B-C (temperature, airway, breathing, circulation). If cold stress occurs, other resuscitative efforts are less successful.

Major Newborn Complications

- **Hypoglycemia**
  - — Assess for risk factors in maternal history (infant of diabetic mother) and environmental factors (cold stress)

Notes

- In general, blood glucose levels <40 mg/dL are considered abnormal and warrant investigation and intervention
- Infant is fed formula or breastfed as soon as the repeat (usually) sample is obtained to prevent a further drop in blood glucose
- Administer IV glucose infusions per HCP prescription for infants with symptomatic hypoglycemia or those too ill to be safely fed orally
- Reduce adverse environmental factors (e.g., irritability and hypothermia)

■ **Respiratory Distress Syndrome (RDS)**
- Caused by inability to produce surfactant
- Resulting in hypoxia and acidosis

■ **Meconium Aspiration Syndrome**
- Fetal distress increases intestinal peristalsis
- Releases meconium into the amniotic fluid

■ **Retinopathy of Prematurity**
- Damage to retinal vessels caused by prolonged use of oxygen (> 30 days)
- Infants receiving oxygen should be examined by an ophthalmologist

■ **Hyperbilirubinemia**
- ↑ Serum levels >12 mg/dL
- Crucial to prevent of kernicterus, which results in permanent neurological damage
- Jaundice starts at the head, spreads to the chest, abdomen, arms, legs, hands, and feet
- Phototherapy: use of fluorescent lights or phototherapy blanket to reduce serum bilirubin levels
  - Possible adverse effects: eye damage, dehydration, or sensory deprivation
  - Expose the skin but cover the genital area
  - Cover eyes with eye shields
  - Monitor skin temperature
  - Increase fluids to compensate for H_2O loss
  - Expect loose green stools and urine
  - Monitor skin color
  - Reposition every 2 hours and as needed (PRN)
  - Provide stimulation
  - Continue monitoring for signs of rebound hyperbilirubinemia

■ **Erythroblastosis Fetalis**
- Results from a Rh-negative mother exposed to RH-positive blood and develops antibodies that are passed to the fetus, destroying fetal red blood cells
- Characterized by hemolytic anemia or hyperbilirubinemia
- Exchange of fetal and maternal blood occurs at birth
- Administer Rho(D) immune globulin (RhoGAM) to a Rh-negative mother to prevent the development of maternal antibodies
- Treatment of newborn includes phototherapy and exchange transfusions

■ **Sepsis**
- Presence of bacteria in the blood
- Prevention—antibiotics in labor for group B Streptococcus (GBS)–positive test
- Assess for maternal, intrapartum, and neonatal risk factors
- Early signs are nonspecific and include lethargy, poor feeding, poor weight gain, and irritability

■ **TORCH Infections**
- Infections that are caused by one of the following:
  - Toxoplasmosis
  - Other infections (e.g., gonorrhea, syphilis, varicella, hepatitis B, HIV, or human parvovirus B19)
  - Rubella
  - Cytomegalovirus
  - Herpes simplex virus

■ **Maternal Substance Abuse**
- Effects on the fetus vary according to substance
- Narcotics cause passive addiction: neonatal abstinence syndrome
- Cocaine is classified as a narcotic but not an opioid; it causes vasoconstriction, preterm birth, poor growth, and neurological problems
- Treatment of drug exposed newborns focuses on reduction of external stimuli, supportive treatment of symptoms, and sedation

■ **Fetal Alcohol Syndrome Disorders (FASDs)**
- Caused by maternal alcohol use during pregnancy
- Associated with neurological problems, IQ deficit, and attention-deficit/hyperactivity disorder
- Craniofacial features include microcephaly, small eyes or short palpebral fissures, a thin upper lip, a flat midface, and an indistinct philtrum

Notes

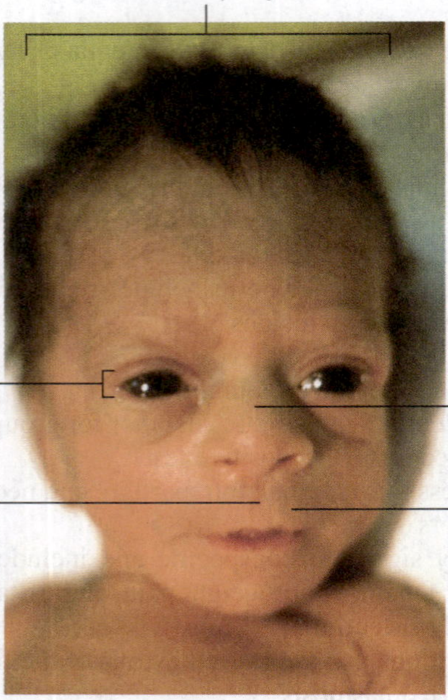

Fetal alcohol syndrome (FAS). (Reprinted with permission from Clark, D.A. [2000]. Atlas of neonatology: A companion to Avery's diseases of the newborn [7th ed.]. Philadelphia: Saunders.)

- **Maternal HIV**
  - — Monitor antibodies closely throughout pregnancy
  - — Testing and treatment in pregnancy greatly reduce risk of transmission to fetus
- **Maternal Diabetes**
  - — Infant born to mother with type 1 or type 2 diabetes or gestational diabetes
  - — Newborn may have hypoglycemia, hypocalcemia, hypomagnesemia, polycythemia, hyperbilirubinemia, cardiomyopathy, Respiratory Distress Syndrome (RDS), birth trauma, and congenital anomalies
  - — Macrosomia: Large for gestational age (LGA) macrosomic infants often have respiratory disorders and other problems

Study Break Box

1. A pregnant client tells the RN that she drinks only one glass of wine a day. Which information would the RN provide the client about the effects of drinking alcohol during pregnancy?

1. Alcohol causes vasoconstriction and decreases placental perfusion.
2. Alcohol decreases the lecithin to sphingomyelin (L:S) ratio, contributing to lung immaturity.
3. Alcohol causes vasodilation and increased fluid overload for the fetus.
4. Alcohol during pregnancy places the fetus at risk for fetal alcohol spectrum disorders.

Correct Answer: 4

Rationale

Alcohol during pregnancy places the fetus at risk for fetal alcohol spectrum disorders. It is not advisable that women drink alcohol during pregnancy. The other information is not accurate.

Test-Taking Strategy

Bowtie questions are unique and can test multiple cognitive skills. First, always read the question carefully and make sure that you have a good understanding of what is being asked. Second, read the scenario and *all* related client information provided in all of the chart tabs. The clue to help you decide which client condition is being experienced may be embedded within the client data that is presented in the chart. Be thorough and don't assume you know what is going on until you carefully read the information presented. Third review the options provided. Hopefully, the disease process you were thinking of is listed. If so, trust your gut. If you were not thinking about one of the options provided, look at each option individually and review the client information. This should assist you in deciding on the correct option. Once you have decided on a client condition, analyze the information you know about the diagnosis to decide which action to take and which parameters to monitor.

Notes

Next-Generation NCLEX® Examination (NGN)–Style Question

Bowtie

Scenario: The RN in the Labor and Delivery unit is caring for a client who is being brought in to triage. The client is arriving via ambulance following an Motor Vehicle Accident (MVA) with airbag deployment. She is reportedly 33 weeks' gestation and is a G1P0. The client reports possibly losing consciousness immediately after the accident. Stated when she awoke, there was a small pool of blood under her. The pants the client is wearing have obvious signs of bleeding. The client appears very anxious and pale. She is not speaking much and only answers yes or no questions. She reports mild continuous "tightness" in abdomen. She denies contractions. She also reports that she may have felt the fetus move earlier that morning but is not sure. She denies any complications with the pregnancy up to this point.

Complete the diagram by choosing from the options below to identify which condition the client is most likely experiencing. Then choose two actions the RN will take to address the identified condition and two parameters that the RN will monitor to assess the client's progress.

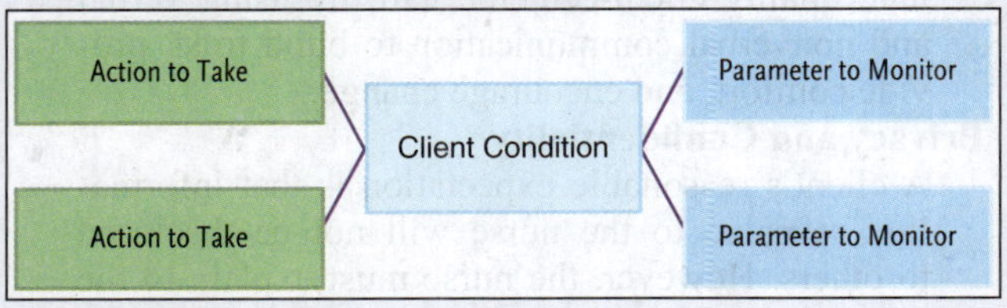

Answer:

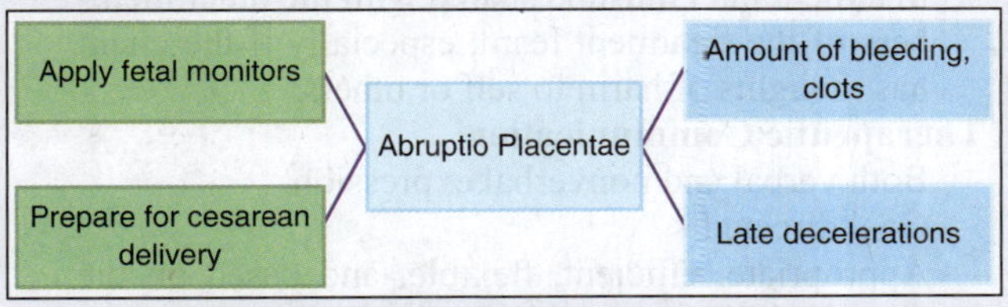

Actions to Take	Potential Conditions	Parameters to Monitor
Apply fetal monitors	Placenta previa	FHR variability
Perform manual vaginal exam	Umbilical cord prolapse	Amount of bleeding, clots
Apply suprapubic pressure	Abruptio placentae	Late decelerations
Prepare for cesarean delivery	Postpartum hemorrhage	Biophysical profile
Place in right lateral position		Uterine atony

Rationale: The client in the scenario is most likely experiencing an abruptio placentae. Actions the RN should take include applying fetal monitors to evaluate fetal heart tones and preparing the client for a probable cesarean delivery. The RN would be diligent in observing the amount of bleeding and the passage of clots. The RN would also evaluate fetal heart tones observing for any signs of fetal distress such as late decelerations. These observations will help determine the degree of abruption, assess the condition of both the mother and the fetus, and determine how quickly the infant should be delivered.

Notes

11 Mental Health Nursing

Mental Health Nursing

- **Nurse-Client Relationship**
  - — The goal of the nurse-client relationship is to facilitate quality client-centered care by using verbal and nonverbal communication to build trust, provide comfort, and encourage change.
- **Privacy and Confidentiality**
  - — A client's reasonable expectation is that information revealed to the nurse will not be disclosed to others. However, the nurse must explain to the client that information relevant to the individual's treatment plan must be shared with the other members of the treatment team, especially if the client has thoughts of harm to self or others.
- **Therapeutic Communication**
  - — Both verbal and nonverbal expression
  - — Goal directed
  - — Appropriate, efficient, flexible, and based on the client's ability to provide feedback
  - — **Principles**
    - Establish trust
    - Demonstrate a nonjudgmental attitude
    - Offer self; be empathetic, not sympathetic
    - Use active listening
    - Accept and support client's feelings
    - Clarify and validate the client's statements
    - Use matter-of-fact approach
  - — **Examples of Therapeutic Communication**
    - **Silence**: sit quietly and wait
    - **Active listening**: give full attention to the client
    - **Open-ended questioning:** promotes sharing
    - **Empathizing**: demonstrates warmth and acknowledgment of feelings
    - **Restating**: repeat what the client says to show understanding and to review what was said

Mental Health Definitions

- **Mental Health**
  - — A lifelong process
  - — Successful adjustment to changing environments (internal and external)
- **Mental Illness**
  - — Defined by clinically significant behavior as a result of the client's distress or disability
  - — An inability to respond to the environment because of mental or medical conditions that affect the client's thinking, ability to relate to others, mood, feeling, and daily functioning (e.g., impaired thinking, poor impulse control, or altered behavior)
  - — In many clients, it is a temporary loss, while in others, it may be a lifelong series of intermittent exacerbations of illness.

Study Break Box

1. An adult client is admitted to the inpatient mental health unit with a diagnosis of severe depression. As the client begins to recover, the client develops rapport with the RN. After being discharged from the hospital, the client and the RN happen to meet in the coffee shop. The client asks the RN if they can schedule future meetings at the coffee shop. Which response by the RN is most therapeutic?

1. I will meet with the nursing supervisor to discuss our plan for routine meetings.
2. "Let's not plan to meet; however, we may inadvertently see each other here."
3. "It's not appropriate for me to discuss therapy with you when I'm off duty."
4. "A social relationship with a former client is not appropriate."

Correct Answer: 4

Rationale

Explain in a matter-of-fact and supportive manner that the nurse-client relationship gives the RN information about the client that creates an uneven balance in a friendly relationship. For example, the client may begin to rely on the RN for emotional support or the RN may inadvertently use information gained during the client's admission in an inappropriate way. The other nurse statements are not therapeutic.

Notes

Coping and Defense Mechanisms

- Primarily unconscious efforts to decrease anxiety.
- Can be constructive or destructive.
- Coping is related to problem solving.
- Defense is related to protecting oneself.
  - — Denial
  - — Displacement
  - — Identification

Therapeutic Treatment Modalities

- **Milieu Therapy**: the physical, social, and therapeutic environment in which the client is receiving treatment.
- **Collaborative Care**: the hallmark of treatment in mental health. The team includes nurses, psychiatrists, social workers, mental health technicians, drug/alcohol therapists, etc.
- **Interpersonal Psychotherapy**: uses a therapeutic relationship to modify the client's feelings, attitudes, and behaviors.
- **Behavior Therapy**: includes many formats that are used to assist the client in changing behavior.
- **Cognitive Therapy**: directive, time-limited approach.
- **Crisis Intervention**: directed at resolution of the immediate crisis and to returning the individual to the precrisis level of functioning.
- **Electroconvulsive Therapy (ECT)**: infrequently used treatment that uses controlled electrically induced seizures to treat severely depressed individuals who fail to respond to antidepressant medications and therapy.

Study Break Box

1. A female client who is a 5-year breast cancer survivor received confirmation that she has a recurrence of breast cancer. She informs her family that the biopsy was negative. Which action would the RN take?

1. Tell the client's family to consult the health care provider.
2. Ask the client to restate what the health care provider told her.
3. Encourage the client to inform her family about the results.
4. Suggest that the client talk to the RN about her fears.

Correct Answer: 4

Rationale
The RN can provide the client with a safe place to share her concerns and obtain support until she is ready to abandon denial as a defense mechanism. The other recommendations do not address the client's concerns.

Group Therapy

- Involves a therapist and five to eight members.
- Provides feedback and support for the individual goals of each member.
- **Group therapy models:**
  - — Cognitive behavioral therapy (CBT)
  - — Interpersonal group therapy
  - — Self-help or support groups
    - Stress management
    - Self-care
    - Medication education
    - Dual diagnosis
  - — Family therapy
    - The member with the presenting symptoms indicates the presence of problems in the entire family
    - A change in one member will bring about changes in other member
- **Therapeutic Factors**
  - — Instillation of hope and optimism about group treatment
  - — **Universality:** Members realize they are not alone with their problems, feelings, or thoughts
  - — **Imparting of information**: Members receive formal teaching by the leader or advice from peers
  - — **Altruism:** Members feel a reward from giving support to others
  - — **Recapitulation:** Members repeat patterns of behavior in the group that they learned in their families; feedback from the leader and peers provides opportunities to learn about their behavior
  - — **Development of socializing techniques:** Members learn new social skills based on feedback from others
  - — **Imitative behavior**: Members copy behavior from the leaders or peers and can adopt healthier habits
  - — **Interpersonal learning:** Members gain insight into themselves based on feedback from others; occurs later in the group after establishing trust
  - — **Group cohesiveness:** In a mature group, members accept positive feedback and constructive criticism
  - — **Catharsis:** Intense feelings, as judged by the member, are shared
  - — **Existential resolution:** Members learn to accept painful aspects of life (i.e., loneliness, death) that affect everyone

Notes

- **Stages of Group Development**
  - — **Initial Stage:** superficial communication; nurse and client orient to parameters of a therapeutic relationship
  - — **Working Stage:** real work is done by the group
  - — **Termination Stage:** provides opportunity to learn to deal with letting go

Study Break Box

1. **During the initial phase of a support group for stress management, a group member, who has a master's degree, states, "My educational background makes it easier for me to help the other group members." Which action would the RN take to assure effective group functioning?**

   1. Reiterating the purpose of the support group sessions.
   2. Asking the group to identify various stressful problems.
   3. Ask members to share stress-reducing strategies.
   4. Terminating the meeting and evaluate the situation.

Correct Answer: 1

Rationale

The group is in the initial phase, so the RN should restate the purpose and goal of the support group. During the middle phase, the RN should solicit problems from the group after trust has been established. During the working middle phase, problem solving is initiated. The RN should not avoid the comments but clarify the focus for group interaction.

Anxiety

- Mild or moderate anxiety is a normal subjective experience that includes feelings of apprehension, uneasiness, uncertainty, or dread.
- Severe stress may create levels of anxiety leading to depression, helplessness, and hopelessness that can end in panic.
- **Types of Anxiety**
  - — Mild: tension of everyday life
  - — Moderate: immediate concerns
  - — Severe: feeling that something bad is about to happen
  - — Panic: terror and a sense of impending doom
- **Anxiety Disorders**
  - — Generalized Anxiety Disorder
    - An unrealistic or persistent anxiety about everyday worries
  - — Panic Disorder
    - Panic disorders produce a sudden feeling of intense apprehension
  - — Phobias
    - Irrational fear of an object, activity, or situation
    - Client may or may not recognize fear as unreasonable
    - Associated with panic-level anxiety
    - Defense mechanisms include repression and displacement (i.e., agoraphobia)
- **Nursing and Collaborative Management**
  - — Reduce environmental stimuli
  - — Provide a calm, quiet environment
  - — Administer antianxiety medications
  - — Administer selective serotonin reuptake inhibitors (SSRIs) and tricyclic antidepressants (TCAs)

Study Break Box

1. **The RN is planning to teach a client strategies for coping with anxiety. The RN finds the client engaged in compulsive handwashing. Which action would the RN take next?**

   1. While the client is handwashing, introduce alternatives to handwashing.
   2. Inform the client they need to immediately stop their handwashing.
   3. Allow the client to complete handwashing; then begin teaching.
   4. Ask the client to describe events that precipitated the handwashing.

Correct Answer: 3

Rationale

The best time for learning occurs at the end of the compulsive behavior when the client's anxiety is lowest. Learning is impaired during compulsive acts that are used to alleviate anxiety, and interrupting the handwashing will only heighten the anxiety. Interrupting the client's behavior will increase his anxiety, which interferes with learning. Compulsions are uncontrollable acts used to deal with anxiety with a subjective feeling of unknown origin. This will not help the RN initiate a teaching plan.

Notes

Study Break Box—cont'd

2. The RN and the unlicensed assistive personnel (UAP) take a group of mental health clients to a baseball game. During the game, a client reports shortness of breath and dizziness. Which intervention would the RN implement first?

1. Have the UAP escort the client back to the unit.
2. Request that the client describes current feelings.
3. Accompany the client to a quiet area.
4. Ask the client if anything untoward occurred.

Correct Answer: 3

Rationale

The RN should take an anxious client to an area where there is reduced environmental stimuli away from the crowd. The client may be experiencing a medical or mental health issue; however, either situation is best assessed in a quiet area away from others. The other interventions are not the priority.

— **Antianxiety (Anxiolytic) Medication**
— Benzodiazepines:
- Recommended for only short-term use because these drugs are addictive and may depress the central nervous system (CNS)
- Have anxiety-reducing (anxiolytic), sedative-hypnotic, muscle-relaxing, and anticonvulsant actions

— Flumazenil (Anexate; Romazicon): a benzodiazepine antagonist administered intravenously that reverses benzodiazepine intoxication in 5 minutes

Somatic Symptom Disorder

- Persistent worry or statements regarding physical illness without physical findings
- Treatment: CBT
- **Types of somatic symptom disorders:**
  - — Illness anxiety disorder or somatic disorder is a preoccupation with complaints about chronic symptoms that cause significant distress
  - — Factitious disorders are self-imposed fabricated symptoms (formerly Munchhausen syndrome).
    - Self-injury, induce or fabricate symptoms without obvious gains such as financial gain
    - Uses medication inappropriately to induce illness
  - — Factitious disorder by proxy occurs when symptoms are imposed on another; e.g., parent induces illness in child (aka, Munchhausen by proxy)
    - when a caregiver (usually the mother) causes a child to need treatment for an illness or injury created or stimulated by the mother

Crisis Intervention

- **Crisis**
  - — Results from experiencing a significant traumatic event or situation that cannot be remedied by the use of previous coping strategies

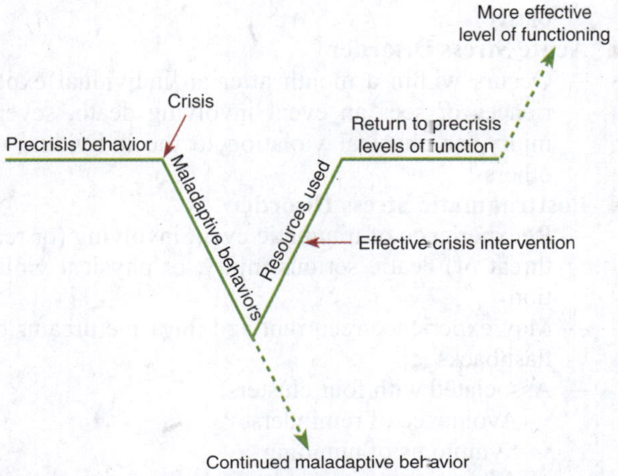

Stages of crisis. (Reprinted with permission from Morrison-Valfre, M. [2017]. Foundations of Mental Health Care [6th ed.]. Elsevier.)

- **Risk Factors**
  - — Multiple comorbidities and losses
  - — Unexpected life changes
  - — Limited coping skills
  - — Chronic pain or disability
  - — Poor social support
  - — Concurrent psychiatric disorders, substance abuse, or disability
  - — Limited access to health care service
- **Goal**
  - — Return the client to precrisis level of functioning
- **Nursing and Collaborative Management**
  - — Assess for suicidal or homicidal thoughts or plans
  - — Help the client feel safe and less anxious

Notes

- — Listen carefully
- — Be directive (e.g., nurse may arrange for shelter or contact a social worker)
- — Mobilize social support
- — Involve the client in identifying realistic, acceptable interventions
- — Regular follow-up is not usually part of crisis intervention
- — Actively listen to the client's description of events to identify the most troubling aspects
- — Assist the client in identifying past successes to promote client's ability to regain control

Trauma Stressor–Related Disorders

- **Acute Stress**
  - — Abnormal response to an extreme abnormal event (witnessing a horrific car accident or war-zone blast)
- **Acute Stress Disorder**
  - — Occurs within a month after an individual experiences or sees an event involving death, severe injury, or physical violation to the individual or others
- **Posttraumatic Stress Disorder**
  - — Reexperience of traumatic event involving (or real threat of) death, serious injury, or physical violation
  - — May experience recurrent and intrusive dreams or flashbacks
  - — Associated with four clusters:
    - Avoidance of reminders
    - Symptoms of numbing
    - Alterations in behavior including self-destructive (suicide), aggression, and irritability
    - Persistent negative mood and alterations in cognition
- **Other Stressor-Related Disorders**
  - — Anxiety displayed in symptoms
    - Intrusive thoughts
    - Nightmares
    - Emotional detachment
    - Flashbacks
  - — Reactions may be triggered by visible reminders of the trauma (e.g., physical disabilities)
  - — Responses include shock, anger, denial or panic, and/or self-destructive behavior (e.g., substance abuse or suicidal ideation)
- **Nursing and Collaborative Management**
  - — Implement suicidal and homicidal precautions as needed
  - — Consistently provide nonthreatening environment

Dissociative Disorders

- These disorders are rarely encountered and are an unconscious defense mechanism that protects the person against overwhelming anxiety.
  - — **Dissociative amnesia**: a sudden temporary inability to recall important personal events following a traumatic event
  - — **Dissociative identity disorder**: two or more distinct identities, at least two of which recurrently take control
  - — **Depersonalization or derealization disorder**: persistent or recurrent episodes of feelings of detachment from oneself that occurs in response to acute stress

Personality Disorders

- Individuals diagnosed with personality disorders have difficulty in work and personal relationships.
  - — Insensitive to the needs of others
  - — Demanding and fault finding
  - — Have inability to trust others
  - — Blur boundaries between themselves and others
  - — Lack individual accountability
  - — Have poor impulse control: engage in self-damaging behaviors (impulsive sexual or suicidal behavior)
- **Obsessive-Compulsive Disorder**
  - — Obsession
    - Persistently intrusive thoughts
  - — Compulsion
    - Repetitive behaviors designed to divert unacceptable thoughts and reduce anxiety (e.g., compulsive handwashing)
- **Antisocial Personality Disorder**
  - — Aggressive toward others without remorse
  - — Is manipulative, self-centered, and impulsive
- **Borderline Personality Disorder**
  - — Highly changeable and intense affect
  - — Poor impulse control, engages in self-damaging behavior (e.g., sexual and/or suicidal)
  - — Pits perceived good person (nurse, friend, family member) against perceived bad person; switches which person is good

Notes

— **Associated behaviors**
- Inflexible maladaptive behavior patterns
- In touch with reality
- Lacks insight into behavior
- Poor impulse control
- Forms of acting out include:
  — Yelling and swearing
  — Cutting own skin
  — Manipulating others
  — Abusing substances
  — Engaging in promiscuous sexual behaviors
  — Attempting suicide

Study Break Box

1. A client diagnosed with borderline personality disorder returns after a weekend pass with lacerations to both wrists. The client complains about how the RN is performing the dressing change. The RN's response would be presented in which manner?

1. Disinterested.
2. Concerned.
3. Matter-of-fact.
4. Empathetic.

Correct Answer: 3

Rationale

If the RN acts as matter-of-fact as possible, there is less likelihood that the client will use splitting to idealize or devalue the RN. The RN should not present the info in a disinterested, concerned, or empathetic manner.

Eating Disorders

- **Compulsive Overeating**
  — Binge-like overeating without purging
  — Lack of control over food consumption
- **Anorexia Nervosa**
  — Onset is often associated with a stressful event
  — Death can occur from starvation, suicide, cardiomyopathies, or electrolyte imbalance
  — The client experiences an altered body image
- **Bulimia Nervosa**
  — Binge-purge syndrome in which eating binges are followed by purging behaviors

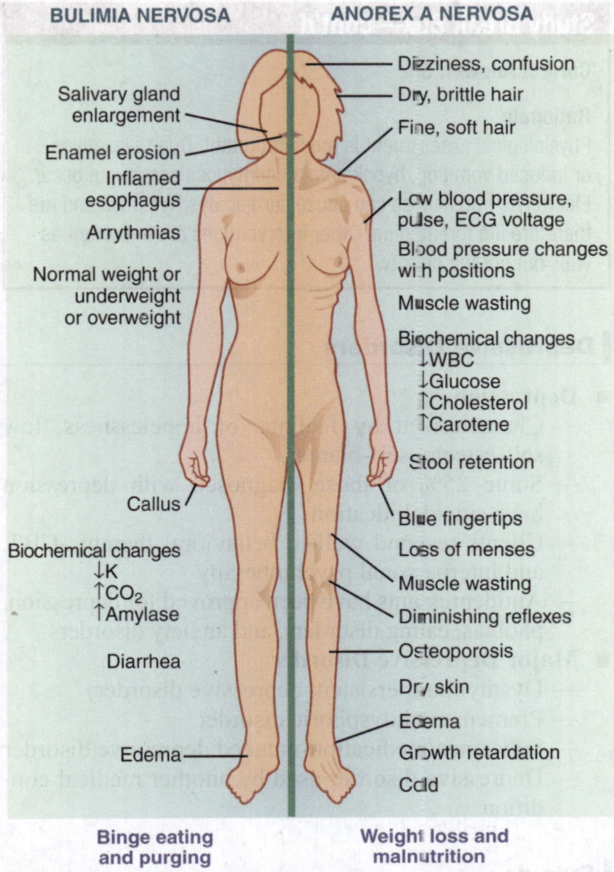

Physical and clinical signs and symptoms of bulimia nervosa and anorexia nervosa. *ECG*, Electrocardiogram; *WBC*, white blood cell count. (Reprinted with permission from Morrison-Valfre, M. [2017]. Foundations of Mental Health Care [6th ed.]. Elsevier.)

Study Break Box

1. A client diagnosed with a history of bulimia is admitted to the mental health unit. Which intervention is most important for the RN to include in the initial treatment plan?

1. Observe the client after meals for purging.
2. Assess daily weight and vital signs.
3. Monitor serum potassium and calcium.
4. Provide a structured environment at mealtime.

Notes

Study Break Box—cont'd

Correct Answer: 3

Rationale

Physiological assessment is most important. Due to laxatives or induced vomiting, hypokalemia and hypocalcemia can occur. Electrolyte imbalances can cause cardiac dysrhythmias and are therefore life threatening. Other interventions are important as well, but not the priority.

Depressive Disorders

- **Depression**
  - — Characterized by feelings of hopelessness, low self-esteem, self-blame
  - — Some 25% of those diagnosed with depression have suicidal ideation
  - — Clients respond well to behavioral therapy, CBT, and interpersonal psychotherapy
  - — Antidepressants have been approved for depression, phobias, eating disorders, and anxiety disorders
- **Major Depressive Disorder**
  - — Dysthymia (persistent depressive disorder)
  - — Premenstrual dysphoric disorder
  - — Substance/medication-induced depressive disorder
  - — Depressive disorder used by another medical condition

Suicide

- A suicide threat is a warning, direct or indirect, verbal or nonverbal, that a person is planning to take his or her own life.
- The person may give away prized possessions, make a will or funeral arrangements, or withdraw from friendships and social activities.
- Assessment includes whether the person has made a specific plan and whether the means to carry out the plan are available.
- **NEVER** leave a suicidal client alone.
- Protect the client from inflicting self-harm, be vigilant, supervise medication administration, and implement strategies to ↑ self-esteem and social support.
- **Suicide Precautions**
  - — Ongoing observations and monitoring of the client
  - — Provide protective environment
  - — Search for weapons or potential weapons.
  - — Be aware of major warning signs of an impending attempt
  - — Client begins to give away possessions
  - — Makes a will or funeral arrangements
  - — Client suddenly becomes "better" or "happy"

Bipolar Disorder

- **Bipolar Disorder**
  - — Characterized by mood swings involving depression, euphoria, grandiosity, and an inflated sense of self-worth
- **Medications (Mood Stabilizers)**
  - — **Lithium carbonate**: medication of choice; can be toxic and requires regular monitoring of serum lithium levels
  - — Toxic level is >1.5 mEq/L
- **Other Medications**
  - — Divalproex (Valproate)
  - — Olanzapine (Zyprexa)
  - — Carbamazepine (Tegretol)
- **Nursing and Collaborative Management: High Alert—Lithium Therapy**
  - — **LITHIUM TOXICITY**
    - **Lithium level range**: 0.4 mEq/L to 1.2 mEq/L
    - **Expected side effects**: fine hand tremor, polyuria, and mild thirst, weight gain, mild nausea
    - Signs of lithium toxicity (level >1.5 mEq/L): N/V, diarrhea, slurred speech, muscle weakness. Withhold medication; obtain lithium blood level
    - **Advanced toxicity:** coarse hand tremor, persistent gastrointestinal (GI) upset, mental confusion, muscle hyperirritability
    - **Severe toxicity:** ataxia, blurred vision, clonic movements, seizures, severe hypotension, death
  - — There is no known antidote for lithium poisoning. The drug is discontinued immediately.

Monoamine Oxidase Inhibitors (MAOIs)

- Use caution when administering MAOIs.
- Inhibit the enzyme monoamine oxidase, which is present in the brain, blood platelets, liver, spleen, and kidneys.
- Administered to clients with depression who have not responded to other antidepressant therapies, including Electroconvulsive Therapy (ETC).

Notes

- There must be a 2-week wash-out period between using MAOIs and SSRIs or serotonin and norepinephrine reuptake inhibitor (SNRIs) (in either direction, i.e., from MAOI to SSRIs, or vice versa); otherwise, the mixture can trigger a hypertensive crisis.
- A hypertensive crisis, or hypotension, coma, or seizures may occur with concurrent use of:
  - Tyramine-containing foods (red wine, aged cheese, raisins)
  - Decongestants, amphetamines
  - Antidepressants, dopamine
  - Opioids epinephrine, guanethidine
  - Levodopa, methyldopa
  - Nasal norepinephrine
  - Reserpine, vasoconstrictors
- Concurrent use with opioid analgesics may cause hyper- or hypotension, coma, or seizures.

Antidepressant Medications

- **SSRIs**
  - Action: Inhibit serotonin reuptake
  - Side Effects/Considerations: Drowsiness, dizziness, headache, insomnia, depressed appetite
    - Citalopram (Celexa)
    - Escitalopram (Lexapro)
    - Fluvoxamine (Luvox)
    - Fluoxetine (Prozac)
    - Paroxetine (Paxil)
    - Sertraline (Zoloft)
- **SNRIs**
  - Action: Block reabsorption of serotonin and norepinephrine
- **TCAs**
  - Action: Block reuptake of norepinephrine (and serotonin) at pre-synaptic neurons
  - Side Effects/Considerations: May take 2 to 4 weeks to produce effect; tachycardia, dizziness, insomnia, drowsiness, fluid retention

    NOTE: Trazodone can cause priapism. Priapism affects the penis and, in rare instances, the clitoris
    - Amitriptyline
    - Clomipramine (Anafranil)
    - Desipramine (Norpramin)
    - Imipramine (Tofranil)
    - Nortriptyline
    - Protriptyline (Vivactil)
    - Trimipramine (Surmontil)
- **Atypical antidepressants**
  - Desvenlafaxine (Pristiq)
  - Duloxetine (Cymbalta)—also approved to treat anxiety and certain types of chronic pain
  - Levomilnacipran (Fetzima)
  - Venlafaxine (Effexor XR)—also approved to treat certain anxiety disorders and panic disorder

HIGH-ALERT Antidepressant Use

- **Serotonin Syndrome**

  Hyperthermia, rigidity, cognitive impairments, and autonomic symptoms
  - Potentially fatal and may occur at any time during therapy with SSRIs or SNRIs (serotonin norepinephrine reuptake inhibitor) combined with MAOIs
  - Treatment is symptomatic with propranolol, cooling blankets, chlorpromazine for hyperthermia, diazepam for muscle rigidity or rigors
- **Antidepressant apathy**: Some clients lose interest in life and the events around them (related to SSRIs)
- **Antidepressant withdrawal syndrome**: Abrupt cessation of antidepressants engenders withdrawal symptoms
- **Antidepressant loss of effectiveness**: Sometimes medications are no longer effective
- **Antidepressant-induced suicide**: Especially 18- to 24-year-olds in the early stages of treatment
- **Lithium toxicity** is potentially fatal:
  - Hyperthermia as high as 108°F (42.2°C), cognitive impairments, and autonomic symptoms
  - Muscular rigidity
  - Altered mental status
  - Irregular pulse
  - Cardiac dysrhythmias
  - Diaphoresis
  - **Nursing and Collaborative Management**
    - Immediately discontinue lithium and notify HCP
    - Client may need to transfer to a critical care unit

Study Break Box

1. Today's lab report of the lithium level is 1.3 mEq/mL for a client diagnosed with bipolar disorder. Which is the first action the RN would take?

1. Withhold the dose until after breakfast.
2. Give the client the prescribed dose.
3. Obtain a prescription to increase the dose.
4. Withhold the dose and notify the health care provider.

Notes

Study Break Box—cont'd

Correct Answer: 4

Rationale

The RN will withhold the dose and notify the health care provider immediately. A lithium level that is >1.2 mEq/mL is considered elevated. All other interventions are inappropriate and would increase the client's lithium level further, which can lead to lithium toxicity.

Schizophrenia Spectrum and Other Psychotic Disorders

- A group of mental disorders characterized by psychotic features
- **Key Symptoms of Schizophrenia**
  - **Negative symptoms**
    - Anhedonia: A reduced ability or inability to experience pleasure in everyday life
    - Avolition: Loss of motivation; difficulty beginning and sustaining goal-directed activities; reduction in motivation or goal-directed behavior
    - Asociality: Decreased desire for, or comfort during, social interaction
    - Affective blunting: Reduced or constricted affect
    - Apathy: A decreased interest in, or attention to, activities or beliefs that would otherwise be interesting or important
    - Alogia: Reduction in speech, sometimes called poverty of speech
  - **Positive Symptoms**
    - Delusions: False beliefs
      - Delusions of persecution
      - Delusions of grandeur
      - Somatic delusions
      - Perceptual delusions
    - Perceptual Distortions
      - Difficulty understanding or using information
    - Illusions
      - Brief experiences of misperception of reality that usually occur with delirium, delirium tremens (DTs), or drug induced
    - Hallucinations
      - Perceptions without a basis in reality
      - Includes five senses (smell, touch, etc.)
- **Nursing and Collaborative Management**
  - Assess for risk of violence to self or others and take appropriate precautions
  - Provide quiet, soothing environment
  - Establish routine and boundaries
  - Provide stable, nonthreatening, brief, social interactions
  - If the client is acting frightened or scared, increase physical space surrounding the client and approach the client calmly
  - Encourage reality-based interests

Antipsychotic Medications

- **Traditional Medications**
  - Chlorpromazine
  - Haloperidol (Haldol)
  - **Purpose**: Treat psychotic behavior
  - Side Effects
    - Extrapyramidal (EPS)
    - Akathisia
    - Acute dystonia
    - Pseudoparkinsonism
    - Anticholinergic
  - **Nursing Assessment**
    - Screen for EPS using Abnormal Involuntary Movement Scale (AIMS)
    - Encourage fluid, gum, and hard candy and increase fiber intake
- **Long-Acting Medications**
  - Clozapine (Clozaril)
  - Risperdal (risperidone) Long-Acting Injection
  - Side Effects
    - Blood dyscrasias and neuroleptic malignant syndrome (NMS) (very high fever)
  - **Nursing and Collaborative Management**
    - Teach the client to change positions slowly to prevent dizziness, and report urinary retention
    - Stress the importance of maintaining medication therapy
- **Atypical Medications**
  - Aripiprazole (Abilify)
    - **Purpose**: treat all positive and negative symptoms
    - **Side effects**: multiple side effects depending on medication
    - **Nursing assessment**: tolerance to effects, NMS

Neuroleptic Malignant Syndrome (NMS)

- Involves autonomic, motor, and behavioral symptoms
- Antipsychotic is stopped immediately if the client develops signs of NMS.
  - Severe muscle rigidity
  - Increased temperature (fever >38°C, as high as 100.4°F), increased pulse, and labile blood pressure

Notes

— Confusion (altered mental status)
— Autonomic dysfunction
— Agitation
— Involves autonomic, motor, and behavioral symptoms

- **Associated medications**
  — Haloperidol, Fluphenazine, Trifluperazine, Thioridazine, Loxapine, Clozaril, Risperidone, Olanzapine, Ziprasidone, Reserpine, Droperidol, Lithium, Levodopa, Desipramine, Amantadine
- **Nursing and Collaborative Management**
  — Assess for risk of violence to self or others and take appropriate precautions
  — Provide quiet, soothing environment
  — Establish routine and boundaries
  — Provide stable, nonthreatening, brief, social interactions
  — If the client is acting frightened or scared, increase your distance of physical space surrounding the client and approach client calmly
  — Encourage reality-based interests

Substance Abuse Disorders

- **Substance dependence**: a pattern of repeated use of a substance.
- **Substance tolerance**: a need for more of the substance to reach the desired effect.
- **Substance abuse**: recurrent use of a substance.
- **Substance withdrawal**: symptoms occur when blood levels of a substance decline.
- **Opioids** are a type of medicine often used to help relieve pain. Signs and symptoms of abuse include:
  — poor coordination
  — drowsiness
  — shallow or slow breathing rate
  — nausea, vomiting
  — constipation
  — physical agitation
  — poor decision making
  — slurred speech
  — mood swings
  — euphoria
  — irritability
  — depression
  — anxiety attacks
- An overdose of opioids requires immediate emergency medical treatment (naloxone).
- **Alcohol Abuse**
  — Alcohol is a CNS depressant
  — **Physical dependence**: a biological need for alcohol to avoid physical withdrawal symptoms
  — **Psychological dependence**: a craving for the subjective effect of alcohol
  — **Intoxication**: blood alcohol level ≥0.1% (21.7 mmol/L [100 mg alcohol/dL] blood])
    - Clients may present to the emergency department with blood alcohol levels as high as 3% to 5% (300 to 500 mg/dL)
  — Alcohol Withdrawal
    - Peaks after 24 to 48 hours
    - Chlordiazepoxide (Librium) is the "gold standard" and most commonly prescribed medication for acute alcohol withdrawal
    - Withdrawal Delirium
      - Peaks 48 to 72 hours after cessation of intake and lasts 2 to 3 days
      - It is a medical emergency
      - At time of admission, always ask clients when their last drink was ingested
      - Death can occur from myocardial infarction, fat emboli, peripheral vascular collapse, electrolyte imbalance, aspiration pneumonia, or suicide
  — **Disulfiram (Antabuse) Therapy**
    - Alcohol deterrent
    - Instruct the client who is on disulfiram therapy to avoid the use of substances that contain alcohol, such as:
      - Cough medicines
      - Mouthwashes
      - Aftershave lotions
  — Other medications used to assist with alcohol cravings:
    - Acamprosate calcium
    - Naltrexone

Study Break Box

1. A client with a history of alcohol abuse is admitted to the medical unit for GI bleeding and pancreatitis. The admission data include BP 156/96 mm Hg, pulse 92 beats/min, and temperature 37.3°C (99.2°F). Which intervention is most important for the RN to implement?

1. Provide quiet, non-threatening and low-stimulus environment.
2. Initiate seizure precautions.
3. Administer as-needed (PRN) lorazepam (Ativan) as prescribed.
4. Determine the time and quantity of the client's last alcohol intake.

Notes

Study Break Box—cont'd

Correct Answer: 4

Rationale
It is most important to determine the time and amount of the client's last alcohol intake to determine the client's risk for withdrawal (4–6 hours after the last drink) or delirium tremens (about 12–36 hours after the last drink). The other nursing interventions are not the priority.

Autism Spectrum Disorder

- **Autism Spectrum Disorder**: a group of developmental disorders that includes autism, Asperger disorder, childhood disintegrative disorder, and pervasive developmental disorder not otherwise specified.
- **Etiology**: no known cause.
- **Clinical Description**
  - — Hyperactivity
  - — Short attention span
  - — Impulsivity
  - — Aggressivity
  - — Self-injurious behavior
  - — Temper tantrums
  - — Repetitive mannerisms
  - — Preoccupation with objects
  - — Absence of spoken language
  - — "Islands of genius" (savant-like syndrome)
- **Prognosis**
  - — No known cure
  - — Language skills and intellectual level are strongest factors related to prognosis
  - — Only a small percentage of individuals with the disorder go on to live and work independently as adults

Attention-Deficit/Hyperactivity Disorder

- **Etiology:** No known cause, but there is a strong correlation between genetic factors and *attention*-deficit/hyperactivity disorder (ADHD).
- **Clinical Description**
  - — Fidgeting in a seat
  - — Getting up when expected to be seated
  - — Excessive running when it is dangerous or inappropriate
  - — Loud and disruptive play during quiet activities
  - — Forgets and misses appointments
  - — Fails to meet deadlines
  - — Loses the train of conversation
  - — Changes topics inappropriately
  - — Does not follow rules of games
- Treatment with CNS stimulants may be required to reduce hyperactive behavior and lengthen attention span.
- **Prognosis**
  - — Continues into adolescence in the majority of children
  - — Many adults with ADHD in childhood report a decrease of hyperactivity but a continuation of difficulty concentrating or attending to complex projects

Neurocognitive Disorders (Not Classified as Mental Illness)

- **Major and Mild Neurocognitive Disorders (NCD)**
  - — Primarily acquired cognitive symptoms that represent a decline
  - — Typically refers to degeneration of younger clients caused by nerve cell deterioration (e.g., traumatic brain injury, HIV)
- **Symptoms**
  - — Significant cognitive decline
  - — Interference with independent functioning
  - — Not caused by other mental disorder
- **Mild NCD**
  - — Does not interfere with independence; not due to delirium
  - — Impairment in judgment, abstract thinking, problem-solving ability, and behavior may also be present.
  - — Providing a safe environment is the priority when cognitive domains are affected.
  - — Cognitive Domains
    - Learning and memory
    - Language
    - Perceptual-motor
    - Social cognition
    - Executive function
    - Complex attention

Dementia

- Dementia is NOT classified by the *Diagnostic and Statistical Manual of Mental Disorders, Fifth Edition (DSM-5)* as mental illness.

Notes

- *DSM-5* refers to major and mild NCD terminology (sometimes referred to as dementia).
- **Dementia:** Progressive deterioration in intellectual functioning secondary to structural or functional changes
  - — Long-term and short-term memory loss
  - — Impairment in judgment, abstract thinking, problem-solving ability, and behavior
  - — Caused by nerve cell deterioration
  - — Providing a safe environment is the priority

Alzheimer's Disease

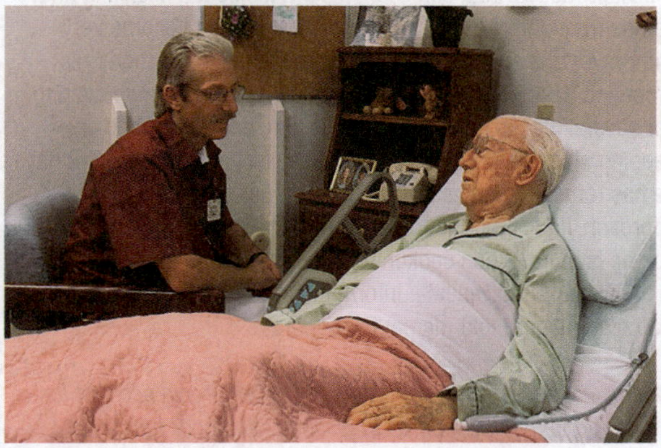

Becoming a client. (Reprinted with permission from Morrison-Valfre, M. [2017]. Foundations of Mental Health Care [6th ed.]. Elsevier.)

- Irreversible form of senile dementia caused by nerve cell deterioration
- Priority is client safety.
- Maintain comfort, toilet as necessary; keep dry.
- Reduce environmental stimulation during late afternoon and evening.
- Maintain daily routine.
- Provide environmental cues; turn on lights before dusk; provide night-light.
- Provide soothing music.
- Provide reassurance and companionship, especially during difficult evening period.

Neurocognitive Disorders: Medications

- Donepezil (Aricept)
- Galantamine (Razadyne)
- Memantine (Namenda)
- Rivastigmine (Exelon)
- Tacrine

Study Break Box

1. A 68-year-old client who is diagnosed with Alzheimer's disease is admitted to the nursing home by the RN. The client does not recognize their spouse or children and forgets how to eat and dress. Which is the RN's priority intervention for the newly admitted client?

1. Establish a daily routine and schedule.
2. Encourage involvement in structured activities.
3. Discuss strategies to coordinate care.
4. Stress the importance of self-nurturing.

Correct Answer: 1

Rationale

Change is difficult for clients diagnosed with Alzheimer's disease. A structured schedule may help the individual maintain their abilities. The other nursing interventions are not the priority.

Test-Taking Strategy

In the NCLEX world (while you are testing), there are some special considerations that you should be aware of. For instance, as the tester, you can assume that you are only caring for this one client that is being presented in the scenario or each individual question. The NCLEX does not account for normal everyday distractions that nurses must deal with in their daily routines. As the nurse in the scenario, you can assume that you have an order from the HCP for any option or options listed in a question. Therefore, do not say that you would not administer a medication or IV fluids because you don't have an order from the HCP. You can safely assume that the options provided in the question are orders from the HCP. Only notify the HCP when an occurrence is an unexpected finding for the disease process. Therefore, you must know the normal (expected) signs and symptoms of disease processes to identify abnormal signs and symptoms that could indicate a potential complication of the disease process.

Notes

Next-Generation NCLEX® Examination (NGN)–Style Question

Highlight in Text

Scenario: The RN in the community mental health hospital is admitting a 21-year-old with a diagnosis of schizophrenia, paranoid type.

Highlight negative symptoms of schizophrenia the client is experiencing.

Nurses Notes:

Client history: He has been working at a local electronics store and lives at home with his parents while attending a local community college. Parents report that he has always been a good student and is socially active. Last semester, his grades began declining and he has frequently been skipping classes. He has become very withdrawn and spends most of his time alone in his room. His grooming has deteriorated; often will go days without showering. For several weeks prior to this admission, he has insisted on keeping all of the curtains in the house closed. For the past 2 days he has refused to eat, saying, "They are poisoning me." Upon approach, it is noted that he appears to be talking to someone, but no one is there. When spoken to, he looks around and answers in a whisper but gives little information. He states, "They are watching me and told me not to cooperate."

Answer:

Client history: He has been working at a local electronics store and lives at home with his parents while attending a local community college. Parents report he has always been a good student and is socially active. Last semester, his grades began declining and he has frequently been skipping classes. He has become very withdrawn and spends most of his time alone in his room. His grooming has deteriorated; often will go days without showering. For several weeks prior to this admission, he has insisted on keeping all of the curtains in the house closed. For the past 2 days he has refused to eat, saying, "They are poisoning me." Upon approach, it is noted that he appears to be talking to someone, but no one is there. When spoken to, he looks around and answers in a whisper but gives little information. He states, "They are watching me and told me not to cooperate."

Rationale: The negative symptoms of schizophrenia account for a large portion of the long-term disability and poor functional outcomes in clients with the disorder and refer to a decreased or absence of motivation and interest, or verbal and emotional expression. Negative symptoms include anhedonia, avolition, asociality, affective blunting, apathy, and alogia. The highlighted items are examples of these negative symptom types. Positive symptoms include delusions, perceptual distortions, illusions, and hallucinations.

Notes

Appendix A
Normal Laboratory Values

Test	Adult	Child	Infant/Newborn	Elderly	Nursing Implications
Hematological					
Hgb (hemoglobin): g/dL or mmol/L (SI units) **Possible critical values: <5.0 or >20 g/dL**	**Male:** 14–18 g/dL or 8.7–11.2 mmol/L **Female:** 12–16 g/dL or 7.4–9.9 mmol/L **Pregnant:** >11 g/dL	**1–6 years:** 9.5–14 g/dL **6–18 years:** 10–15.5 g/dL	**Newborn:** 14–24 g/dL **0–2 weeks:** 12–20 g/dL **2–6 months:** 10–17 g/dL **6 months–1 year:** 9.5–14 g/dL	Values slightly decreased	High-altitude living increases values. Drug therapy can alter values. Slight Hgb decreases normally occur during pregnancy.
Hct (hematocrit): volume fraction (SI units) or % **Possible critical values: <15% or >60%**	**Male:** 0.42–0.52 volume fraction or 42%–52% **Female:** 0.37–0.47 volume fraction or 37%–47% **Pregnant:** >33%	**1–6 years:** 30–40 **6–18 years:** 32–44	**Newborn:** 44–64 **2–8 weeks:** 39–59 **2–6 months:** 35–50 **6 months–1 year:** 29–43	Values slightly decreased	Prolonged tourniquet application can cause stasis and alter values. Abnormalities in RBC size may alter Hct values.
RBC (red blood cell) count: RBC × 1012/L (SI units)	**Male:** 4.7–6.1 **Female:** 4.2–5.4	**1–6 years:** 4–5.5 **6–18 years:** 4–5.5	**Newborn:** 4.8–7.1 **2–8 weeks:** 4–6 **2–6 months:** 3.5–5.5 **6 months– 1 year:** 3.5–5.2	Same as adult	Never craw a specimen from an arm with an infusing IV. Exercise and high altitudes can cause an increase in values. Values are usually lower during pregnancy. Drug therapy can alter values.
WBC (white blood cell) count: WBC × 109/L (SI units) **Possible critical values: <2500 or >30,000 mm^3**	**Both sexes:** 5000–10,000 mm^3 or 5–10 × 109/L	**≤2 years:** 6200–17,000 mm^3 **>2 years:** 5000–10,000 mm^3 or 5–10 × 109/L	**Newborn:** 9000–30,000/mm^3	Same as adult	Anesthetics, stress, exercise, and seizures can cause increased values. Certain types of drugs can increase or decrease WBC levels. The final month of pregnancy and labor may cause increased WBC levels.

Notes

Test	Adult	Child	Infant/Newborn	Elderly	Nursing Implications
Platelet count: × 109/L (mm^3) **Possible critical values: <50,000 or >1 million/mm^3**	**Both sexes:** 150,000–400,000 mm^3 or 150–400 × 109/L (SI units)	150,000–400,000 mm^3	**Premature infant:** 100,000–300,000 mm^3 **Newborn:** 150,000–300,000 mm^3 **Infant:** 200,000–475,000 mm^3	Same as adult	Living at high altitudes, exercising strenuously, or taking oral contraceptives may increase values. Decreased values may be caused by hemorrhage, DIC, reduced production of platelets, infections, use of prosthetic heart valves, and drugs (e.g., chemotherapy, H2 blockers, INH, levofloxacin, streptomycin, sulfonamides, thiazide diuretics).

HESI Hint: *The laboratory values that are most important to know for the NCLEX-RN exam are Hgb, Hct, WBCs, Na+, K+, BUN, blood glucose, ABGs (arterial blood gases), bilirubin for newborns, and therapeutic range for PT and PTT.*

Test	Adult	Child	Infant/Newborn	Elderly	Nursing Implications
SED rate, ESR (erythrocyte sedimentation rate): mm/hr	**Male:** up to 15 mm/hr **Female:** up to 20 mm/hr	Up to 10 mm/hr	**Newborn:** 0–2 mm/hr	Same as adult	Pregnancy (second and third trimester) can cause elevations in ESR.
PT (prothrombin time): sec	**Both sexes:** 11–12.5	Same as adult	Same as adult	Same as adult	PT is monitored to help regulate warfarin (Coumadin) dosages. Therapeutic range: 1.5–2 times normal or control
PTT (partial thromboplastin time): sec (see APTT, later)	**Both sexes:** 60–70	Same as adult	Same as adult	Same as adult	PTT is monitored to help regulate heparin dosages. Therapeutic range: 1.5–2.5 times normal or control
INR (international normalized ratio)	**Both sexes:** 0.8–1.1	Same as adult	Same as adult	Same as adult	Ideal INR value must be individualized. Typical values for certain clients: Clients with atrial fibrillation and deep vein thrombosis, between 2.0 and 3.0. Clients with mechanical heart valves, between 3.0 and 4.0
APTT (activated partial thromboplastin time): sec	**Both sexes:** 30–40 **Pregnancy:** may prolong APTT	Same as adult	Same as adult	Same as adult	APTT is used to help partially regulate heparin dosages. Therapeutic range: 1.5–2.5 times normal or control

Notes

Test	Adult	Child	Infant/Newborn	Elderly	Nursing Implications
Blood Chemistry					
Alkaline phosphatase: units/L	**Both sexes:** 30–120	**<2 years:** 85–235 **2–8 years:** 65–210 **9–15 years:** 60–300 **16–21 years:** 30–200	**Newborn male:** 75–375 **Newborn female:** 65–350	Slightly higher than adult	Hemolysis of specimen can cause falsely elevated values.
Albumin: g/dL or g/L (SI units)	**Both sexes:** 3.5–5 g/dL or 35–50 g/L	4.5–9 g/dL	**Premature infant:** 3–4.2 g/dL **Newborn:** 3.5–5.4 g/dL **Infant:** 4.4–5.4 g/dL	Same as adult	No special preparation is needed.
Bilirubin total: mg/dL or µmol/L (SI units)	**Total:** 0.3–1.0 mg/dL or 5.1–17 µmol/L **Indirect:** 0.2–0.8 mg/dL or 3.4–12.0 µmol/L **Direct:** 0.1–0.3 mg/dL or 1.7–5.1 µmol/L	Same as adult	**Newborn:** Total bilirubin: 1.0–12.0 mg/dL or 17.1–205 µmol/L	Same as adult	Prevent hemolysis of blood during venipuncture. Do not shake tube; this can cause inaccurate values. Protect blood sample from bright light.
Calcium: mmol/L (mg/dL)	**Both sexes:** 2.25–2.75 (9–10.5)	2.2–2.7 (8.8–10.8)	**<10 days:** 1.9–2.60 (7.6–10.4) **Cord:** 2.25–2.88 (9–11.5) **10 days–2 years:** 2.3–2.65 (9–10.6)	Values tend to decrease.	No special preparation is needed. Use of thiazide diuretics can cause increased calcium values.
Chloride: mmol/L (SI units) or mEq/L	**Both sexes:** 98–106	90–110	**Newborn:** 96–106 **Premature infant:** 95–110	Same as adult	Do not collect from an arm with an infusing IV solution.
Cholesterol: mmol/L (SI units) or mg/dL	**Both sexes:** <5.2 mmol/L or <200 mg/dL	120–200 mg/dL	**Infant:** 70–175 mg/dL **Newborn:** 53–135 mg/dL	Same as adult	Do not collect from an arm with an infusing IV solution.
CPK (creatine phosphokinase): units/L	**Male:** 55–170 **Female:** 30–135	Same as adult	**Newborn:** 65–580	Same as adult	Values are higher after exercise. Early pregnancy may cause decreased levels.

Notes

Test	Adult	Child	Infant/Newborn	Elderly	Nursing Implications
Creatinine: µmol/L (SI units) or mg/dL	**Male:** 0.6–1.2 mg/dL or 53–106 µmol/L **Female:** 0.5–1.1 mg/dL or 44–97 µmol/L	**Adolescent:** 0.5–1.0 mg/dL **Child:** 0.3–0.7 mg/dL	**Infant:** 0.2–0.4 mg/dL **Newborn:** 0.3–1.2 mg/dL	Decrease in muscle mass may cause decreased values.	NPO for 8 hours before testing is preferred but not required. BUN-to-creatinine ratio of 20:1 indicates adequate kidney functioning.
Glucose: mmol/L (SI units) or mg/dL	**Both sexes:** 74–106 mg/dL or 4.1–5.9 mmol/L	**Child <2 years:** 60–100 mg/dL or 3.3–5.5 mmol/L **Child >2 years to adult:** **Fasting (no caloric intake for at least 8 hours):** 70–110 mg/dL or <6.1 mmol/L **Nonfasting:** ≤200 mg/dL (<11.1 mmol/L)	**Cord:** 45–96 mg/dL or 2.5–5.3 mmol/L **Premature infant:** 20–60 mg/dL or 1.1–3.3 mmol/L **Neonate:** 30–60 mg/dL or 1.7–3.3 mmol/L **Infant:** 40–90 mg/dL or 2.2–5.0 mmol/L	**60–90 years:** 82–115 mg/dL or 4.6–6.4 mmol/L **>90 years:** 75–121 mg/dL or 4.2–6.7 mmol/L	Client is kept NPO, except for water, for 8 hours before testing. Stress, infection, and caffeine can cause increased values.
HCO_3–: mmol/L (mEq/L)	**Both sexes:** 21–28	21–28	**Newborn/infant:** 16–24	Same as adult	None
Iron: µmol/L (SI units) or mcg/dL	**Male:** 80–180 mcg/dL or 14–32 µmol/L **Female:** 60–160 mcg/dL or 11–29 µmol/L	50–120 mcg/dL	100–250 mcg/dL	Same as adult	NPO for 12 hours before test.
TIBC (total iron binding capacity): µmol/L (SI units) or mcg/dL	**Both sexes:** 250–460 mcg/dL or 45–82 µmol/L	Same as adult	Same as adult	Same as adult	None
LDH (lactic dehydrogenase): units/L	**Both sexes:** 100–190	60–170	**Newborn:** 160–450 **Infant:** 100–250	Same as adult	Do not give IM injections for 8–12 hours before test. Hemolysis of blood causes a false-positive result.
Potassium: mmol/L (SI units) or mEq/L	**Both sexes:** 3.5–5	3.4–4.7	**Newborn:** 3.9–5.9 **Infant:** 4.1–5.3	Same as adult	Hemolysis of specimen can result in falsely elevated values. Exercise of the forearm with tourniquet in place may cause an increased potassium level.

Notes

Test	Adult	Child	Infant/Newborn	Elderly	Nursing Implications
Protein total: g/L (SI units) or g/dL	**Both sexes:** 6.4–8.3 g/dL or 64–83 g/L	6.2–8 g/dL	**Premature infant:** 4.2–7.6 g/dL **Newborn:** 4.6–7.4 g/dL **Infant:** 6–6.7 g/dL	Same as adult	NPO for 8 hours before test is preferred but not required.
AST/SGOT (aspartate aminotransferase): units/L	0–35 (Female slightly lower than adult male)	**3–6 years:** 15–50 **6–12 years:** 10–50 **12–18 years:** 10–40	**0–5 days:** 35–140 **<3 years:** 15–60	Slightly higher than adult	Exercise may cause an increased value. If possible, avoid giving any IM injection because increased enzyme levels may result.
ALT/SGPT (alanine aminotransferase): units/L	**Both sexes:** 4–36	Similar to adult	Values may be 2× as high as adults.	Slightly higher than adult	Previous IM injections may cause elevated levels.
Sodium: mEq/L	**Both sexes:** 136–145	136–145	**Newborn:** 134–144 **Infant:** 134–150	Same as adult	Recent trauma, surgery, or shock may cause increased levels.
Triglycerides: mmol/L (SI units) or mg/dL	**Male:** 40–160 mg/dL or 0.45–1.81 mmol/L **Female:** 35–135 mg/dL or 0.40–1.52 mmol/L	**Male:** **6–11 years:** 31–108 mg/dL **12–15 years:** 36–138 mg/dL **16–19 years:** 40–163 mg/dL **Female** **6–11 years:** 35–114 mg/dL **12–15 years:** 41–138 mg/dL **16–19 years:** 40–128 mg/dL	**Male** **0–5:** 30–86 mg/dL **Female** **0–5:** 32–99 mg/dL	Same as adult	Client is kept NPO for 12 hours before test. No alcohol for 24 hours before test
BUN (blood urea nitrogen): mmol/L (SI units) or mg/dL	**Both sexes:** 10–20 mg/dL or 3.6–7.1 mmol/L	5–18 mg/dL	**Infant:** 5–18 mg/dL **Newborn:** 3–12 mg/dL **Cord:** 21–40 mg/dL	Slightly higher	None

Notes

Test	Adult	Child	Infant/Newborn	Elderly	Nursing Implications
Arterial Blood Chemistry					
pH	**Both sexes:** 7.35–7.45	**Child >2 years:** same as adult	**Newborn:** 7.32–7.49 **2 months–2 years:** 7.34–7.46	Same as adult	Specimen must be heparinized. Specimen must be iced for transport. All air bubbles must be expelled from sample. Direct pressure to puncture site must be maintained.
PCO_2: mm Hg	**Both sexes:** 35–45	Same as adult	**<2 years:** 26–41	Same as adult	See earlier.
PO_2: mm Hg	**Both sexes:** 80–100	Same as adult	**Newborn/Infant:** 60–70	Same as adult	See earlier.
HCO_3^-: mmol/L (mEq/L)	**Both sexes:** 21–28	Same as adult	**Newborn/Infant:** 16–24	Same as adult	See earlier.
O_2 saturation: %	**Both sexes:** 95–100	Same as adult	**Newborn:** 40–90	95	See earlier.

DIC, Disseminated intravascular coagulation; *IM*, intramuscular; *INH*, isoniazid; *NPO*, nothing by mouth; *PCO_2*, carbon dioxide partial pressure; *PO_2*, oxygen partial pressure; *HCO_3^-*, bicarbonate.

From Pagana, K. D., Pagana, T. J., & Pagana T. N. (2019). *Mosby's diagnostic and laboratory test reference* (14th ed). St. Louis, MO: Elsevier.

Notes

Appendix B
Comparison of Three Types of Hepatitis

Characteristics	Hepatitis A (Infectious Hepatitis)	Hepatitis B (Serum Hepatitis)	Hepatitis C
Source of Infection	Contaminated food Contaminated water or shellfish	Contaminated blood products Contaminated needles or surgical instruments Mother to child at birth	Contaminated blood products Contaminated needles Intravenous (IV) drug use Dialysis
Route of Infection	Oral Fecal Parenteral Person to person	Parenteral Oral Fecal Direct contact Breast milk Sexual contact	Parenteral Sexual contact
Incubation Period	15–50 days	14–180 days	14–180 days (average)
Onset	Abrupt	Insidious	Insidious
Seasonal Variation	Autumn Winter	All year	All year
Age Group Affected	Children Young adults	Any age	Any age
Vaccine	Yes	Yes	No
Inoculation	Yes	Yes	Yes
Potential for Chronic Liver Disease	No	Yes	Yes
Immunity	Yes	Yes	No
Treatment	Prevention—hepatitis A (HAV) vaccine Proper hand washing Avoid contaminated food or water. Obtain immunoglobulin within 14 days if exposed to the virus.	Prevention—hepatitis B (HBV) vaccine for high-risk groups Antiviral and immunomodulating drugs	Subcutaneous pegylated interferon alpha once a week and oral ribavirin (Copegus, Rebetol) daily
Complications	Very few	Chronic hepatitis Cirrhosis Hepatitis D Liver cancer	Chronic hepatitis Cirrhosis Liver cancer

Notes

Appendix C
Compare and Contrast: Parkinson's Disease, Myasthenia Gravis, and Multiple Sclerosis

	Parkinson Disease	Myasthenia Gravis	Multiple Sclerosis
Definition	Chronic, progressive neurodegenerative disorder	Autoimmune disorder of the neuromuscular junction with fluctuating weakness of some skeletal muscles	Chronic, progressive, degenerative disorder Demyelination of nerve fibers of the brain and spinal cord
Client	Peak onset in 70s, men	Onset between 10 and 65 years; women more common	Young to middle age, female, temperate climates
Etiology	Unknown but with genetic and environmental components	Antibodies attack acetylcholine receptors, which prevents stimulation of muscle contraction	Unknown; may be related to viral, immunologic, and genetic factors
Signs and Symptoms	Gradual, insidious; may be unilateral; tremor more pronounced at rest Rigidity, bradykinesia, stooped posture, drooling, masked face, shuffling gait, and jerky movements	Fluctuating weakness of skeletal muscles; strength restored after period of rest Primarily muscles of the eyes, mouth, and respiratory system Highly variable disorder	Insidious, gradual onset Remissions and exacerbations: limb weakness, diplopia, numbness, tingling, and neuropathic pain Decreased bowel, bladder function Sexual dysfunction Short-term memory and cognitive changes
Nursing Management	Safety Maximize neurologic function Maintain independence in ADL Optimize psychosocial aspects	Safety Optimize endurance Manage fatigue Avoid complications Maintain quality of life	Safety Maintain independence in ADL Maximize neuromuscular function Manage disabling fatigue Optimize psychosocial adjustment to illness Reduce exacerbating factors
Medications	Dopaminergics Anticholinergics Antihistamine Monoamine oxidase inhibitors (MAIOs) Catechol-*O*-methyltransferase (COMT) inhibitors	Anticholinesterase drugs Corticosteroids Immunosuppressants	Corticosteroids Immunomodulators Cholinergics, anticholinergics Muscle relaxants Acetylcholinesterase inhibitors

ADL, Activities of daily living.

Notes

Appendix D Practice Questions for the NCLEX-RN® Examination with NGN–Style Case Studies

NCLEX-RN® Examination Practice Questions

Management/Leadership

1. Which activity would the RN delegate to an unlicensed assistive personnel (UAP)?

1. Assist a client to ambulate who was just admitted with stroke symptoms.
2. Encourage additional oral fluids for an elderly client with pneumonia who has developed a fever.
3. Report the ability of a client with myasthenia gravis to manage the supper tray independently.
4. Record the number of liquid stools of a client who received lactulose for an elevated NH_3 level.

2. Which client situation requires the registered RN (RN) to intervene? A client with:

1. active tuberculosis who is leaving the room without a mask.
2. end-stage renal disease requesting orange juice to drink.
3. anemia who is complaining of fatigue and asking for help getting dressed to go home.
4. chronic obstructive pulmonary disorder who removes his oxygen and is leaving the unit to smoke.

3. When entering a client's room, the RN finds the client threatening to cut herself. Which is the priority intervention?

1. Call in an extra RN or UAP for the next shift.
2. Assign one of the current UAPs to sit with the client.
3. Move the client to another room with a roommate.
4. Administer an as-needed (PRN) dose of lorazepam.

4. A UAP is assisting with the care of several clients on a postpartum unit. Which assignment would the RN delegate to the UAP?

1. Check fundal firmness and lochia for the clients who delivered vaginally.
2. Take vital signs every 15 minutes for a client with preeclampsia.
3. Provide breastfeeding instructions for a primigravida.
4. Assist with daily care activities for all clients as needed.

Advanced Clinical Concepts

5. Which client is at the highest risk for respiratory complications?

1. A 21-year-old client with dehydration and cerebral palsy who is dependent in daily activities.
2. A 60-year-old client who has had type 2 diabetes for 20 years and was admitted with cellulitis.
3. An obese 30-year-old client with hypertension who is noncompliant with the medication regimen.
4. A 40-year-old client who takes a loop diuretic, has a serum K^+ of 3.4 mmol/L (mEq/L), and complains of fatigue.

6. A RN working at a clinic finds a client in one of the examination rooms slumped over and apneic. The RN notes an empty syringe and needle still in the client's arm. Which action has the highest priority?

1. Call 911.
2. Remove the syringe and needle.
3. Assess for a pulse.
4. Obtain the automated external defibrillator (AED).

Notes

7. A client who is immediately postoperative for abdominal aortic aneurysm repair has been receiving normal saline intravenously at 125 mL/hr. The RN observes dark yellow urine. The hourly output for the past 3 hours was 30 mL, 18 mL, and 10 mL. What action would the RN take?

1. Administer a bolus D_5 ½ normal saline at 200 mL/hr.
2. Contact the health care provider (HCP).
3. Monitor output for another 2 hours.
4. Draw blood samples for blood urea nitrogen (BUN) and creatinine levels.

8. The RN is evaluating the effects of the administration of fresh frozen plasma (FFP) on a client diagnosed with cirrhosis. Which finding would indicate a positive outcome? (Select all that apply.)

1. BUN 3.9 mmol/L (11 mg/dL); creatinine 62 mcmol/L (0.7 mg/dL)
2. Hemoglobin level of 100 mmol/L (10 gm/dL).
3. Return of temperature to normal.
4. Decreased bleeding from the gums.
5. Negative guaiac for occult bleeding.

9. A client's arterial blood gas (ABG) results are as follows: pH 7.29, PCO_2 55 mm Hg, and HCO_3 26 mEq/L. Which compensatory response would the RN expect to see?

1. Respiratory rate of 30 breaths/min.
2. Apical rate of 120 beats/minute.
3. Potassium level of 5.8 mmol/L (mEq/L).
4. Complaints of pounding headache.

10. A client with chronic back pain is not receiving adequate pain relief from oral analgesics. Which alternative action would the RN explore to promote the client's independence?

1. Ask the HCP to increase the analgesic dosage.
2. Obtain a prescription for a second analgesic to be given by the IV route.
3. Consider the client's receptivity to complementary therapy.
4. Encourage counseling to prevent future addiction.

Maternal/Newborn Nursing

11. A client at 41 weeks' gestation who is in active labor calls the RN to report that her membranes have ruptured. The RN performs a vaginal examination and discovers that the umbilical cord has prolapsed. Which intervention would the RN implement first?

1. Move the presenting fetal part off the cord.
2. Cover the cord with sterile moist saline gauze.
3. Prepare for an emergency cesarean delivery.
4. Administer O_2 by face mask at 10 L/min.

12. A client at 39 weeks' gestation plans to have an epidural block when labor is established. Which intervention would the RN implement to prevent side effects? (Select all that apply.)

1. Teach about the procedure and effects of the epidural.
2. Place the client in a chair next to the bed.
3. Administer a bolus of 500 mL of normal saline solution.
4. Monitor the fetal heart rate and contractions continuously.
5. Assist the client to empty her bladder every 2 hours.

13. A female client presents in the emergency department with right lower quadrant abdominal pain and pain in her right shoulder. She has no vaginal bleeding, and her last menses was 6 weeks ago. Which action would the RN take first?

1. Assess for abdominal rebound pain, distention, and fever.
2. Obtain a complete set of vital signs and establish IV access.
3. Observe for recent musculoskeletal injury, bruising, or abuse.
4. Collect specimens for pregnancy test, hemoglobin, and white blood cell count.

Notes

14. A RN has been assigned a pregnant client who has heart disease. The client's condition has been diagnosed as New York Heart Association (NYHA) class II cardiac disease. Which important fact about activities of daily living while pregnant would the RN teach this client? (Select all that apply.)
1. Increase fiber in the diet.
2. Anticipate the need for rest breaks after activity.
3. Notify the HCP if her rings do not fit.
4. Maintain bed rest with bathroom privileges.
5. Start a low-impact aerobic exercise program.

Medical-Surgical

15. A client with type II diabetes is scheduled for an intravenous pyelogram (IVP). Which assessment is most important for the RN to complete before the test is performed?
1. Baseline vital signs.
2. Current medication list.
3. Coagulation status.
4. Electrolyte levels.

16. The RN is teaching a client who has chronic urinary tract infections about a prescription for ciprofloxacin 500 mg PO bid (twice daily). Which side effect could the client expect while taking this medication? (Select all that apply.)
1. Photosensitivity.
2. Dyspepsia.
3. Diarrhea.
4. Urinary frequency.
5. Anemia.

17. A RN working on a hospice unit finds a client crying. The client states that he is afraid to die. Which action would the RN implement? (Select all that apply.)
1. Sit quietly with the client and listen to his or her concerns.
2. Provide the client with privacy.
3. Give the client an antianxiety medication.
4. Contact the client's spiritual counselor or pastor.
5. Assess the client for signs of impending death.

18. A male client with a peritoneal dialysis (PD) catheter calls the clinic to report that he feels poorly and has a fever. Which is the best response by the RN?
1. Encourage him to come to the clinic today for assessment.
2. Instruct him to increase his fluid intake to 3 L/day.
3. Review his PD regimen.
4. Inquire about his recent dietary intake of protein and iron.

19. The RN is reviewing the cardiac markers for a client who was admitted with the diagnosis of chest pain. Which marker is best to determine cardiac damage?
1. Troponin levels.
2. Myoglobin level.
3. Creatine kinase myocardial band (CK-MB) level.
4. Lactate dehydrogenase (LDH) level.

20. The RN is providing discharge instructions to a client who has been diagnosed with angina pectoris. Which instruction is most important?
1. Avoid activity that involves the Valsalva maneuver.
2. Seek emergency treatment if chest pain persists after the third nitroglycerin dose.
3. Rest for 30 minutes after having chest pain before resuming activity.
4. Keep extra nitroglycerin in an airtight, light-resistant bottle.

21. The RN is providing discharge teaching for a client who has been prescribed diltiazem. Which dietary instruction has the highest priority?
1. Maintain a low-sodium diet.
2. Eat a banana each morning.
3. Ingest high-fiber foods daily.
4. Avoid grapefruit products.

Notes

22. The RN is teaching a young adult female who has a history of Raynaud disease how to control her pain. What information should the RN offer?
1. Take oral analgesics at regularly spaced intervals.
2. Avoid extremes of heat and cold.
3. Limit foods and fluids that contain caffeine.
4. Keep the affected extremities in a dependent position.

23. The clinic nurse is caring for a client taking argatroban for atrial fibrillation. Which information is essential for the clinic nurse to include in the client's teaching plan? (Select all that apply.)
1. Have protamine sulfate available.
2. Notify the HCP of any unusual bleeding.
3. Eat a diet high in green leafy vegetables.
4. Keep the medication in a dark, dry container.
5. Avoid aspirin or aspirin-containing medications.

24. A client who was admitted to the hospital with cancer of the larynx is scheduled for a laryngectomy tomorrow. What is the client's priority learning need tonight?
1. Anticipated body image changes.
2. Pain management expectations.
3. Communication techniques.
4. Postoperative nutritional needs.

Psychiatric Nursing

25. A victim of a motor vehicle collision is dead on arrival at the emergency department. The significant other arrives and is noticeably upset. Which action would the RN take to assist the significant other with this crisis?
1. Ask whether there are family, friends, or clergy to call.
2. Inform the significant about the treatment the victim received.
3. Provide education about the stages of grief and loss.
4. Assess the significant other's level of anxiety.

26. The RN is planning to lead a seminar for community health RNs on violence against women during pregnancy. Which statement describes an appropriate technique for assessing for violence?
1. Women should be assessed only if they are part of a high-risk group.
2. Women may be assessed in the presence of young children but not intimate partners.
3. The assessment only needs to be completed at the beginning of the pregnancy.
4. Women should be reassessed face to face by a RN as the pregnancy progresses.

27. The charge nurse reminds clients on the mental health unit that breakfast is at 8 AM, medications are given at 9 AM, and group therapy sessions begin at 10 AM. Which treatment modality has been implemented?
1. Milieu therapy.
2. Behavior modification.
3. Peer therapy.
4. Problem-solving.

28. The RN is accompanying a male client to the radiography department when he becomes panic stricken at the elevator and states, "I can't get on that elevator." Which action would the RN take first?
1. Ask one more staff member to ride in the elevator.
2. Offer a prescribed anti-anxiety medication.
3. Begin desensitization about riding the elevator.
4. Affirm the client's fears about riding the elevator.

29. A male client suffering from posttraumatic stress disorder (PTSD) is found one night trying to strangle his roommate. Which intervention is the RN's highest priority?
1. Give the client a sedative or hypnotic.
2. Administer an antipsychotic.
3. Assign a UAP to sit with the client.
4. Process with both clients about event.

Notes

30. The RN is updating the plan of care for a client who has a borderline personality disorder. Which intervention is most important to implement?
1. Assign the same RN to care for the client.
2. Avoid challenging inappropriate behavior.
3. Limit the client's contact with other clients.
4. Remove consequences for acting-out behaviors.

31. A female adolescent is admitted to the mental health unit for anorexia nervosa. In planning care, which is the RN's highest priority?
1. Teach the client the importance of self-expression.
2. Supervise the client's activities closely.
3. Include the client in daily group therapy.
4. Facilitate social interactions with others.

32. The charge RN is planning the daily schedule for clients on the mental health unit. A male client who is manic should be assigned to which activity?
1. A basketball game in the gym.
2. Jogging at least 1 mile.
3. A table tennis game with a peer.
4. Group activity with the art therapist.

Leadership and Delegation

33. A RN is planning the client assignments for the night shift. The nursing team includes an RN, a licensed practical RN (LPN), and two UAPs. Which duty would be delegated to the UAPs? (Select all that apply.)
1. Transport a client to the radiology department for a computed tomography (CT) scan.
2. Bathe a client with sickle cell disease who has multiple IV lines and a client-controlled analgesia pump.
3. Turn a 92-year-old client who has end-stage heart failure and a do-not-resuscitate order.
4. Report to the HCP the fingerstick blood glucose level of 2.72 mmol/L (49 mg/dL).
5. Feed a female client her first meal after she experienced a stroke.

34. A hospitalized client has been newly diagnosed with type 2 diabetes. Which task can the RN delegate to the UAP? (Select all that apply.)
1. Contacting the dietitian for a prescribed consult.
2. Reviewing the client's insulin injection technique.
3. Obtaining the fingerstick blood glucose level before each meal and at bedtime.
4. Reminding the client to dry the toes carefully after a shower.
5. Talking to the client about foods that raise the blood glucose level.

35. The home health RN evaluates the insulin preparation and administration technique of a 36-year-old male client newly diagnosed with diabetes. The client has been prescribed lispro insulin before meals and glargine insulin once daily in the morning. Which finding indicates that the client needs further education?
1. He mixes glargine and lispro in the same syringe for the morning dose.
2. He leaves the insulin syringe in place for 10 seconds after injection.
3. He stores the opened insulin vials at room temperature in the cabinet.
4. He recaps and disposes of the single-use insulin syringe.

36. At change of shift, the charge nurse assigns the UAP four clients. The charge nurse would direct the UAP to take vital signs on which client first?
1. The 89-year-old with chronic obstructive pulmonary disease who is resting quietly on 2 L of oxygen and who needs assistance with a bath.
2. The client who returned from surgery and needs their second set of every-15-minute vital signs taken.
3. The client newly diagnosed with type 2 diabetes who had a fingerstick glucose level of 5.0 mmol/L (90 mg/dL) and needs help with breakfast.
4. The newly admitted client with rheumatoid arthritis who needs hand splints reapplied to both hands.

Notes

37. **The arrhythmia alarm sounds on a client on the telemetry unit, indicating that the client is in ventricular tachycardia. Place the RN's actions for this client in order of priority from first to last.**
1. Call the rapid response team.
2. Assess for a pulse and blood pressure.
3. Give oxygen via nasal cannula.
4. Bring defibrillator/crash car to the bedside.
5. Document the incident.

38. **The RN is reviewing the laboratory values for their assigned clients. Which client has an abnormal laboratory report that the RN would immediately call to the HCP?**
1. The client who is postsplenectomy after a motor vehicle accident and has a hemoglobin of 109 mmol/L (10.9 g/dL).
2. The client receiving warfarin (Coumadin) who has an international normalized ratio (INR) of 2.3.
3. The 38-year-old client who is 24 hours postthyroidectomy and has a total calcium level of 2.35 mmol/L (9.4 mg/dL).
4. The newly admitted client with bipolar disorder with a lithium level of 2.5 mEq/L.

39. **The RN receives a change-of-shift report on their four acute care clients. Which action would the RN take first?**
1. Administer an antiemetic to a postoperative client who has been nauseated and is now vomiting.
2. Notify a family member of a client's impending transfer to the intensive care unit for angina and ST-segment changes.
3. Inform the HCP of a potassium level of 5.2 mmol/L (mEq/L) in the client with end-stage renal disease.
4. Begin assessment rounds, starting with the palliative care client having a diagnosis of congestive failure.

40. **The emergency department staff RN is assigned four clients. Which client would the RN assess first?**
1. A preschooler with a barking cough, an O_2 saturation of 93% on room air, and occasional inspiratory stridor.
2. A 10-month-old infant with a tympanic temperature of 38.9°C (102°F) and green nasal drainage who is pulling at her ears.
3. A crying 8-month-old with a harsh, paroxysmal cough; an audible expiratory wheeze; and mild retractions.
4. A clingy 3-year-old who has a sore throat and drooling and whose tongue is slightly protruding from his mouth.

41. **The outpatient clinic nurse is reviewing phone messages from the previous night. Which client would the RN call back first?**
1. A woman at 30 weeks' gestation who has been diagnosed with mild preeclampsia and was unable to relieve her heartburn.
2. A woman at 24 weeks' gestation who was crying about painful vulvar lesions and urinary frequency for the past 8 hours.
3. A woman at 12 weeks' gestation who was recently discharged from the hospital with hyperemesis gravidarum and has had two episodes of vomiting in 6 hours.
4. A woman with type 1 diabetes who tested positive with a home pregnancy kit and was worried about managing her diabetes.

42. **The clinic nurse suspects that a 2-year-old child is being abused. Which assessment finding would support this? (Select all that apply.)**
1. Petechiae in a straight line on the chest.
2. Gray-blue pigmented areas on the sacral region.
3. Bald patches on the scalp.
4. Ear tugging and crying.
5. Symmetrical burns on the hands.

Notes

43. The RN is caring for a client who had a thoracotomy 48 hours earlier and now has left lower lobe chest tubes. The RN notes that a chest tube is not tidaling. Which action would the RN take first?

1. Check for kinks in the chest drainage system.
2. Assess the heart rate and blood pressure.
3. Notify the rapid response team immediately.
4. Reconnect the chest tube to wall suction.

44. While the RN is caring for a client who has had a myocardial infarction, the monitor alarm sounds, and the RN notes ventricular fibrillation. Which is the RN's first course of action?

1. Notify the HCP.
2. Increase the oxygen concentration.
3. Assess the client.
4. Prepare to defibrillate the client.

45. The HCP has prescribed the removal of a client's internal jugular central line catheter. To remove the catheter safely, the RN should give which intervention(s) the highest priority? (Select all that apply.)

1. Carefully remove the bio-occlusive dressing.
2. Place the client in the Trendelenburg position.
3. Send the catheter tip to the laboratory for a culture and sensitivity.
4. Have the client hold a deep breath during removal.
5. Apply pressure for 20 minutes after removal of the catheter.

46. The RN who usually works on the orthopedic surgery unit is floating to a cardiovascular unit. Which client would be best to assign to the float RN?

1. Client scheduled for a heart catheterization this morning.
2. Client admitted last night for chest pain.
3. Client who is 1 day postoperative for popliteal bypass surgery.
4. Client with heart failure and scheduled for a stress test today.

47. The RN is admitting a client who is a paraplegic and has a nonhealing pressure injury with a possible methicillin-resistant Staphylococcus aureus infection. A practical RN (PN) and UAP are assigned to the RN's team. Which task would be delegated to the PN? (Select all that apply.)

1. Place the client in isolation.
2. Complete a dressing change.
3. Assess and document the wound.
4. Insert a urinary catheter.
5. Administer oral pain medications.

48. The nursing supervisor calls the charge nurse on a step-down unit about the need for a bed for an unstable client from the medical unit. Which client would the RN anticipate to be transferred to the medical unit to receive this unstable client?

1. A client admitted for an ST-elevation myocardial infarction (STEMI) who just returned from having a cardiac catheterization performed.
2. A client diagnosed with congestive heart failure who is receiving an IV infusion of furosemide.
3. A client with possible Guillain-Barré syndrome who may need an exchange transfusion.
4. A client in hypertensive crisis who is prescribed a sodium nitroprusside drip.

49. When accessing the medication-dispensing system (Pyxis), the RN finds chlorpropamide in the drawer instead of the expected chlorpromazine. Which action would the RN take? (Select all that apply.)

1. Remove the tablets of chlorpropamide.
2. Notify the pharmacy about the mistake.
3. Complete an incident occurrence report.
4. Be extra vigilant because pharmacy is making mistakes.
5. Place a warning note on the Pyxis machine.

Notes

50. The RN is calling the HCP about a client's current needs. Which is the best way to communicate?

1. Call the HCP with the request and a recommendation.
2. Use the SBAR (situation, background, assessment, recommendation) tool for communication.
3. Send a text message or page with the needed order.
4. Ask the HCP to come back to the unit to discuss the client's needs.

51. The HCP plans to do a paracentesis on a client with cirrhosis in 1 hour. In what order would the RN perform the following activities?

1. Ensure that the informed consent has been obtained.
2. Measure the client's abdominal girth.
3. Have the client empty his or her bladder.
4. Assemble needed equipment.
5. Administer oral pain medication.

52. The RN receives report on a client from the emergency department with a diagnosis of pneumonia. Which intervention has the highest priority?

1. Obtain blood cultures.
2. Initiate prescribed antibiotics.
3. Place the client in isolation.
4. Obtain an accurate weight.

53. The RN is part of the triage team at a disaster. Which client would be treated first?

1. A 90-year-old woman with a crushed pelvis and head injuries.
2. A 21-year-old man screaming in pain from a broken leg.
3. A 30-year-old woman with a flail chest secondary to a puncture wound to the chest.
4. A 12-year-old crying with multiple lacerations to both legs.

54. The triage RN in the emergency room is assessing four clients. Which client requires the most immediate intervention?

1. The adult client who arrived via ambulance with numbness and tingling of his left arm and face.
2. The adult client who had a seizure at home who is sleeping on his left side.
3. The 60-year-old client who complains of frequent urination and has a blood sugar of 16.7 mmol/L (300 mg/dL).
4. The middle-aged client who presents with severe unilateral back pain and previous history of kidney stones.

55. After the change-of-shift report on an orthopedic floor, which client would the RN assess first?

1. A client who had surgery yesterday and has a temperature of 37.6°C (99.7°F).
2. A client who is complaining of numbness and tingling distal to the fracture site.
3. A client who had a left leg amputation and states he is experiencing pain in the left foot.
4. A client who is extremely upset with their care and is requesting to speak to the manager.

56. The RN is administering medications to a client admitted for an overdose and a history of substance abuse. Which intervention is a priority to include in this client's plan of care? (Select all that apply.)

1. Allow the client to take medications independently.
2. Ensure that all medications have been swallowed before leaving the client's room.
3. Request that oral pain medications be changed from tablet to oral suspension.
4. Administer flumazenil as prescribed every 6 hours around the clock.
5. Administer all medications to the client via the intravenous route.

Notes

57. The RN is returning phone calls to clients who are cared for at an outpatient mental health center. Which client would the RN call first?

1. The young mother diagnosed with schizophrenia who is hearing voices saying that they are pursuing her children.
2. The elderly man at an assisted living facility who says he wants to end it all.
3. The female client diagnosed with bipolar disorder who has not slept for 48 hours.
4. The teenager diagnosed with bulimia whose mother called and reported that she found her daughter purging.

58. An 18-year-old woman is being discharged after delivering a healthy baby. She has a cousin whose baby died from sudden infant death syndrome (SIDS). The client seems to know many of the precautions to take. Which information does the RN need to correct?

1. Always place infants on their backs to sleep.
2. Room sharing has been shown to decrease SIDS.
3. Keep the crib free of stuffed animals and crib pads.
4. Sleeping with the baby can alert the mother to changes.

59. A 4-year-old admitted with pneumonia weighs 18 kg. The HCP has prescribed vancomycin 40 mg/kg/day IV. The order states to divide the dose and give it three times daily. How many milligrams of vancomycin should the child receive in each dose? (Round the answer to the nearest whole number.)

______________________ mg/dose

60. The RN needs to initiate an IV on an 8-year-old child. Which intervention(s) is/are appropriate? (Select all that apply).

1. Start the IV in the treatment room, not the child's room.
2. Apply a lidocaine-based cream for a few minutes before starting the IV.
3. Ask the parents to leave the room while performing the procedure.
4. Encourage the child to use guided imagery to cope.
5. Offer the child a reward if they cooperate during the procedure.

Notes

Answers and Rationales

(Correct answers are underlined.)

Management/Leadership

1. Which activity would the RN delegate to an unlicensed assistive personnel (UAP)?

Rationales

1. ***Assist a client to ambulate who was just admitted with stroke symptoms.***
   This requires assessment of the client's ability to ambulate safely, which is beyond the scope of practice of a UAP.
2. ***Encourage additional PO (by mouth) fluids for an elderly client with pneumonia who has developed a fever.***
   These directions are not sufficiently clear and detailed for the UAP to perform the task.
3. ***Report the ability of a client with myasthenia gravis to manage the supper tray independently.***
   This requires assessment of the client's clinical status, which is beyond the scope of the UAP.
4. ***Record the number of liquid stools of a client who has received lactulose for an increased NH_3 level.***
   This task encompasses basic care, elimination, and intake and output; it does not require judgment or the expertise of the RN and can be performed by the UAP.

2. The RN is assigning tasks to the UAP. Which client situation requires the RN to intervene? A client with:

Rationales

1. ***active TB who is leaving the room without a mask.***
   A UAP can be delegated to provide a box of masks or to direct the client back to the room.
2. ***end-stage renal disease requesting orange juice to drink.***
   A UAP can be directed to provide specific types and amounts of fluids, but orange juice is high in potassium, which is contraindicated for clients in end-stage renal disease.
3. ***anemia who is complaining of fatigue and asking for help getting dressed to go home.***
   A UAP can assist a client to get dressed. Fatigue is an expected finding with anemia.
4. ***chronic obstructive pulmonary disorder removes his oxygen and is leaving the unit to smoke.***
   A UAP can ask the client to not leave the unit to smoke.

3. When entering a client's room, the RN finds the client threatening to cut herself. Which is the priority intervention?

Rationales

1. ***Call in an extra RN or UAP for the next shift.***
   The charge nurse should plan ahead for staffing, but the immediate focus should be the client's safety now.
2. ***Assign one of the current UAPs to sit with the client.***
   Because the client is at risk for self-harm, the charge nurse should assign a staff member to stay with the client.
3. ***Move the client to another room with a roommate.***
   This will not ensure the client's safety; also, a staff member, not another client, must always be present with the client.
4. ***Administer an as-needed (PRN) dose of lorazepam as prescribed.***
   Although the client may be anxious, this is not a priority intervention that would ensure her safety.

4. A UAP is assisting with the care of several clients on a postpartum unit. Which assignment would the RN delegate to the UAP?

Rationales

1. ***Check fundal firmness and lochia for the clients who delivered vaginally.***
   Assessment is a responsibility of the RN.
2. ***Take vital signs every 15 minutes for a client with preeclampsia.***
   This is a high-risk client who needs to be evaluated by a licensed RN.

Notes

3. ***Provide breastfeeding instructions for a primigravida.***
   Teaching is the responsibility of the RN.
4. ***Assist with daily care activities for all clients as needed.***
   This is the most appropriate assignment for the UAP. The RN should delegate daily care activities to the UAP based on the RN's assessments of each client's needs.

Advanced Clinical Concepts

5. Which client is at the highest risk for respiratory complications?

Rationales

1. ***A 21-year-old client with dehydration and cerebral palsy who is dependent in daily activities***
   A client with dehydration and cerebral palsy, characterized by uncoordinated, spastic muscle movements, is at increased risk for respiratory problems because of impaired mobility and impaired swallowing.
2. ***A 60-year-old client who has had type 2 diabetes for 20 years and was admitted with cellulitis.***
   This older client is more at risk for renal, cardiac, and vascular complications.
3. ***An obese 30-year-old client with hypertension who is noncompliant with the medication regimen.***
   An obese adult who is noncompliant with antihypertensive medications is more at risk for cardiac or cerebral events than for respiratory problems.
4. ***A 40-year-old client who takes a loop diuretic, has a serum K+ of 3.4 mmol/L (mEq/L), and complains of fatigue.***
   This middle-aged adult is hypokalemic and fatigued but is not at high risk for respiratory problems.

6. A RN working at a clinic finds a client in one of the examination rooms slumped over and apneic. The RN notes an empty syringe and needle still in the client's arm. Which action has the highest priority?

Rationales

1. ***Call 911.***
   Calling for assistance is a high priority but not the highest.
2. ***Remove the syringe and needle.***
   The syringe and needle should be removed and possibly sent to a laboratory for analysis of the contents, but this is not a priority.
3. ***Assess for a pulse.***
   Assessing for a pulse is the highest priority to determine whether cardiopulmonary resuscitation (CPR) needs to be initiated.
4. ***Obtain the AED.***
   This action is needed only if there is no pulse detected.

7. A client who is immediately postoperative for abdominal aortic aneurysm repair has been receiving normal saline intravenously at 125 mL/hr. The RN observes dark yellow urine. The hourly output for the past 3 hours was 30 mL, 18 mL, and 10 mL. What action would the RN take?

Rationales

1. ***Administer a bolus D5 ½ normal saline at 200 mL/hr.***
   The decreasing urine output may be a sign of acute renal failure, a complication of aortic aneurysm repair. Giving more fluids may cause the client's condition to deteriorate.
2. ***Contact the HCP.***
   Acute renal failure can result from interruption of blood flow during an aortic aneurysm repair. Low urinary output may indicate acute renal failure and requires more immediate intervention from the HCP.
3. ***Monitor output for another 2 hours.***
   Urine output has been monitored, and further intervention is needed.
4. ***Draw blood samples for BUN and creatinine levels.***
   The BUN and creatinine should be evaluated, but these tests are not the immediate priority.

Notes

8. The RN is evaluating the effects of the administration of fresh frozen plasma (FFP) on a client diagnosed with cirrhosis. Which finding would indicate a positive outcome? (Select all that apply.)

Rationales

1. ***BUN 3.9 mmol/L (11 mg/dL); creatinine 62 mcmol/L (0.7 mg/dL).***
   These values are not affected by administration of FFP. They assess renal function.
2. ***Hemoglobin level of 100 mmol/L (10 gm/dL).***
   FFP does not affect hemoglobin levels.
3. ***Return of temperature to normal.***
   Although monitoring the client's temperature is important, FFP does not have a direct effect on this parameter.
4. ***Decreased bleeding from the gums.***
   FFP replaces clotting factors; therefore, a decrease in bleeding is an expected, positive outcome.
5. ***Negative guaiac for occult bleeding.***
   FFP replaces clotting factors; therefore, no occult (hidden) bleeding would be an expected, positive outcome.

9. A client's arterial blood gas (ABG) results are as follows: pH 7.29, PCO_2 55 mm Hg, and HCO_3 26 mEq/L. Which compensatory response would the RN expect to see?

Rationales

1. ***Respiratory rate of 30 breaths/min.***
   The client is experiencing respiratory acidosis. In addition to the metabolic system compensating, the respiratory system may also compensate.
2. ***Apical rate of 120 beat/min.***
   Acid-base imbalances are compensated primarily by the lungs and the renal system. Plasma proteins and ionic shifts (intracellular) also serve as buffering systems. Tachycardia does not serve as a compensatory mechanism.
3. ***Potassium level of 5.8 mmol/L (mEq/L).***
   To compensate for the acidosis created by increased CO_2, K^+ ions are released from cellular proteins and H^+ ions take their place, bound to the proteins. The result is frequently serum hyperkalemia.
4. ***Complaints of a pounding headache.***
   Headache may be a manifestation of CO_2 retention, but it is not a compensatory mechanism for respiratory acidosis.

10. A client with chronic back pain is not receiving adequate pain relief from oral analgesics. Which alternative action would the RN explore to promote the client's independence?

Rationales

1. ***Ask the HCP to increase the analgesic dosage.***
   Although this intervention may improve pain relief, it may not promote self-care without increasing side effects that could affect the client's independence.
2. ***Obtain a prescription for a second analgesic to be given by the IV route.***
   The IV route does not promote self-care and may cause additional side effects that interfere with the client's ability to carry out activities of daily living independently.
3. ***Consider the client's receptivity to complementary therapy.***
   This action supports self-care without the high level of adverse effects associated with additional medication. It is the least invasive measure, and it promotes the active participation (self-care) of the client.
4. ***Encourage counseling to prevent future addiction.***
   Referrals may be needed, but the RN should teach clients about potential problems with medications and measures to manage pain and maintain self-care.

Notes

Maternal-Newborn Nursing

11. A client at 41 weeks' gestation who is in active labor calls the RN to report that her membranes have ruptured. The RN performs a vaginal examination and discovers that the umbilical cord has prolapsed. Which intervention would the RN implement first?

Rationales

1. ***Move the presenting fetal part off the cord.***
   This action is the most critical intervention. The RN must prevent compression of the cord by the presenting part because that would impair fetal circulation, leading to morbidity and, possibly, death.
2. ***Cover the cord with sterile moist saline gauze.***
   If the cord is protruding outside the vagina, this action should be taken to prevent drying of the Wharton's jelly. However, another RN should do this while the first RN maintains elevation of the presenting part off the cord.
3. ***Prepare for an emergency cesarean delivery.***
   This is implemented by the staff while the RN keeps the presenting part elevated off the cord.
4. ***Start O_2 by face mask at 10 L/min.***
   Oxygen should be provided to the mother to increase oxygen delivery to the fetus via the placenta; however, another RN should do this while first the RN keeps the presenting part elevated off the cord.

12. A client at 39 weeks' gestation plans to have an epidural block when labor is established. Which intervention would the RN be prepared to implement to prevent side effects? (Select all that apply.)

Rationales

1. ***Teach the client about the procedure and the effects of the epidural.***
   Teaching is an important nursing intervention to alleviate anxiety, but it does not prevent any of the possible side effects.
2. ***Place the client in a chair next to the bed.***
   Epidural block reduces lower extremity sensation and movement to varying degrees. Any upright positions such as walking and standing may not be possible during epidural pain management and may not prevent side effects.
3. ***Administer a bolus of 500 mL of normal saline solution.***
   Prehydration increases maternal blood volume and prevents hypotension, which occurs as a result of vasodilation, a side effect of epidural anesthesia. A saline solution is used to prevent fetal secretion of insulin that later places the neonate at risk for hypoglycemia.
4. ***Monitor the fetal heart rate and contractions continuously.***
   Vital signs should be monitored every 5 minutes immediately after the initial epidural dose, and if the client's condition is stable, then every 15 minutes. Continuous fetal heart rate and contraction monitors should be applied during this time also.
5. ***Assist the client to empty her bladder every 2 hours.***
   Assisting the client to void every 2 hours prevents bladder distention.

13. A female client presents in the emergency department with right lower quadrant abdominal pain and pain in her right shoulder. She has no vaginal bleeding, and her last menses was 6 weeks ago. Which action would the RN take first?

Rationales

1. ***Assess for abdominal rebound pain, distention, and fever.***
   Bleeding related to an ectopic pregnancy (based on the client's history) may present these manifestations, but the RN should first assess the client for early signs of hypovolemic shock.
2. ***Obtain a complete set of vital signs and establish IV access.***
   The RN should first evaluate the client for vital sign changes related to blood loss due to a possible ruptured ectopic pregnancy (an obstetrical emergency). Vascular access is vital in an emergency situation.
3. ***Observe for recent musculoskeletal injury, bruising, or abuse.***
   This may be part of the assessment if a life-threatening situation is ruled out first.

Notes

4. ***Collect specimens for pregnancy test, hemoglobin, and white blood cell count.*** Specimens for a pregnancy test and complete blood count should be collected. However, the RN should first notify the HCP of the client's status, based on the presenting vital signs and symptoms.

14. A RN has been assigned a pregnant client who has heart disease. The client's condition has been diagnosed as New York Heart Association (NYHA) class II cardiac disease. Which important fact about activities of daily living while pregnant would the RN teach this client? (Select all that apply.)

Rationales

1. ***Increase fiber in the diet.*** Restrictions in activities of daily living for clients with NYHA Class II cardiac disease create a risk factor for constipation.
2. ***Anticipate the need for rest breaks after activity.*** Individuals with NYHA Class II cardiac disease may have limitations on activity and need periods of rest throughout the day, but especially after periods of activity.
3. ***Notify the HCP if her rings do not fit.*** Tight rings may indicate weight gain, and the client is at risk for congestive heart failure.
4. ***Maintain bed rest with bathroom privileges.*** It is not necessary to maintain bed rest for a client with NYHA Class II cardiac disease.
5. ***Start a low-impact aerobic exercise program.*** Individuals with NYHA class II cardiac disease may have some slight limitation of activity. Additionally, during pregnancy is not an ideal time to start a new exercise program.

Medical-Surgical

15. A client with type II diabetes is scheduled for an intravenous pyelogram (IVP). Which assessment is most important for the RN to complete before the test is performed?

Rationales

1. ***Baseline vital signs.*** Baseline values are important but there is a higher priority.
2. ***Current medication list.*** This is a priority. If the client is taking an oral diabetic agent with metformin, the RN may need to hold the medication for 48 hours before the IVP because of potentially decreased kidney function.
3. ***Coagulation status.*** There is no risk of bleeding related to an IVP.
4. ***Electrolyte levels.*** Electrolyte levels are not affected by an IVP, and high or low levels are not considered a contraindication for completing the test.

16. The RN is teaching a client who has chronic urinary tract infections about a prescription for ciprofloxacin 500 mg PO bid (twice daily). Which side effect could the client expect while taking this medication? (Select all that apply.)

Rationales

1. ***Photosensitivity.*** This is a side effect of ciprofloxacin; exposure to sunlight or tanning beds should be avoided. The client should be instructed to use sunscreen and protective clothing.
2. ***Dyspepsia.*** Ciprofloxacin causes gastrointestinal (GI) irritation, nausea and vomiting, and abdominal pain, which should be reported.
3. ***Diarrhea.*** Watery, foul-smelling diarrhea is an adverse reaction to ciprofloxacin that indicates pseudomembranous colitis; this should be reported and requires immediate intervention. This is not an expected side effect.

Notes

4. ***Urinary frequency.***
   Urinary frequency may indicate that the medication is ineffective and should be reported, but it is not an expected side effect.
5. ***Anemia.***
   This is not a side effect of ciprofloxacin.

17. A RN working on a hospice unit finds a client crying. The client states that he is afraid to die. Which action would the RN implement? (Select all that apply).

Rationales

1. ***<u>Sit quietly with the client and listen to his or her concerns.</u>***
   Silence, or offering one's presence, is an effective technique that lets the client share as he or she desires and also indicates that the RN cares.
2. ***Provide the client with privacy.***
   The client has shared that he or she is afraid. Further isolating the client from others will not address this need.
3. ***Give the client an antianxiety medication.***
   The RN may eventually decide to give the client a medication to help with his or her anxiety, but this should not be the first action.
4. ***<u>Contact the client's spiritual counselor or minister.</u>***
   Facing death is a spiritual issue. Requesting help from the client's spiritual provider is appropriate.
5. ***Assess the client for signs of impending death.***
   The client is awake and oriented. There is no indication that the client's death is imminent.

18. A male client with a peritoneal dialysis (PD) catheter calls the clinic to report he feels poorly and has a fever. Which is the best response by the RN?

Rationales

1. ***<u>Encourage him to come to the clinic today for assessment.</u>***
   PD catheters are used in PD. They are often used at home by the client, placing the client at risk for peritoneal infection. Because dialysis clients usually have some degree of compromised immunity, the client should come to the clinic for assessment.
2. ***Instruct him to increase his fluid intake to 3 L/day.***
   Clients who need dialysis retain fluid and usually are restricted to an intake that is only 300 mL greater than output.
3. ***Review his PD regimen.***
   The RN should evaluate the client's PD regimen, but assessing him for infection is a higher priority.
4. ***Inquire about his recent dietary intake of protein and iron.***
   Iron deficiency and protein loss are common problems in clients who are receiving PD. Dietary intake is important, but it is not a higher priority than possible infection.

19. The RN is reviewing the cardiac markers for a client who was admitted with the diagnosis of chest pain. Which marker is best to determine cardiac damage?

Rationales

1. ***<u>Troponin levels.</u>***
   A rise in the troponin levels is diagnostic of myocardial injury and is considered the gold standard.
2. ***Myoglobin level.***
   An increase in myoglobin is indicative of muscle damage but is not specific to cardiac damage.
3. ***CK-MB level.***
   This isoenzyme is useful for supporting a diagnosis of myocardial infarction and in determining the extent and time of the infarct.
4. ***LDH level.***
   The LDH level is not currently used to determine recent cardiac damage.

20. The RN is providing discharge instructions to a client who has been diagnosed with angina pectoris. Which instruction is most important?

Rationales

1. ***Avoid activity that involves the Valsalva maneuver.***
   Although minimizing or avoiding the Valsalva maneuver decreases anginal pain, this is not the most important factor.

Notes

2. ***Seek emergency treatment if chest pain persists after the third nitroglycerin dose.***
This instruction is most important because chest pain characteristic of acute myocardial infarction persists longer than 15 minutes, and delaying medical treatment can be life-threatening.
3. ***Rest for 30 minutes after having chest pain before resuming activity.***
Waiting 30 minutes may be recommended, but the need to call 911 if chest pain persists is more important.
4. ***Keep extra nitroglycerin in an airtight, light-resistant bottle.***
This is excellent medication teaching, but it does not have the same urgency as seeking emergency care.

21. The RN is providing discharge teaching for a client who has been prescribed diltiazem. Which dietary instruction has the highest priority?

Rationales

1. ***Maintain a low-sodium diet.***
The client may need to restrict sodium intake, but it is not specific for diltiazem.
2. ***Eat a banana each morning.***
If the client has low potassium, this should be recommended.
3. ***Ingest high-fiber foods daily.***
This is an excellent teaching point for everyone, but it is not specific for diltiazem.
4. ***Avoid grapefruit products.***
Grapefruit should be avoided during therapy with calcium channel blockers because it can cause an increase in the serum drug level, predisposing the client to hypotension.

22. The RN is teaching a young adult female who has a history of Raynaud disease how to control her pain. Which information would the RN offer?

Rationales

1. ***Take oral analgesics at regularly spaced intervals.***
Pain is not always associated with Raynaud disease, as is the feeling of cold hands and fingers and pallor. If pain is sporadic or situational, it should not require regular use of analgesics.
2. ***Avoid extremes of heat and cold.***
In Raynaud disease, vascular spasms of the hands and fingers are triggered by exposure to extremes of heat or cold, which causes the characteristic pallor and cold-to-the-touch symptoms of the upper extremities.
3. ***Limit food and fluids that contain caffeine.***
Caffeine is not the primary trigger of the episodes; however, if the client notes that caffeine contributes to the blanching and coldness, it should be avoided.
4. ***Keep the affected extremities in a dependent position.***
This is not effective for a client with Raynaud disease.

23. The clinic nurse is caring for a client taking argatroban for atrial fibrillation. Which information is essential for the RN to include in the client's teaching plan? (Select all that apply.)

Rationales

1. ***Have protamine sulfate available.***
Protamine sulfate is the antidote for heparin, not argatroban.
2. ***Notify the HCP of any unusual bleeding.***
GI bleeding or excessive bleeding is an adverse effect. The client needs to notify their HCP immediately.
3. ***Eat a diet high in green leafy vegetables.***
This is a good recommendation for clients low in vitamin K but is not an issue for clients on argatroban.
4. ***Keep the medication in a dark, dry container.***
This is essential for nitroglycerin and some other medications but not for argatroban.
5. ***Avoid aspirin or aspirin-containing medications***
Aspirin and argatroban can have an additive effect and result in bleeding.

Notes

24. A client who was admitted to the hospital with cancer of the larynx is scheduled for a laryngectomy tomorrow. Which is the client's priority learning need tonight?

Rationales

1. ***Anticipated body image changes.***
This is a concern after surgery, when the immediate life-threatening insult of cancer has been assimilated and basic needs have been met.
2. ***Pain management expectations.***
Pain relief expectations are a priority, but the inability to convey (communicate) a subjective symptom, such as pain, is the fear the client perceives first.
3. ***Communication techniques.***
A client who is in crisis and anticipating the immediate postoperative period is concerned with immediate needs, such as the ability to express and convey a subjective symptom (e.g., pain) and obtain the needed intervention.
4. ***Postoperative nutritional needs.***
Nutrition is important to promote healing, but the ability to communicate subjective needs is a higher priority.

Psychiatric Nursing

25. A victim of a motor vehicle collision is dead on arrival at the emergency department. The victim's significant other arrives and is noticeably upset. Which action would the RN implement to assist the significant other?

Rationales

1. ***Ask whether there are family, friends, or clergy to call.***
The RN should help the significant other identify support systems and resources that are helpful in coping with a crisis situation, such as the sudden death of a spouse.
2. ***Inform the significant about the treatment the victim received.***
The significant other may be unable to process information during the crisis, and the RN should focus on immediate needs for coping and support.
3. ***Provide education about the stages of grief and loss.***
Educating the significant other about grief and loss is not an immediate priority in a crisis and should be provided after they begin to cope with the situation.
4. ***Assess the significant other's level of anxiety.***
Although the RN should assess the significant other for anxiety, the immediate intervention should include a directive approach to assist the spouse in dealing with the stressful event.

26. The RN is planning to lead a seminar for community health RNs on violence against women during pregnancy. Which statement describes an appropriate technique for assessing for violence?

Rationales

1. ***Women should be assessed only if they are part of high-risk groups.***
Violence against women occurs in all ethnic groups and at all income levels.
2. ***Women may be assessed in the presence of young children but not intimate partners.***
It is important to assess women without their partners present; it is also important that verbal children not be present because they may repeat what is heard. Infants may be present.
3. ***The assessment only needs to be completed at the beginning of the pregnancy.***
Many women do not reveal violence the first time they are asked. As trust develops between the RN and the client, the woman may be more comfortable sharing her story. Also, violence may start later in the pregnancy.
4. ***Women should be reassessed face to face by a RN as the pregnancy progresses.***
More than one face-to-face interview elicits the highest reports of violence during pregnancy.

Notes

27. The charge nurse reminds clients on the mental health unit that breakfast is at 8 AM, medications are given at 9 AM, and group therapy sessions begin at 10 AM. Which treatment modality has been implemented?

Rationales

1. ***Milieu therapy.***
Milieu therapy uses resources and activities in the environment to assist with improving social functioning and activities of daily living.
2. ***Behavior modification.***
Behavior modification involves changing behaviors using positive and negative reinforcements to allow desired activities or remove privileges.
3. ***Peer therapy.***
Peer therapy is not a single therapeutic modality; it involves the interaction of peers who are responsible for supporting, sharing, and compromising within their peer group and milieu.
4. ***Problem-solving.***
Problem-solving is used in crisis intervention; it focuses on problem identification and ways to return to previous levels of functioning.

28. The RN is accompanying a male client to the radiography department when he becomes panic stricken at the elevator and states, "I can't get on that elevator." Which action would the RN take first?

Rationales

1. ***Ask one more staff member to ride the elevator.***
One more staff member will not be able to mobilize the client to ride the elevator. The client must first recognize his feelings about the phobia and accept the need to change his behavior. Additional individuals in the elevator may actually increase the client's anxiety.
2. ***Offer a prescribed antianxiety medication.***
Offering an antianxiety medication may be needed to proceed with desensitization, but it not the first action.
3. ***Begin desensitization about riding the elevator.***
Desensitizing the client may be implemented, but first the client should identify his fears and recognize his anxiety.
4. ***Affirm the client's fears about riding the elevator.***
The RN should first validate and allow the client to affirm his anxiety and fears about riding the elevator. Then options to initiate desensitization may be considered.

29. A male client suffering from posttraumatic stress disorder (PTSD) is found one night trying to strangle his roommate. Which intervention is the RN's highest priority?

Rationales

1. ***Give the client a sedative or hypnotic.***
While this may help the client with anxiety, safety is the priority.
2. ***Administer an antipsychotic medication.***
An antipsychotic medication is indicated if the client is psychotic and agitated; however, the RN should ensure the safety of both clients first.
3. ***Assign a UAP to sit with the client.***
The RN should implement safety precautions immediately and place a sitter with the client.
4. ***Process with both clients about the event.***
Although both clients should talk about the incident, this is not an opportune time, and the clients should be separated to provide a safe environment.

30. The RN is updating the plan of care for a client who has a borderline personality disorder. Which intervention is most important to implement?

Rationales

1. ***Assign the same RN to care for the client.***
The best intervention is to provide consistency and avoid splitting the staff by assigning the client to only one RN.
2. ***Avoid challenging inappropriate behavior.***
The RN should assist the client to recognize manipulative behavior and set limits on manipulative behaviors as necessary.
3. ***Limit the client's contact with other clients.***
Socialization should be encouraged to improve the client's social skills.
4. ***Remove consequences for acting-out behavior.***
Firm limits with clear expectations and consequences are needed for manipulative clients.

Notes

31. A female adolescent is admitted to the mental health unit for anorexia nervosa. In planning care, which is the RN's highest priority?

Rationales

1. ***Teach the client the importance of self-expression.***
Self-expression of feelings is important, but reestablishing normal eating habits and physiological integrity is the priority intervention.
2. ***Supervise the client's activities during the day.***
The RN should monitor and supervise the client's activities to prevent binging, purging, or avoiding meals.
3. ***Include the client in daily group therapy.***
The client should be included in daily groups, but the priority is physiological needs and monitoring meals.
4. ***Facilitate social interactions with others.***
The client should be given opportunities to socialize, but monitoring activities during the day, especially meals, is the priority.

32. The charge nurse is planning the daily schedule for clients on the mental health unit. A male client who is manic would be assigned to which activity?

Rationales

1. ***A basketball game in the gym.***
The client should avoid any potentially competitive physical activity, especially contact sports, that can stimulate aggressive acting out.
2. ***Jogging at least 1 mile.***
Jogging is the best activity for this client because it is a noncompetitive physical activity, and it requires the use of large muscle groups that expend energy associated with mania.
3. ***A table tennis game with a peer.***
The client should not be assigned to any competitive activities that can frustrate him and stimulate mood swings.
4. ***Group therapy with the art therapist.***
A manic client may become disruptive and distracted in an art group; physical activity using large muscle groups is more effective in expending energy.

Leadership and Delegation

33. A RN is planning the client assignments for the night shift. The nursing team includes an RN, a licensed practical RN (LPN), and two UAPs. Which duties would be delegated to the UAPs? (Select all that apply.)

Rationales

1. ***Transport a client to the radiology department for a CT scan.***
2. ***Bathe a client with sickle cell disease who has multiple IV lines and a client-controlled analgesia pump.***
3. ***Turn a 92-year-old client who has end-stage heart failure and a do-not-resuscitate order.***
4. ***Report to the HCP the fingerstick blood glucose level of 2.72 mmol/L (49 mg/dL).***
5. ***Feed a female client her first meal after she experienced a stroke.***
The UAP can perform noninvasive and nonsterile activities (options A, B, and C).

34. A hospitalized client has been newly diagnosed with type 2 diabetes. Which task can the RN delegate to the UAP? (Select all that apply.)

Rationales

1. ***Contacting the dietitian for a prescribed consult.***
2. ***Reviewing the client's insulin injection technique.***
3. ***Obtaining the fingerstick blood glucose level before each meal and at bedtime.***
4. ***Reminding the client to dry their toes carefully after a shower.***
5. ***Talking to the client about foods that raise the blood glucose level.***
The UAP can collect and report data such as vital signs, height and weight, and capillary blood sugar results; perform hygiene tasks; and carry out clerical duties. Clients who need education or reinforcement of education require intervention by the RN or LPN.

Notes

35. The home health RN evaluates the insulin preparation and administration technique of a 36-year-old male client newly diagnosed with diabetes. The client has been prescribed lispro insulin before meals and glargine insulin once daily in the morning. Which finding indicates that the client needs further education?

Rationales

1. ***He mixes glargine and lispro in the same syringe for the morning doses.***
   Glargine and lispro must not be mixed with any other insulin.
2. ***He leaves the insulin syringe in place for 10 seconds after injection.***
   This ensures that all of the insulin is absorbed.
3. ***He stores the opened insulin vials at room temperature in the cabinet.***
   Insulin is stored at room temperature, out of direct sunlight.
4. ***He recaps and disposes of the single-use insulin syringe.***
   Clients may recap needles, but HCPs may not to reduce the risk of needlestick injury.

36. At change of shift, the charge nurse assigns the UAP four clients. The RN would direct the UAP to take vital signs on which client first?

Rationales

1. ***The 89-year-old with chronic obstructive pulmonary disease who is resting quietly on 2 L of oxygen and who needs assistance with a bath***
   This client is stable.
2. ***The client who returned from surgery and needs their second set of every-15-minute vital signs taken.***
   This client has a set of time-sensitive vital signs, so this is a priority.
3. ***The client newly diagnosed with type 2 diabetes who had a fingerstick blood glucose level of 5.0 mmol/L (90 mg/dL) and who needs help with breakfast.***
   This client is stable.
4. ***The newly admitted client with rheumatoid arthritis who needs to have hand splints reapplied to both hands.***
   This client is stable.

37. The arrhythmia alarm sounds on a client on the telemetry unit, indicating that the client is in ventricular tachycardia. Place the RN's actions for this client in order of priority from first to last.

Rationales

1. ***Call the rapid response team.***
2. ***Assess for a pulse and blood pressure.***
3. ***Give oxygen via nasal cannula.***
4. ***Bring defibrillator/crash cart to bedside.***
5. ***Document the incident.***
   Correct order: 2, 1, 3, 4, 5. The RN needs to first assess the client before calling the rapid response team. Also, if the client is truly in ventricular tachycardia, it needs to be determined if it is pulseless v-tach or if the client has a pulse and blood pressure. If there is a pulse, the second action would be to call the rapid response team so that additional help is available. Then, the client needs to have oxygen to maximize oxygenation of the circulating blood. The defibrillator needs to be brought to the bedside to be used for cardioversion. The final activity is to document the findings.

38. The RN is reviewing the laboratory values for their assigned clients. Which client has an abnormal laboratory report that the RN would immediately call to the HCP?

Rationales

1. ***The client who is postsplenectomy after a motor vehicle accident and has a hemoglobin of 109 mmol/L (10.9 g/dL).***
   This hemoglobin level is low but not at a critical level. This is not the priority.
2. ***The client receiving warfarin (Coumadin) who has an INR of 2.3.***
   This lab value is therapeutic and expected.
3. ***The 38-year-old client who is 24 hours postthyroidectomy and has a total calcium level of 2.35 mmol/L (9.4 mg/dL).***
   This lab value is within normal limits.
4. ***The newly admitted client with bipolar disorder with a lithium level of 2.5 mEq/L.***
   Severe lithium toxicity occurs at 2.0 mEq/L; the RN should notify the HCP immediately.

Notes

39. The RN receives a change-of-shift report on their four acute care clients. Which action would the RN take first?

Rationales

1. ***Administer an antiemetic to a postoperative client who has been nauseated and is now vomiting.***
   Postoperative nausea and vomiting (PONV) are among the most common reactions after surgery. PONV can stress and irritate abdominal and GI wounds, increase intracranial pressure in clients who had head and neck surgery, elevate intraocular pressure in clients who had eye surgery, and increase the risk for aspiration. Obtaining a prescription for relieving PONV will decrease these risks.
2. ***Notify a family member of a client's impending transfer to the intensive care unit for angina and ST-segment changes.***
   This is a change in status and should be performed after managing the PONV.
3. ***Inform the HCP of a potassium level of 5.2 mmol/L (mEq/L) in the client with end-stage renal disease.***
   This is an expected finding in end-stage renal disease.
4. ***Begin assessment rounds, starting with the palliative care client having a diagnosis of congestive failure.***
   Assessing the client receiving palliative care is important; however, managing the client with PONV is the priority.

40. The emergency department staff RN is assigned four clients. Which client would the RN assess first?

Rationales

1. ***A preschooler with a barking cough, an O_2 saturation of 93% on room air, and occasional inspiratory stridor.***
   This is not a medical emergency. With an O_2 saturation of 93%, the child is not in acute respiratory distress.
2. ***A 10-month-old with a tympanic temperature of 38.9°C (102°F) and green nasal drainage and who is pulling at her ears.***
   The child has an infection and probably needs antibiotics, but this is not a medical emergency.
3. ***A crying 8-month-old with a harsh, paroxysmal cough; an audible expiratory wheeze; and mild retractions.***
   These symptoms are often seen with children with croup. While the child does need humidified air, they are not in acute respiratory distress.
4. ***A clingy 3-year-old who has a sore throat and drooling and whose tongue slightly protrudes from his mouth.***
   Drooling, a history of sore throat, and a protruding tongue are classic manifestations of epiglottitis; this is a medical emergency. The throat can quickly occlude and cause respiratory arrest.

41. The outpatient clinic nurse is reviewing phone messages from the previous night. Which client would the RN call back first?

Rationales

1. ***A woman at 30 weeks' gestation who has been diagnosed with mild preeclampsia who was unable to relieve her heartburn.***
   A sign of a potential complication of eclampsia is epigastric pain, which may be indicative of liver damage and HELLP (hemolysis, elevated liver enzymes, low platelet count) syndrome, a medical emergency.
2. ***A woman at 24 weeks' gestation who was crying about painful vulvar lesions and urinary frequency for the past 8 hours.***
   This are concerns, possibly indications of a sexually transmitted disease. But these concerns do not take priority over the client with possible HELLP syndrome.
3. ***A woman at 12 weeks' gestation who was recently discharged from the hospital with hyperemesis gravidarum and has had two episodes of vomiting in 6 hours.***
   This client does need to be followed up with for possible dehydration, but the client with possible HELLP syndrome takes precedence.
4. ***A woman with type 1 diabetes who tested positive with a home pregnancy kit and was worried about managing her diabetes.***
   This client needs education, but this is not a priority.

Notes

42. The clinic nurse suspects that a 2-year-old child is being abused. Which assessment finding would support this? (Select all that apply.)

Rationales

1. ***Petechiae in a straight line on the chest.***
Petechiae on the chest may be the result of the coining procedure, a cultural practice among Southeast Asian populations.
2. ***Gray-blue pigmented areas on the sacral region.***
These are Mongolian spots, blue areas commonly located on the sacral region that are consistent in shape and color.
3. ***<u>Bald patches on the scalp.</u>***
Bald patches typically are symmetrical and are indicative of physical abuse.
4. ***Ear tugging and crying.***
Ear tugging and crying are typical signs of otitis media.
5. ***<u>Symmetrical burns on the hands.</u>***
Symmetrical burns are indicative of physical abuse.

43. The RN is caring for a client who had a thoracotomy 48 hours earlier and now has left lower lobe chest tubes. The RN notes that a chest tube is not tidaling. Which action would the RN take first?

Rationales

1. ***<u>Check for kinks in the chest drainage system.</u>***
Normal fluctuation of the water, called tidaling, reflects the intrapleural pressure during inspiration and expiration. If no tidaling is observed (rising with inspiration and falling with expiration in a spontaneously breathing client), the drainage system may be blocked. An absence of fluctuation may mean that the lung has fully healed (which is unlikely at 48 hours), or it can mean that there is an obstruction in the chest tube. A simple step is to ensure that there are no kinks that would occlude the chest tube and prevent lung drainage and expansion.
2. ***Assess the heart rate and blood pressure.***
Checking the heart rate and blood pressure is not directly related to the lack of chest tube drainage.
3. ***Notify the rapid response team immediately.***
Although the RN should immediately notify the rapid response team for tracheal deviation, sudden onset of dyspnea, or mediastinal shift, the absence of tidaling may not be a medical emergency.
4. ***Reconnect the chest tube to wall suction.***
When a chest tube is connected to wall suction, tidaling may stop. The RN should disconnect the tube, not reconnect it, to observe for tidaling.

44. While the RN is caring for a client who has had a myocardial infarction, the monitor alarm sounds, and the RN notes ventricular fibrillation. Which is the RN's first course of action?

Rationales

1. ***Notify the HCP.***
This may be an appropriate action after assessment of the client's clinical status.
2. ***Increase the oxygen concentration.***
This may be an appropriate action after assessment of the client's clinical status.
3. ***<u>Assess the client.</u>***
If a monitor alarm sounds, the RN should first assess the client's clinical status to see whether the problem is an actual dysrhythmia or a monitoring system malfunction.
4. ***Prepare to defibrillate the client.***
This may be an appropriate action after assessment of the client's clinical status.

45. The HCP has prescribed the removal of a client's internal jugular central line catheter. To remove the catheter safely, the RN should give which intervention(s) the highest priority? (Select all that apply.)

Rationales

1. ***Carefully remove the bio-occlusive dressing.***
Removing the bio-occlusive dressing is important, but it is not a safety priority.
2. ***<u>Place the client in the Trendelenburg position.</u>***
The procedure for removing the catheter safely is (1) place the client in the Trendelenburg position, (2) have the client take a deep breath and hold it, and (3) gently withdraw the catheter while applying direct pressure with sterile gauze.

Notes

Holding the breath creates positive pressure in the intrathoracic space, and the Trendelenburg position minimizes the risk of air entering the catheter.

3. ***Send the catheter tip to the lab for culture and sensitivity.***
   The catheter tip may or may not be sent to the lab, depending on the protocol of the facility.
4. ***Have the client hold a deep breath during removal.***
   See the explanation for B.
5. ***Apply pressure for 20 minutes after removal of the catheter.***
   Applying pressure for 20 minutes is a technique used in arterial line withdrawal to prevent bleeding.

46. The RN who usually works on the orthopedic surgery unit is floating to a cardiovascular unit. Which client would be best to assign to the float RN?

Rationales

1. ***Client scheduled for a heart catheterization this morning.***
   Preparing the client for a cardiac catheterization requires specialized information, and it would be best to assign to the RN who usually works on the cardiovascular unit.
2. ***Client admitted last night for chest pain.***
   This client requires close monitoring by the RN who has additional education about cardiac issues.
3. ***<u>Client who is 1 day postoperative for popliteal bypass surgery.</u>***
   This would require similar care to a client who had just had lower extremity orthopedic surgery and would be the safest assignment for this RN.
4. ***Client who has heart failure and is scheduled for a stress test today.***
   Preparing the client for a stress test requires specialized information and would be best to assign to the RN who usually works on the cardiovascular unit.

47. The RN is admitting a client who is a paraplegic and has a nonhealing pressure injury with a possible methicillin-resistant Staphylococcus aureus infection. A practical RN (PN) and UAP are assigned to the RN's team. Which task would be delegated to the PN? (Select all that apply.)

Rationales

1. ***Place the client in isolation.***
   This task can be safely assigned to the UAP.
2. ***<u>Complete a dressing change.</u>***
   This task is within the scope of practice for the PN.
3. ***Assess and document the wound.***
   Initial assessment of a wound should be completed by the RN.
4. ***<u>Insert a urinary catheter.</u>***
   This task is within the scope of practice for the PN.
5. ***<u>Administer oral pain medications.</u>***
   This task is within the scope of practice for the PN.

48. The nursing supervisor calls the charge nurse on a step-down unit about the need for a bed for an unstable client from the medical unit. Which client would the RN anticipate to be transferred to the medical unit to receive this unstable client?

Rationales

1. ***A client admitted for a STEMI who just returned from having a cardiac catheterization performed***
   This client needs close monitoring for the first 24 hours and should remain on the step-down unit.
2. ***<u>A client diagnosed with congestive heart failure who is receiving IV infusion of furosemide</u>***
   This client could be safely taken care of on a medical-surgical unit.
3. ***A client with possible Guillain-Barré syndrome who may need an exchange transfusion***
   This client needs close monitoring and should remain in the step-down unit.
4. ***A client in hypertensive crisis who is on a sodium nitroprusside drip***
   Clients on a nitroprusside drip need frequent vital signs and close monitoring. This client should remain on the step-down unit.

Notes

49. When accessing the medication dispensing system (Pyxis), the RN finds chlorpropamide in the drawer instead of the expected chlorpromazine. Which action would the RN take? (Select all that apply.)

Rationales

1. ***Remove the tablets of chlorpropamide.***
2. ***Notify the pharmacy about the mistake.***
3. ***Complete an incident or occurrence report.***
4. ***Be extra vigilant because the pharmacy is making mistakes.***
5. ***Place a warning note on the Pyxis machine.***
   The RN needs to ensure that others do not give the wrong medication, so the tablets of chlorpropamide need to be removed and returned to the pharmacy (1). The pharmacy needs to be made aware of the error (2) and an incident (also called an occurrence) report completed (3) to help prevent the error in the future. The other options (4 and 5) are not needed at this time.

50. The RN is calling the HCP about a client's current needs. Which is the best way to communicate?

Rationales

1. ***Call the HCP with the request and a recommendation.***
   Letting the physician know the needs of the client is important, but key information may be missed using this way to communicate.
2. ***Use the SBAR (situation, background, assessment, recommendation) tool for communication.***
   Using the SBAR format ensures that all key information is given and is the best way to communicate.
3. ***Send a text message or page with the needed order.***
   This may be an ineffective way to communicate and may not ensure that all key information is given. Additionally, if both phones are not encrypted, this may place the client's information at risk.
4. ***Ask the HCP to come back to the unit to discuss the client's needs.***
   Although face-to-face communication is often valuable, this does not ensure that all key information is communicated.

51. The HCP plans to do a paracentesis on a client with cirrhosis in 1 hour. In what order would the RN perform the following activities?

Rationales

1. ***Ensure that the informed consent has been obtained.***
2. ***Measure the client's abdominal girth.***
3. ***Have the client empty his or her bladder.***
4. ***Assemble needed equipment.***
5. ***Administer oral pain medication.***
   Correct order: 1, 5, 3, 2, 4
   Before a procedure can be completed, it is essential to have an informed consent (1). Oral pain medication can then be given (after the consent has been obtained) to help the client relax during the procedure (5). The client then needs to empty his or her bladder before the procedure to prevent accidentally puncturing the bladder (3). After the bladder is empty, a baseline abdominal girth is obtained (2). Finally, the RN needs to assemble the correct equipment for the procedure (4).

52. The RN receives report on a client from the emergency department with a diagnosis of pneumonia. Which intervention has the highest priority?

Rationales

1. ***Obtain blood cultures.***
   Blood cultures are not needed unless the client is suspected of being septic.
2. ***Initiate prescribed antibiotics.***
   Studies have shown that the sooner antibiotics are started, the better the outcomes. Current requirements include antibiotic administration within 2 hours of diagnosis. This is the priority.
3. ***Place the client in isolation.***
   The question does not state what organism is causing the pneumonia, so this may not be needed.
4. ***Obtain an accurate weight.***
   This would be needed if the antibiotic is weight based but is not usually a priority.

Notes

53. The RN is part of the triage team at a disaster. Which client would be treated first?

Rationales

1. ***A 90-year-old woman with a crushed pelvis and head injuries.***
   This client would be triaged black.
2. ***A 21-year-old male screaming in pain from a broken leg.***
   This client's injuries are not life-threatening, and he can wait to be seen.
3. ***A 30-year-old woman with a flail chest secondary to a puncture wound to the chest.***
   The flail chest causes the heart to become unstable and is life-threatening. This client needs to be seen immediately.
4. ***A 12-year-old crying with multiple lacerations to the legs.***
   Although the child needs to be comforted, the injuries are not life-threatening, and this client can wait for treatment.

54. The triage RN in the emergency room is assessing four clients. Which client requires the most immediate intervention?

Rationales

1. ***The client who arrived via ambulance with numbness and tingling of his left arm and face.***
   The client may be experiencing a stroke and requires immediate assessment and interventions. If interventions are initiated quickly, the complications may be mitigated.
2. ***The adult client who had a seizure at home who is sleeping on his left side.***
   While a seizure is highly concerning, the priority is the client who may be diagnosed with a stroke.
3. ***The 60-year-old client who complains of frequent urination and has a blood sugar of 16.7 mmol/L (300 mg/dL).***
   An elevated blood sugar may indicate diabetes, and polyuria is an expected symptom. It is considered urgent and not emergent.
4. ***The middle-aged client who presents with severe unilateral back pain and previous history of kidney stones.***
   Although this is highly concerning, the client exhibiting symptoms of a stroke is a higher priority.

55. After the change-of-shift report on an orthopedic floor, which client would the RN assess first?

Rationales

1. ***A client who had surgery yesterday and has a temperature of 37.6°C (99.7°F)***
   A slight increase in temperature is expected postoperatively.
2. ***A client who is complaining of numbness and tingling distal to the fracture site***
   This is a sign of compartment syndrome. This client needs to be assessed first.
3. ***A client who had a left leg amputation and states he is experiencing pain in the left foot.***
   Phantom pain is expected after an amputation and should be treated but is not as critical as assessing for compartment syndrome.
4. ***A client who is extremely upset with their care and is requesting to speak with the manager.***
   This is a customer service issue and needs to be addressed but is not a high priority.

56. The nurse is administering medications to a client admitted for an overdose and a history of substance abuse. Which intervention is a priority to include in this client's plan of care? (Select all that apply.)

Rationales

1. ***Allow the client to take medications independently.***
   With a history of substance abuse, the RN needs to observe the client as medications are taken.
2. ***Ensure that all medications have been swallowed before leaving the client's room.***
   To ensure that medications are not being hoarded or kept to be taken at a later time, the RN needs to watch the client swallow his or her medications.
3. ***Request that oral pain medications be changed from tablet to oral suspension.***
   Liquid forms of medications are harder to save to be taken later so are often used for clients with a history of substance abuse.
4. ***Give flumazenil every 6 hours around the clock.***
   Flumazenil is used to reverse benzodiazepine overdose and is given as needed, not around the clock.
5. ***Only give medications to the client via the intravenous route.***
   There is no indication to give medications intravenously.

Notes

57. The RN is returning phone calls to clients who are cared for at an outpatient mental health center. Which client would the RN call first?

Rationales

1. ***The young mother diagnosed with schizophrenia who is hearing voices say that they are pursuing her children.***
This client is at risk for hurting herself or her children. She needs to be seen first.
2. ***The elderly male at an assisted living facility who says he wants to end it all.***
This client is at risk for committing suicide, but he lives in a facility where there is staff that the RN can notify about his thoughts. The staff can stay with him until he can be brought into the clinic.
3. ***The female client diagnosed with bipolar disorder who is manic and has not slept for 48 hours***
Although this client needs to be seen to have her medications adjusted, she is not the priority client.
4. ***The teenager diagnosed with bulimia whose mother called and reported that she found her daughter purging.***
This client does need to be seen but is not in imminent danger

58. An 18-year-old female is being discharged after delivering a healthy baby. She has a cousin whose baby died from sudden infant death syndrome (SIDS). The client seems to know many of the precautions to take. Which information does the RN need to correct?

Rationales

1. ***Always place infants on their backs to sleep.***
This is correct. Babies should be placed on their backs.
2. ***Room sharing has been shown to decrease SIDS.***
This is correct. Studies show that room sharing does decrease SIDS.
3. ***Keep the crib free of stuffed animals and crib pads.***
This is correct. The bed should be free of items that could cause suffocation.
4. ***Sleeping with the baby can alert the mother to changes.***
Sleeping with the baby increases the risk for injury and SIDS for infants.

59. A 4-year-old admitted with pneumonia weighs 18 kg. The HCP has prescribed vancomycin 40 mg/kg/day IV. The order states to divide the dose and give it three times daily. How many mg of vancomycin should the child receive in each dose? (Round the answer to the nearest whole number.)

Answer: 240 mg/dose

Rationale

$$\frac{180\text{ mg} \times 40\text{ mg}}{\text{kg}} = \frac{720\text{ mg}}{\text{kg}}$$

$$\frac{720\text{ mg}}{3} = \frac{240\text{ mg}}{\text{dose}}$$

60. The RN needs to initiate an IV on an 8-year-old child. Which intervention(s) is/are appropriate? (Select all that apply).

Rationales

1. ***Start the IV in the treatment room, not the child's room.***
The child's room is a safe zone, and painful treatments should not be performed in the child's room.
2. ***Apply a lidocaine-based cream for a few minutes before starting the IV.***
To be effective, the cream needs to be applied for about 1 hour before the IV is started.
3. ***Ask the parents to leave the room while performing the procedure.***
Having parents present can help the child cope with this procedure.
4. ***Encourage the child to use guided imagery to cope.***
Children at this age can understand and participate in guided imagery.
5. ***Offer the child a reward if they cooperate during the procedure.***
Offering the child a reward does not help the child to cope with the IV insertion.

Notes

Next-Generation NCLEX® Examination–Style Unfolding Case Studies

Unfolding Case Study 1

The RN is caring for a 63-year-old client complaining of occasional chest discomfort for approximately 1 week. Also complains of frequent fatigue.

History and Physical: The client is a business owner who has hypertension and a history of angina pectoris x3 years, treated with sublingual nitroglycerin. Reports taking SL NTG 8–10 times over the last week for midchest discomfort. History of cardiac catheterization several years ago that showed 50% stenosis of the right descending coronary artery and 40% of the left descending coronary artery. Reports smoking one pack per day for over 40 years.

Home medication list: metoprolol 50 mg PO daily, atorvastatin 20 mg PO daily, aspirin (ASA) 81 mg PO daily, amlodipine 5 mg PO daily.

Question 1 (Multiple Response Select N): Select four findings that require immediate follow-up.

1. Pain level of 2/10 after SL NTG
2. Apical pulse is bounding
3. BP: 154/92 mmHg
4. Shortness of breath with exertion
5. SpO_2 96% on room air
6. Complains of dizziness and light-headedness
7. Weight gain of 25 pounds over the last 2 months
8. Potassium level is 4.7 mEq/L

Question 2 (Matrix Multiple Choice): For each risk factor for coronary artery disease (CAD) listed, specify whether the risk factor is modifiable or nonmodifiable by placing a mark in the appropriate column.

Risk Factor	Modifiable	Non-modifiable
Stress level		
Gender		
Obesity		
Smoking		
Hypertension		
Diabetes mellitus		
Alcohol use		
Physical inactivity		
Hyperlipidemia		
Family Hx of CAD		

Notes

Case Study cont'd:

An electrocardiogram (ECG) is performed. The following cardiac rhythm is observed on the monitor.

Diagnostic:

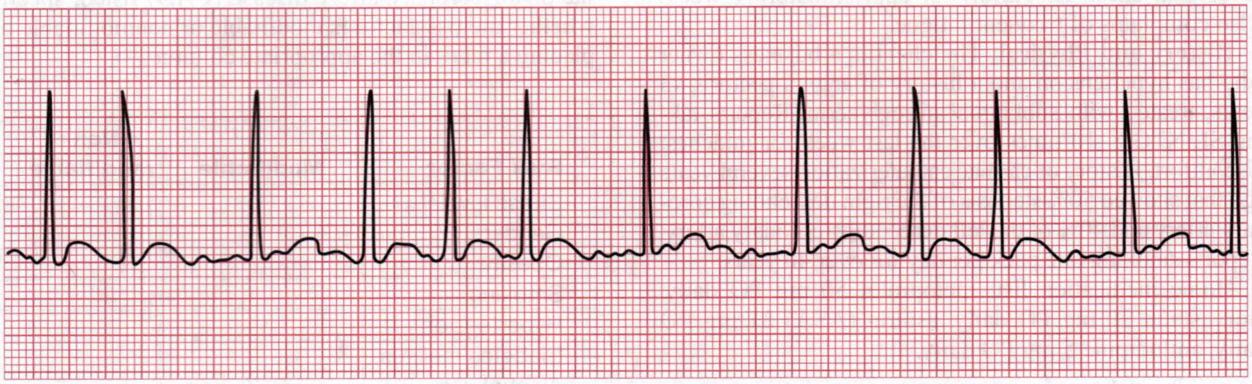

Question 3 (Drop-Down Cloze): Complete the following statements.

The RN identifies this rhythm as________(1)_________. The RN places the client on continuous telemetry.

The RN would prioritize the client problem __________(2)_____________ associated with this rhythm.

Drop-Down Option 1	Drop-Down Option 2
Atrial flutter	High blood pressure
Supraventricular tachycardia	Risk for stroke
Atrial fibrillation	Need for health teaching
Complete heart block	Decreased clotting

Notes

Case Study cont'd:

The client is admitted to the telemetry unit for continuous cardiac monitoring. The client is prescribed diltiazem to treat the dysrhthmia. The RN plans to monitor for signs and symptoms of adverse reactions when starting any new medications. While monitoring the client, the RN notes the following findings.

Question 4 (Highlight Text): Highlight the six RN findings that indicate an adverse reaction to diltiazem that the RN will plan to notify the healthcare provider of immediately.

RN's Notes

1642: Client received from ED in stable condition. A&O x4. Speech is clear. PERRLA. Sclera yellow. Vitals= BP: 96/46, P: 69, R: 21, T: 99.2°F. Reports pain level of 4/10. Reports having moderate fatigue with activity over the last week. Lung sounds: crackles in the lower lobes with nonproductive cough. O_2 @ 2 L/min via nasal cannula. SpO_2 is 96%. Bowels hypoactive in all 4 quadrants. Reports normal BM yesterday. Peripheral pulses palpable, strong. 3+ pitting edema to lower extremities. IV to Left AC, 20g catheter. Site has blood under occlusive dressing. IVFs: Normal Saline at 75 mL/hr and diltiazem at 10 mg/hr. Reports feeling nauseated, emesis basin given. No emesis at this time. Bruising noted to bilateral arms and legs. Skin is warm, pink, and moist.

Question 5 (Matrix Multiple Choice): The RN is planning care for the client. For each potential nursing action, mark the column to specify whether the intervention is indicated or contraindicated.

Potential Action	Indicated	Contraindicated
Evaluate client reports of fatigue		
Keep room temperature warm		
Maintain strict bed rest		
Restrict PO fluid intake		
Hold stool softener		
Review lifestyle changes		
Consult the facility social worker		

The RN chooses to address smoking cessation with the client as a priority teaching intervention. The RN uses knowledge about basic physiological responses to nicotine ingestion to enhance understanding in the teaching performed for the client. The RN would identify that the client has correct understanding of the teaching if the client can correctly complete the following statement.

Question 6 (Drag-and-drop Rationale): Drag the options to complete the sentence.

Cigarette smoking causes peripheral _______ (1)_______, which leads to increased peripheral vascular resistance and _______(2)_______ peripheral tissue and organ perfusion.

Drag-and-drop Options	
Vasoconstriction	Decreased
Vasodilation	Increased
Hypoxia	Unaffected
Hypercapnia	

Answers and Rationales

Unfolding Case Study 1

Rationales

Question 1 (Multiple Response Select N):
Answer: 3, 4, 6, 7.

Rationale

Hypertension is a risk factor for CAD. An elevated blood pressure (BP) increases cardiac workload, which can cause ischemia to the heart muscle in clients with significant atherosclerosis. Shortness of breath with exertion is another sign of increased workload of the heart and decreased perfusion of the cardiac muscle. Dizziness and light-headedness could be a result of decreased blood flow from narrowing of the arteries supplying oxygen to the brain. New onset or worsening of these symptoms could indicate a neurological complication and require further assessment. Weight gain of 25 pounds in a 2-month period is a significant amount of weight gain and can put excessive strain on the heart. This weight gain could also be an indication that the client may be experiencing other complications such as congestive heart

Notes

failure or kidney injury. The other findings do not require immediate follow-up.

Question 2 (Matrix Multiple Choice):

Answer:

Risk Factor	Modifiable	Nonmodifiable
Stress level	x	
Gender		x
Obesity	x	
Smoking	x	
Hypertension	x	
Diabetes mellitus	x	
Alcohol use	x	
Physical inactivity	x	
Hyperlipidemia	x	
Family Hx of CAD		x

Rationale

There are many risk factors for CAD. Risk factors that can be controlled are considered to be modifiable. These include hypertension, elevated cholesterol levels, smoking, diabetes mellitus, overweight or obesity, lack of physical activity, unhealthy diet, and stress. Those that cannot be controlled are considered nonmodifiable and include age, sex (men are generally at greater risk of CAD), family history, and race.

Question 3 (Drop-Down Cloze):

Option 1 Answer: Atrial Fibrillation.

Option 2 Answer: Risk for stroke

Rationale

Risk for stroke is the priority client problem when experiencing atrial fibrillation. Clients have an increased likelihood of developing a clot within the atria due to incomplete emptying of blood from the heart chambers. If the clot leaves the atria, it can travel through the circulatory system to the brain and cause a stroke. Treatment for atrial fibrillation is most likely to cause Low blood pressure, not high. The client will require health teaching, but this is not the priority nursing problem. Atrial fibrillation causes increased risk of clotting, not decreased.

Question 4 (Highlight in Text):

Answer: 1642: Client received from ED in stable condition. A&O x4. Speech is clear. PERRLA. Vitals= BP: 86/46, P: 69, R: 21, T: 99.2°F. Reports pain level of 4/10. Reports having moderate fatigue with activity over the last week. Lung sounds: crackles in the lower lobes with nonproductive cough. O_2 @ 2 L/min via nasal cannula. SpO_2 is 96%. Bowels hypoactive in all 4 quadrants. Reports normal BM yesterday. Peripheral pulses palpable, strong. 3+ pitting edema to lower extremities. IV to Left AC, 20g catheter. Site has blood under occlusive dressing. IVFs: Normal Saline at 75 mL/hr and diltiazem at 10 mg/hr. Reports feeling nauseated, emesis basin given. No emesis at this time. Bruising noted to bilateral arms and legs. Skin is warm, pink, and moist.

Rationale

Hypotension is an adverse reaction of diltiazem caused by systemic vasodilation. Diltiazem is contraindicated in clients with a systolic BP (SBP) <90 mm Hg. A cough, constipation, and peripheral edema are also adverse reactions associated with diltiazem use. Bleeding and bruising may be signs of thrombocytopenia which is also an adverse reaction to diltiazem.

Question 5 (Matrix Multiple Choice):

Answer:

Potential Action	Indicated	Contraindicated
Evaluate client reports of fatigue	x	
Keep room temperature warm	x	
Maintain strict bed rest		x
Restrict PO fluid intake	x	
Hold stool softener		x
Review lifestyle changes	x	
Consult the facility social worker		x

Notes

Rationale
The nurse should thoroughly evaluate client reports of fatigue and its precipitating factors. This is essential to monitor the client's condition. Keeping the room temperature at a comfortable level is necessary to address client comfort and avoid added stress. It is also important to restrict PO fluid intake because this client is showing signs of fluid volume excess (crackles and edema). There are many modifiable risk factors for CAD, and these factors need to be reviewed with the client. Smoking cessation is very important for clients with hypertension and CAD. Assist the client in making a plan for reducing these risk factors. It is important to increase activity levels gradually. Maintaining strict bed rest is contraindicated and could lead to other complications. Stool softeners should be administered to help the client avoid bearing down for a bowel movement which could stimulate the Valsalva response. Consulting the facility social worker is also unnecessary. A consult with a case manager to arrange home care and follow-up care will be more beneficial to this client.

Question 6 (Drag-and-Drop Rationale):
Answer:
Cigarette smoking causes peripheral vasoconstriction, which leads to increased peripheral vascular resistance and decreased peripheral tissue and organ perfusion.

Unfolding Case Study 2

The RN is caring for a 73-year-old client. The client is postoperative day 2 after an Open reduction and internal fixation (ORIF) for a fractured right femur. He has been on bed rest since surgery.

RNs Notes
0800: VSs= BP: 138/86 mmHg, P: 70 BPM—regular rhythm, R: 18/min unlabored, and T: 99.1°F, and SpO_2 97% on room air. He is awake and A&Ox4. No adventitious heart sounds noted. Breath sounds are clear but diminished in bases bilaterally. Bowel sounds hypoactive in all quadrants. Tolerating clear liquids. IV of D5LR at 75 mL/hr in left hand and orders have been received to change it to a S/L this AM if able to maintain adequate oral fluid intake. Orders for O_2 to maintain SpO_2 >92%, but he is refusing to wear the NC while sleeping. Pain is controlled with morphine sulfate 4 mg IV Q4H PRN.

At 06:30 PM you answer MM's call light and find him lying in bed breathing rapidly and rubbing the right side of his chest. He is reporting right-sided chest pain and appears to be restless.

Question 1 (Highlight in Table): Which information, based on the findings listed in the table, will the RN report to the HCP? Highlight the findings that need to be reported.

Client Assessment Findings		
BP: 98/60, P: 120, RR: 24 labored	Telemetry shows nonspecific T wave changes on Lead II	Restless and slightly confused
SpO_2= 86%	Faint crackles in the posterior bases bilaterally	Bowel sounds hypoactive
Pain = 7/10 (number scale)	No JVD noted	Nonpitting edema to BLE

After calling the client's HCP, an order is received to collect an ABG.

Lab Results
Arterial Blood Gas

pH 7.55
$PaCO_2$ 24 mm Hg
HCO_3 24 mEq/L
PaO_2 56 mm Hg
SaO_2 86% (RA)

Question 2 (Drop-Down Rationale): Complete the following sentence using the options in the drop-down lists.

The client is experiencing ____(1)____, as evidenced by ____(2)____ amount of ____(3)____.

Drop-Down Option 1	Drop-Down Option 2	Drop-Down Option 3
Respiratory acidosis	increased	$PaCO_2$
Respiratory alkalosis	decreased	HCO_3
Metabolic acidosis	Normal	PaO_2
Metabolic alkalosis		SaO_2

The HCP orders a chest x-ray and CT of the lungs.

Imaging
Moderate pleural effusions noted to bilateral lung bases. A wedge-shaped, pleura-based triangular opacity

Notes

with an apex pointing toward the hilus (Hampton hump) and decreased vascularity (Westermark sign) are present.

Impression: These findings are suggestive of pulmonary embolism (PE).

Question 3 (Matrix Multiple Response): For each risk factor for PE in the following list, note whether the client is most likely at risk of experiencing a fat embolus, a thromboembolism in the lungs, or both by placing a mark in the corresponding column or columns.

Risk Factor	Fat Embolus	Thromboembolism
Prolonged immobility		
Skeletal injury		
Post cardiopulmonary resuscitation		
Sickle cell disease		
Cancer		
Pancreatitis		
Obesity		
Parenteral feeding through central venous catheter		

The client is transferred to the intensive care unit. The HCP orders heparin following the facility's heparin protocol.

Orders

Heparin Protocol

Initial bolus: Give 80 units/kg.

Initial infusion: 18 units/kg/hr.

Every 6 hours, check partial thromboplastin time (PTT). Follow titration instructions:

a. PTT less than 55 seconds—Give bolus of 80 units/kg and increase infusion rate by 4 units/kg/hr.

b. 55–70 seconds—Give 40 units/kg bolus and increase infusion rate by 2 units/kg/hr.

c. 71–105 seconds—No change in rate

d. 106–140 seconds—Decrease infusion rate by 2 units/kg/hr from previous rate.

e. Greater than 140 seconds—Reduce infusion by 3 units/kg/hr and notify MD.

Question 4 Drag & Drop Table: Using the heparin protocol described, complete the table with the appropriate heparin dosages the RN will implement in the plan of care for this client who weighs 76 kg using the client information that is collected.

Initial bolus (units)	
Initial infusion (units/hr)	
6-hour PTT result of 63 seconds: Infusion rate (units/hr)	
12-hour PTT result of 144 seconds: Infusion rate (units/hr)	
18-hour PTT result of 109 seconds: Infusion rate (units/hr)	

Drag & Drop Options

1292	2764	6080	1672	5320	4788
1520	1216	3040	1140	1368	1064

Two days after admission to the intensive care unit, the client is transferred to the medical-surgical unit for continued medication and physical therapy. After 4 days of continued care, the client is preparing for transfer to a rehabilitation center. The RN is preparing education for the list of medications the HCP has prescribed for the client. The RN will base the client education on knowledge of the different drug classifications and implement this information into the teaching session.

Orders

docusate sodium 100 mg PO daily
rivaroxaban 10 mg PO daily
oxycodone 10 mg PO BID
gabapentin 300 mg PO TID
celecoxib 200 mg PO daily

Question 5 (Drop-Down Table): Complete the following table by choosing the medication classification for each medication ordered for the client to incorporate into the client teaching to be performed.

Medication Name	Therapeutic Drug Classification
Docusate sodium	
Rivaroxaban	
Oxycodone	
Gabapentin	
Celecoxib	

Notes

Drop-Down Options (Therapeutic Drug Classifications)		
Skeletal muscle relaxant	Anticoagulant	Therapeutic analgesic adjunct
Laxative	Nonsteroidal anti-inflammatory agent	Opioid analgesic

After the RN performs the discharge medication teaching, the nurse will evaluate client understanding. The RN will conclude that the client has attained correct understanding of the dietary restrictions associated with anticoagulant therapy when they can identify 5 Vitamin K-rich foods from the provided list that should be consumed in moderation.

Question 6 (Multiple Response Select N): Select 5 vitamin K-rich foods from the provided food list.

1. **asparagus**
2. **kale**
3. **bananas**
4. **vanilla bean**
5. **broccoli**
6. **ginger**
7. **garlic**
8. **spinach**
9. **swiss chard**
10. **iceberg lettuce**

Answers and Rationales

Unfolding Case Study 2

Rationales

Question 1 (Highlight Table):

Answer:

Client Assessment Findings		
BP: 98/60, P: 120, RR: 24 labored SpO_2 = 86%	Telemetry shows nonspecific T wave changes on Lead II Faint crackles in the posterior bases bilaterally	Restless and slightly confused Bowel sounds hypoactive
Pain = 7/10 (Number scale)	No JVD noted	Nonpitting edema to BLE

Rationale

The vital signs including BP, P, RR, and SpO_2 listed indicate client distress and represent a deviation from baseline vitals from earlier in the day. These vitals could indicate a serious medical condition. The pain level reported regarding the chest pain describes its intensity and should be reported to the HCP for further evaluation. Any new-onset changes noted to the ECG, especially those related to T wave abnormalities, must be reported to the HCP. Faint crackles in the bases of the lungs and finding the client to be restless and slightly confused could indicate decreased oxygenation. The cause of these findings should be evaluated. The client's bowel activity has not changed since the previous assessment and is not pertinent to the client assessment findings at this time. Therefore, this information does not need to be reported. Having no JVD is a normal physiological finding. Nonpitting edema to the bilateral lower extremities (BLE) is also not a priority concern at this time.

Question 2 (Drop-Down Rationale):

Answer:

The client is experiencing **respiratory alkalosis**, as evidenced by **decreased** amount of **$PaCO_2$**.

Rationale

$PaCO_2$ levels below 35 mm Hg indicate respiratory alkalosis. Normal levels of $PaCO_2$ are 35–45 mm Hg. This ABG shows that the client is hyperventilating and blowing off too much CO_2, which is leading to an alkalotic state. This is also evident with the previous assessment findings documenting a RR of 24 breaths/min.

Question 3 (Matrix Multiple Response):

Answer:

Risk Factor	Fat Embolus	Thromboembolism
Prolonged immobility		X
Skeletal injury	X	X
Post cardiopulmonary resuscitation	X	
Sickle cell disease		X
Cancer		X
Pancreatitis	X	
Obesity		X
Parenteral feeding through central venous catheter	X	X

Notes

Rationale

Risk factors for fat emboli include severe skeletal injuries, parenteral feeding with lipid infusion, liposuction, and pancreatitis and can be seen following cardiopulmonary resuscitation. Risk factors for thromboembolism include prolonged immobility, central venous catheters, surgery, pregnancy, obesity, advancing age, general and genetic conditions that increase blood clotting, history of thromboembolism, varicose veins, sickle cell disease, certain cancers, and trauma such as a broken hip or femur.

Question 4 (Drag & Drop Table):

Answer:

Initial bolus (units)	6080
Initial infusion (units/hr)	1368
6-hour PTT result of 63 seconds: Infusion rate (units/hr)	1520
12-hour PTT result of 144 seconds: Infusion rate (units/hr)	1292
18-hour PTT result of 109 seconds: Infusion rate (units/hr)	1140

Rationale

$$1:80 \text{ units} \times 76 \text{ kg} = 6080 \text{ units}$$
$$2:18 \text{ units} \times 76 \text{ kg} = 1368 \text{ units/hr}$$
$$3:20 \text{ units} \times 76 \text{ kg} = 1520 \text{ units/hr}$$
$$4:17 \text{ units} \times 76 \text{ kg} = 1292 \text{ units/hr}$$
$$5:15 \text{ units} \times 76 \text{ kg} = 1140 \text{ units/hr}$$

Question 5 (Drop-Down Table):

Answer:

Medication Name	Therapeutic Drug Classification
Docusate sodium	Laxative
Rivaroxaban	Anticoagulant
Oxycodone	Opioid analgesic
Gabapentin	Therapeutic analgesic adjunct
Celecoxib	Nonsteroidal anti-inflammatory agent

Question 6 (Multiple Response Select N):

Answer: 1, 2, 5, 8, 9

Rationale:

It has long been stated that clients that are receiving anticoagulant therapy should avoid or not eat vitamin K-rich foods. However, small amounts of these foods are acceptable in the diet in moderation and while remaining proportionate to the client's dosage of medication. Foods that are rich in vitamin K include asparagus, kale, broccoli, spinach, and swiss chard among other green leafy vegatables. The other foods listed may contain very little of no vitamin K and are safe to eat in larger amounts. Iceberg lettuce is one of the only lettuce varieties that do not contain vitamin K and is a great alternative for dark greens.

Unfolding Case Study 3

The RN is admitting a 12-year-old client with cystic fibrosis (CF) to the pediatric medical-surgical unit. The client is admitted with a diagnosis of suspected lower respiratory infection and exacerbation of CF.

RNs Notes

Vital signs: BP = 125/79, P = 88, R = 30, T = 102.4°F (oral) and SpO_2 = 87% on room air. The client weighs 30 kg. A&O x4. Skin Color: pale and dry with bluish-tinged nail beds and clubbing noted to all fingertips; capillary refill <3 seconds. Respiratory effort labored; coarse productive cough with green sputum; rhonchi noted throughout; states pain of 4/10 with coughing. Thorax has a barrel-chest appearance. Client is thin with decreased muscle mass. Abdomen scaphoid, non-tender; bowel sounds hyperactive in all quadrants. Reports last void and bowel movement this morning with no problems. Client anxious and easily fatigued; only able to answer questions in short phrases. Parents at bedside, attentive to child's needs and helping answer history and medication questions.

Notes

Question 1 (Extended Drag-and-Drop) Drag the assessment findings which require immediate follow-up to the box on the right.

Assessment Findings:	Assessment Findings That Require Immediate Follow-up.
Vital signs	
Skin color	
Capillary refill	
Pain	
Sputum appearance	
Elimination patterns	
Fatigue	
Family support	

Question 2 (Multiple Response—Grouping): Select which physician orders the RN would anticipate for each of the following categories after reporting the previous finding to the HCP. (Note: each category must have **at least** one option selected.)

Category		Orders
Imaging		Chest x-ray CT of abdomen MRI of the chest Lung perfusion scan
Laboratory		Arterial blood gas Sputum culture Sweat chloride level Complete blood count with automatic differential
Medications		Gentamicin Ipratropium bromide and albuterol sulfate Dornase alfa Ivacaftor

Question 3 (Multiple Response—Select all that apply): Which of the following nursing diagnoses would the RN include in the client's plan of care? **Select all that apply**.

1. Ineffective airway clearance
2. Imbalanced nutrition: less than body requirements
3. Ineffective family coping
4. Sedentary lifestyle
5. Impaired gas exchange
6. Risk for injury
7. Impaired comfort
8. Risk for infection
9. Powerlessness
10. Constipation

The client's weight is below the 5th percentile for that age group. A dietary consultation is ordered for this client and the dietician recommends a high-protein, high-calorie diet for this client.

Question 4 (Matrix Multiple Choice): Choose the appropriate food options to include in the diet order for this client following the dietician's recommendations. Check whether the food is recommended or contraindicated for this client.

Food Options	Recommended	Contraindicated
Sausage biscuit		
Scrambled eggs		
Tomatoes		
Brown rice		
Ground beef		
Cheddar cheese		
Greek yogurt		
Baked sweet potato		

Five hours after admission to the pediatric unit, the doctor comes to evaluate client. The RN reviews the new physician orders.

Question 5 (Highlight Table): Highlight the three orders the RN will perform immediately.

Physician Orders

1. Acetaminophen 325 mg PO now and Q6H PRN fever >100.4°F or mild pain.
2. Respiratory consult for chest physiotherapy.
3. Titrate O_2 via NC to keep SpO_2 above 95%.
4. DuoNeb 3 mL INH nebulizer Q4H.
5. 3000-calorie, high-protein det.
6. 1800 lipase units per gram of fat ingested.
7. Repeat ABG, CBC, CMP.
8. Daily weight and strict I&Os.

Notes

In addition to reviewing dietary recommendations, the RN wants to evaluate the client's understanding of administration of pancreatic enzyme replacement therapy (PERT).

Question 6 (Drop-Down Rationale):

Effective dosing of PERT is determined by observing the client's ______(1)______. If therapy is sufficient, then the RN will see it ______(2)______.

Drop-Down Option 1	Drop-Down Option 2
Urine	Contains glucose
Feces	Contains protein
Emesis	Sink
Sweat	Float
Saliva	Increase
Sputum	Decrease

Answers and Rationales

Unfolding Case Study 3

Rationales

Question 1 (Extended Drag-and-Drop):
Answer:

Assessment Findings:	Assessment Findings That Require Immediate Follow-up:
	Vital signs
	Skin color
Capillary refill	
Pain	
	Sputum appearance
Elimination patterns	
	Fatigue
Family support	

The client's vital signs require immediate follow-up because of the elevated temperature and SpO_2. These values indicate possible severe infection and respiratory complications in a client with CF and must be reported immediately to the HCP. The client's skin color is highly indicative of respiratory distress and also requires immediate follow-up. Green sputum is an indication that the client may be experiencing a respiratory infection which can be a life-threatening occurrence in a client with CF. Also, the fact that the client is anxious and easily fatigued; only able to answer questions in short phrases is further signs of respiratory distress. The other findings listed are within normal limits for a client with this disorder and do not require immediate follow-up.

Question 2 (Multiple Response—Grouping):
Answer:

Category	Orders	
Imaging	X	Chest x-ray
		CT of abdomen
		MRI of the chest
		Lung ventilation scan
Laboratory	X	Arterial blood gas
	X	Sputum culture
		Sweat chloride level
	X	Complete blood count with automatic differential
Medications	X	Gentamicin
	X	Ipratropium bromide and Albuterol sulfate
	X	Dornase alfa
	X	Ivacaftor

Rationale

Imaging: A chest x-ray will help to diagnose and grade the severity of pneumonia present for this client. Laboratory: ABG tests will help to evaluate the severity of ineffective gas exchange and respiratory acid-base imbalance. A sputum culture will help to identify the type of bacteria, fungus, virus, or parasite that is causing the lower respiratory infection in this client. A complete blood count (CBC) with automatic differential will help to evaluate the extent and what type of infection could be present. Medications: Gentamicin is effective in the treatment of serious Gram-negative bacteria, which are common in pneumonia infections. Duoneb (ipratropium bromide and albuterol sulfate) nebulizer treatments are effective bronchodilators, which will help to relax the bronchioles and decrease respiratory effort. Dornase alfa is a mucus thinner that is most effective when used after bronchodilators. Ivacaftor is a CF transmembrane conductance

Notes

regulator that is designed to correct the malfunctioning protein in clients with CF. A CT of the abdomen and magnetic resonance imaging (MRI) are not necessary for this condition. A chest x-ray will be sufficient to provide the information needed to diagnose the client's lower respiratory infection without exposing the client to unnecessary radiation or costs of the procedures. Lung ventilation scans can be diagnostic of CF. However, this diagnosis already exists for this client and the scan is not necessary. A sweat chloride level is a test also used to diagnose CF and is unnecessary at this time.

Question 3 (Multiple Response—Select all that apply):
Answer: 1, 2, 5, 7, 9, 10.

Rationale

Ineffective airway clearance: Persons with CF have increased mucus production. The excessive amount of mucus and retained secretions are difficult to clear from the airway and are a chronic complication associated with this disorder.

Imbalanced nutrition: less than body requirements: CF impairs the digestive process and absorption of nutrients. Without adequate ingestion of pancreatic enzymes, the client is unable to digest food and absorb nutrients effectively.

Impaired gas exchange: This client is being admitted for a suspected lower respiratory infection, which can decrease the lung's ability to exchange oxygen and carbon dioxide in the alveoli due to an accumulation of fluid and exudate.

Impaired comfort: The client is reporting a pain level of 4/10 with coughing. CF clients have a constant need to clear secretions from their airway, which results in frequent coughing. This will cause the client to have a perceived lack of ease or relief from the pain.

Powerlessness: Clients (especially children and adolescents) may feel a sense of powerlessness and lack of control over their own bodies. They frequently can feel frustration about inability to perform and participate in activities like other children their age due to their inherited disorder.

Constipation: Constipation is a frequent complication associated with CF. Clients often experience greasy or bulky stools, difficult bowel movements, and constipation due to difficulty digesting fat in their diet (particularly if they are fighting an infection). There is no evidence given in the scenario of RN's assessment to support any of the other diagnoses listed.

Question 4 (Matrix Multiple Choice):
Answer:

Food Options	Recommended	Contraindicated
Sausage biscuit	X	
Scrambled eggs	X	
Tomatoes		X
Brown rice		X
Ground beef	X	
Cheddar cheese	X	
Greek yogurt	X	
Baked sweet potato		X

Rationale

Breakfast sausage, eggs, ground beef, cheese products, and yogurt are foods high in protein and calories. These foods will meet the dietician's recommendations. Fruits, vegetables, and rice are foods that are high in nutrients but not high in protein and calories. Although these foods are beneficial for a well-balanced diet, they will not help this client gain weight as needed.

Question 5 (Highlight Table):
Answer:

Physician Orders

1. Acetaminophen 325 mg PO now and Q6H PRN fever >100.4°F or mild pain.
2. Respiratory consult for chest physiotherapy.
3. Titrate O_2 via NC to keep SpO_2 above 95%.
4. DuoNeb 3 mL INH nebulizer Q4H.
5. 3000-calorie, high-protein diet
6. 1800 lipase units per gram of fat ingested.
7. Repeat ABG, CBC, CMP.
8. Daily weight and strict I&Os.

Notes

Rationale

The RN should prioritize tasks that address a client's airway or breathing efforts. The RN should first obtain an SpO_2 reading and apply O_2 if indicated. Administration of the nebulizer treatment will dilate the bronchioles and increase airflow in and out of the lungs, which will decrease respiratory effort. Next the RN should consult the respiratory therapist to perform chest physiotherapy. This intervention will break up secretions and mucus and make them easier to expel. Once these have been completed, the RN can follow through with the other orders.

Question 6 (Drop-Down Rationale):

Answer:

Effective dosing of PERT is determined by observing the client's feces. If therapy is sufficient, then the RN will see it sink.

Rationale

Feces from a client who is receiving adequate PERT will sink to the bottom of the toilet. Feces that contains fat will float to the surface of the water in the toilet. Undigested fat in the stool indicates insufficient PERT in clients with CF. This is an easily observable indication of therapeutic medication dosing for clients. PERT will not affect the other body fluids mentioned.

Notes